THE TRYST BETRAYED

The Tryst Betrayed
*Reflections on Diplomacy
and Development*

JAGAT S. MEHTA

VIKING
Published by the Penguin Group
Penguin Books India Pvt. Ltd, 11 Community Centre, Panchsheel Park, New Delhi 110 017, India
Penguin Group (USA) Inc., 375 Hudson Street, New York, New York 10014, USA
Penguin Group (Canada), 90 Eglinton Avenue East, Suite 700, Toronto, Ontario, M4P 2Y3, Canada (a division of Pearson Penguin Canada Inc.)
Penguin Books Ltd, 80 Strand, London WC2R 0RL, England
Penguin Ireland, 25 St Stephen's Green, Dublin 2, Ireland (a division of Penguin Books Ltd)
Penguin Group (Australia), 250 Camberwell Road, Camberwell, Victoria 3124, Australia (a division of Pearson Australia Group Pty Ltd)
Penguin Group (NZ), 67 Apollo Drive, Rosedale, North Shore 0632, New Zealand (a division of Pearson New Zealand Ltd)
Penguin Group (South Africa) (Pty) Ltd, 24 Sturdee Avenue, Rosebank, Johannesburg 2196, South Africa

Penguin Books Ltd, Registered Offices: 80 Strand, London WC2R 0RL, England

First published in Viking by Penguin Books India 2010

Copyright © Jagat Singh Mehta 2010

All photogaphs provided by the author from his personal collection.

All rights reserved

10 9 8 7 6 5 4 3 2 1

The views and opinions expressed in this book are the author's own and the facts are as reported by him which have been verified to the extent possible, and the publishers are not in any way liable for the same.

ISBN: 9780670082469

Typeset in Sabon MT by Eleven Arts, New Delhi

Printed at Replika Press Pvt. Ltd, Kundli, Haryana

This book is sold subject to the condition that it shall not, by way of trade or otherwise, be lent, resold, hired out, or otherwise circulated without the publisher's prior written consent in any form of binding or cover other than that in which it is published and without a similar condition including this condition being imposed on the subsequent purchaser and without limiting the rights under copyright reserved above, no part of this publication may be reproduced, stored in or introduced into a retrieval system, or transmitted in any form or by any means (electronic, mechanical, photocopying, recording or otherwise), without the prior written permission of both the copyright owner and the above-mentioned publisher of this book.

In memory of

Rama

who remains an inspiration for her affections and
integrity to me, our four children,
and seven grandchildren who came after she was gone

Contents

ACKNOWLEDGEMENTS ix

PROLOGUE: THE PITFALLS OF EGOTISM IN A MEMOIR 1

1. THE FEUDAL BACKDROP: A FAMILY BONDED TO MEWAR 7
2. THE EDUCATIONAL EMANCIPATION OF A SPOILT ONLY SON (1928–47) 17
3. STARTING SERVICE ON THE FIRST FLOOR OF SOUTH BLOCK (1947–49) 31
4. RAMA 48
5. INDUCTION INTO THE ADMINISTRATION (1949–51) 64
6. BERN AND VIENNA: NEHRU IN BURGENSTOCK (1951–54) 73
7. LONDON AND THE SUEZ (1954–56) 91
8. THE NORTH-EASTERN LIMITROPHE: BOGGED DOWN BY THE INDIA–CHINA BOUNDARY QUESTION (1956–61) 102
9. DIVIDED GERMANY: 'ICH BIN EIN BERLINER'; FRANCO–GERMAN RECONCILIATION (1961–63) 122
10. ENJOYING THE PEKING 'DOGHOUSE': OBSERVING THE SINO–SOVIET RIFT AND RECEIVING AN ULTIMATUM THREATENING WAR (1963–66) 131
11. POLICY PLANNING AND ITS SUBJECTIVE BENEFITS; INTERLUDE AT HARVARD (1966–70) 164
12. EXHILARATING IN THE BANISHMENT TO TANZANIA (1970–74) 183

13. BACK TO DELHI UNDER SUBTERFUGE: ADDITIONAL SECRETARY ADMINISTRATION (1974–76)   **199**

14. CATAPULTED TO FOREIGN SECRETARY; THE EMERGENCY; UNPRECEDENTED FRUITFUL NEGOTIATIONS (1976–77)   **210**

15. STRADDLING THE CHANGE IN GOVERNMENT: BIPARTISANSHIP CONTINUES IN FOREIGN POLICY (1977–79)   **225**

16. REMOVED WITHOUT REASON BY A GOVERNMENT WITHOUT A MANDATE   **251**

17. LEARNING THROUGH TEACHING: ACADEMIA (1980–96)   **260**

18. BACK TO THE ORIGINS: VOLUNTARISM IN DEVELOPMENT, EDUCATION AND GRASS-ROOTS DEMOCRACY (1985 TO DATE)   **270**

19. PROFESSIONALISM IN DIPLOMACY: BOUQUETS AND BRICKBATS   **288**

20. WHY HAS INDIA UNDERPERFORMED AFTER INDEPENDENCE?   **303**

INDEX   **322**

Acknowledgements

It is after much delay and protracted reluctance that I have decided to write down my life story. My generation witnessed the historic 'Tryst with Destiny', but many have already forgotten the principles which inspired the struggle. It placed an obligation upon all of us to uphold the values which permeated the quest for Independence.

As I write this with the Mumbai terrorist attacks of November 2008 still fresh in our minds, and a populist desire for retaliation, there is danger of obscuring the distant vision of functional cooperation between all South Asian countries. Notwithstanding the ugly past, it is only through a forward-looking diplomacy that compromises can be reached. We led the process of decolonization and we must contribute equally to safeguarding the planet's future. Sincere voluntarism can supplement the state's responsibility to ease the poverty of two-thirds of our people; otherwise terror, homegrown, as well as imported malevolence, can overwhelm national integrity.

I did not keep a diary or even a record of all my engagements, and my memory frequently lets me down. I showed the manuscript to some friends, to whom I must acknowledge my gratitude. Arun Singh spent weeks of his holiday in Singapore reading the text, and gave me invaluable suggestions. Deepika Roy corrected some quotes. I also want to thank my colleague, Kiran Doshi, who plodded through many chapters and gave me the benefit of his thoughtful scrutiny. I consulted Neelima Khetan, the Chief Executive of Seva Mandir, and Riaz Tehsin, the President of Vidya Bhawan, for the accuracy of my recall about their institutions. Vijay, my daughter, read the chapter on Rama. Vikram, my son, went through most of the draft and though he had reservations on the suggested ethics of civil servants, he thought there were bigger flaws in the working of the political system. There were many to whom I posed the question—the subject of my concluding chapter—Why has India underperformed? The answers were diverse, but the final version is my own.

Much of this story pertains to my years in the Ministry of External Affairs (MEA). It may not be inappropriate to pay tribute to the supporting infrastructure of the Ministry. I worked with many stenographers and do not recall a single one who was lagging in patriotic zest, or lacked the capacity to work long hours, sharing my responsibilities. I specially recall the late Kashi Chakravarty, G.S. Mehta, A.S. Bedi; others like Kailash Srivastava, Katial, Vaidya and Priti Sircar who are still with us and who were real partners. I would like to pay special tribute to S. Amrik Singh, who started as a lower division clerk in the twenties. He was an expert on Tibet. Later in life, he lost his eyesight totally and the administration considered retiring him prematurely. I knew he was an invaluable asset who could recall pages of files. I provided him with a stenotypist to facilitate his office work. He, more than anyone else, was a mental custodian of our Tibetan archives. He was among the unsung heroes in the lower deck.

Incidentally, after I retired, I suggested to the Foreign Minister that, facing the main staircase, a commemorative plaque should be put up for those of the Foreign Service, regardless of rank, who died only because they were serving India abroad. It would, for example, include P.P. Pillai, then First Secretary in Ottawa, who was shot at his desk for not obtaining a residence permit for a mad Yugoslav, (the High Commissioner was out of the office and Pillai was number two); A.K. Sen who, despite his heart condition, accepted Consul Generalship in Lhasa and had a stroke at that height; S.L. Bhalla, whose aircraft was shot down while serving the International Control Commission for Vietnam and whose body to this day, has not been found. There must be many others whom I do not recall, but just like the army, the Foreign Service too, should honour those who died serving India.

My deteriorating handwriting and slow-witted thinking required repeated drafts and typing. I must acknowledge the unwavering help of S.S. Bolia. I was also helped cheerfully by H. Venkatachalam and K.J. Baskaran, whenever required.

Finally, I am grateful to Ranjana Sengupta, Saroja Khanna and the editorial staff at Penguin for their patience.

October 2009   Jagat S. Mehta

Prologue: The Pitfalls of Egotism in a Memoir

Writing a memoir is a perilous exercise strewn with pitfalls of egotism. I resisted the temptation for more than two decades. However, as one grows older, reaches beyond expectations of recognition, and develops immunity against envy and ill-informed affronts, one begins to surmise that an honest recall could prove a small corrective for the national future. It is part of a citizen's obligation to reinforce faith in the working of our democracy.

I retired in 1980 after an exceptionally eventful career in the Foreign Service. However, it ended not with a bang, but with a whimper. My fidelity to India was never questioned. Years later, I came across officers who had joined the service after I had retired, and was flattered when told that they had heard of me and how I had been summarily displaced. I had tried to remain true to civil service ethics as I understood them, and the totality of my experience has been a mix of bouquets and brickbats. Loyalty to the long-term interest of the country is essential to professionalism but it demands character and integrity even more than training.

As it happened, my foreign service career started in August 1947, on almost the first working day after the Union Jack ceased to fly from the twin towers of North and South Blocks. I was probably the first officer to sign a charge report in the central government after India attained Independence. Unlike anyone I know or have heard of, my first room was on the first floor of the South Block (room 151A), which had been vacated by Creighton, the outgoing Acting British Foreign Secretary, on 14 August. It is next to room 152 which, since 1952 has been the office of successive prime ministers. My father, then a nominated member representing southern Rajputana in the Constituent Assembly, because of his friendship with B.F.H.B. Tyabji, who was Joint Secretary, got me a pass for the visitors' gallery. Aside from Fori Nehru, the wife of the late B.K. Nehru, who just crossed one hundred, I could be the only survivor who saw and heard Panditji when, without a scrap of paper, he declared, 'Long ago we made a Tryst with Destiny and now we must redeem our pledge . . . Such moments come rarely in history . . . at the midnight hour India awakes to life and freedom.' Many years later, I found a photograph in the Assembly records and saw my father standing in the row behind the Prime Minister—who earlier the same morning had been sworn to that office by the Governor General—when all members of the assembly were swearing allegiance to Independent India. I also happened to be standing on one of the chairs, witnessing the greatest parade of the British Empire, which took place near India Gate the same afternoon. The Governor General—no longer Viceroy—and Lady Mountbatten, escorted by a squadron of bodyguards in full uniform and with pennants flying, had come down from the Raisina Hill Lodge to unfurl the Indian national tricolour. There were nearly half a million people creating a friendly bedlam around the British-built memorial to the Indian army. I recall Panditji making his way through the milling crowd to rescue Pamela Mountbatten who was standing not far from me and he managed to put her in the Governor General's carriage.

It was the greatest parade of the British Empire, not because India, 'the jewel in the imperial crown' had started the process of decolonization, but because the ceremony could not take place! The ground was overrun in amity and exuberance, with the crowd shouting 'Mahatma Gandhi ki jai,' 'Jawaharlal Nehru ki jai' but also 'Pandit Mountbatten ki jai.' On Panditji's advice, the Governor General's four-horse-drawn carriage, with caparisoned grooms, gingerly made its way back. Panditji energetically tried to control the crowd and rescue women in danger of being crushed. Years later, in the Chelsea home of Michael Hadow, overlooking the Thames, I saw a photograph of Marie, Hadow's wife, who was one of the women saved by Nehru. In the photograph, Nehru himself is sitting on the folded rear cover of the viceregal carriage and she is seated next to the ADC opposite the Mountbattens! Michael Hadow belonged to the Indian Political Service and until 14 August he was in the External Affairs department, but he crossed over to join the British High Commission as First Secretary to deal with post-Independence internal politics of India. He was eventually knighted as British Ambassador to Mexico.

After 200 years of imperial imposition, this friendly parting between India and the UK was a unique symbol of forgiveness—only replicated when Nelson Mandela was released forty-four years later. It was all due to a frail little man, who was dousing the flames of hatred in faraway Noakhali in Bengal. I now realize how fortunate I was to have been witness to these historic events.

After retirement, I have written three books and many articles, but they have been on problems and issues with minimal, or at best essential, relevant personal reflections. What follow are mostly personal recollections of my experiences, but they may provide a small brick in the vast edifice of the ongoing story of India at a historic moment of its rebirth. Anyway, these vignettes, even if much is forgotten, could interest and amuse my grandchildren!

I will, however, not dare discuss Gandhiji's *Experiments with Truth* which provides the kernel of the philosophy of Swaraj, of ends and means, the evolution of defiant non-violence and the disarming strength of non-retaliation. Nehru's autobiography too, belongs to the history of Independence. The life of Sardar Vallabhbhai Patel by B. Krishna is a faithful account of his statesmanship and his far-sighted pragmatism. V.P. Menon's classic on the story of the integration of India will remain invaluable for historians. Many other stories of our times provide useful supplementary bits and pieces of information, but often there is a little too much subjective rationalization of the writer's role.

My problem therefore remains. I have acquired many books written by contemporaries whom I have known and whose memoirs cover grounds similar to mine. I ask myself, can one write a memoir and resist the pitfalls of egotism?

B.K. Nehru started his memoirs at eighty, but he had assistants and yet it was only published nine years later. In Udaipur, I am on my own. There must be errors of all kinds. I do refer to national penalties which can be traced to the lack of courage in professional advice by civil servants. I repeat I had exceptional and, perhaps undeserved, opportunities. I had one of the longest tenures as Foreign Secretary starting at a young age and was entrusted with many negotiating assignments. I do not envy any others who were given ambassadorial assignments, sometimes several, or the comfort and prestige of the Raj Bhavan. I have an inner satisfaction that, at times tactfully and discreetly but at others risking criticism and displeasure, I gave my views and remained true to my conscience with a long-term vision on foreign policy for India. It is therefore gratifying for me to be sometimes held up as a legend of professional values and receiving some stray encouragement to write my memoir.

My last few years have been in association with volunteerism and the occasional writing of articles and even publishing books on international affairs. But what follows is a personal account of a man with a fading memory, whose exciting career is being recorded for the general public, on the sidelines of life after Independence.

George Kennan in one of his last books, *Around the Cragged Hill: A Personal and Political Philosophy*, mentions that heredity and environment are relevant, and helped by education which determines a person's approach to public life. It was my father who enabled me to see some traces of democratic idealism beyond feudalism. I was reminded of this when Mrs Gandhi was compelled to disclose in Parliament the names of the people whose telephones were being tapped. I was the only ex-civil servant in that tally of suspects! An old friend, the late Nikhil Chakravarty, told me that, one evening at P.N. Haksar's house, T.N. Kaul had said, 'Jagat's independence is dangerous.' I suppose he meant in not joining those who belonged to the ranks of the 'committed' bureaucracy. That was about fifteen years ago. When I was at Allahabad University's Muir Hostel—now Amar Nath Jha Hostel—we enacted parts of Macbeth and I was assigned to do Lady Macbeth. I still remember holding a candle during the sleepwalking scene and saying about Duncan, 'Yet who would have thought the old man to have had so much blood in him?' Being listed with the Opposition political heavyweights is unmerited flattery.

As I approach the end of my life, I truly believe that major conflicts in the twenty-first century can only be constructively resolved through diplomacy; and if they cannot be solved, then it is our professional duty to prevent deterioration, at least for the time being. India must seek to set an example by proving that democracy and development can be blended. Hard power must be limited to 'sufficiency' (a Soviet phrase). Soft power must eventually have the upper hand. We have had ups and downs in our defence policy, but Gandhi has been vindicated and now, equitable justice for the people will defy violence. With technology having internationalized awareness, for a poor country the real security is in distributional justice. With President Obama in the White House, neo-liberalism has been given a new lease on life. India must revert to its original asset of plurality and tolerance. We had a needless setback after the impetuous Partition. We were greatly respected when India was considered principled and world-centred, but our reputation suffered after Partition by becoming hyphenated with Pakistan. This was in large part due to the voluntary adoption of the paranoia of the Cold War. Terrorism is now internationalized, but we continue to believe that subcontinental tensions were unique. Public opinion in India, perhaps understandably, attributed the attacks in Mumbai not to the militancy of a small group of Lashkar-e-Toiba, but to Pakistan as a whole. For professionals, it should have been evident that the newly elected government in Pakistan was not in a position to exercise authority over intelligence organizations or the army; it continued with the knee-jerk habit of denial simply because it could not confess to acquiescence as the group had started with a commitment to liberate Kashmir by all possible means. In the twenty-first century, we must get out of the imprisonment of the Cold War mindset of suspicion and scapegoatism. India must look ahead and mould public opinion as, perhaps, is being attempted by Obama.

My selfish satisfaction, I realize, borders on egotism, but it is coupled with great gratitude to several political leaders and some eminent civil servants. It was a privilege to serve with Nehru, Shastri, Mrs Gandhi and Morarji Desai; A.B. Vajpayee as Foreign Minister; Sir G.S. Bajpai as Secretary General; S. Dutt, C.S. Jha and Rajeshwar Dayal as Foreign Secretaries, and P.N. Dhar, Secretary to the PM. They gave me confidence which spurred me on.

1

The Feudal Backdrop:
A Family Bonded to Mewar

On the edge of the western ramparts of the Aravallis stand the ruins of the vast fort of Kumbhalgarh. On a bright day when the sun is behind it in the east, from the topmost floor of the old palace built by Rana Kumbha, they say it is possible to see across the vast desert of Marwar, and even the city of Jodhpur. Kumbhalgarh was the unconquered bastion of Sisodia Mewar against the onslaughts of the Rathores of Marwar and the siege by the Mughals in Aurangzeb's time. We Mewaris are familiar with the story of how the future Rana Uday Singhji was saved because Panna Dhay, the attending nurse, pointed to her own son sleeping nearby who was then killed by the ambitious impostor Balbir. Later, Uday Singhji was smuggled out of Chittor fort. Rana Pratap, the hero of Haldighati, the son of Maharana Uday Singh, was born in Kumbhalgarh.

An ancestor is banished after having been dewan of Mewar for twenty years

On the climb to the Kumbhalgarh palace, now visited by a constant stream of tourists, few are told that one of the gates used to be called the Mehta gate. The gate was so named not because of any commemorative honour, but until fifteen years ago, it carried a stone plaque in running Mewari, installed in the time of Maharana

Bhim Singhji in the early nineteenth century, announcing the banishment of Mehta Ram Singhji who, for over twenty years had been the dewan (equivalent to Prime Minister in today's parlance) of Mewar. Col. James Tod, in his Gibbon-like two-volume history titled *The Annals and Antiquities of Rajasthan*, in the appendix, describes encountering Mehta Ram Singhji on his way from 'Oodipore' to Marwar. Apparently, Ram Singhji had a strikingly handsome personality and was something of a dandy. As the dewan rode a famous Mewari breed of horse to the palace, the people who were lined along his route saw him throw cotton wool doused with attar (perfume). In his prime, Col Tod records, Ram Singhji was the 'right hand man' of the Maharana.

However, as in feudal courts, there was constant rivalry for favour, and intrigue for displacement of the incumbent. The contention was between different families, who were often related to one another through marriage. The rulers were Rajputs, but the dewans were from a few families belonging to the same subcaste of Oswals, many bearing the surname Mehta. Originally they were Rajputs who had been given refuge by a Jain muni and who then pledged to give up meat, hunting and drinking. Mehta Sher Singhji's family was the rival of Ram Singhji. According to the poet-historian Shyamaldas in *Veer Vinod*, a respected history of Mewar, Sher Singh intrigued against Ram Singh that he had favoured another contender to the throne and so Ram Singh was summarily dismissed. He had to take refuge in the residency and managed to escape to Ajmer, which was then directly administered by the East India Company.

Sher Singh must have put up plaques to placate the Maharana in all the principal forts of Mewar including the one in Chittor. The others were probably removed, but this particular tablet at the Mehta gate of Kumbhalgarh remained embedded. An English friend of mine with a powerful telescopic camera took a photograph of the stone tablet and brought it back for me. The inscription is vicious. It *inter alia* states, 'Anyone who gives refuge to Ram Singh or his progeny will be punished as if he had been responsible for slaughtering a sacred cow.'

In Mandalgarh fort, there was an identical scurrilous plaque, which a rival dignitary—another Mehta—had reinstalled because it had been removed!

Some time after Ram Singhji's exile, it was discovered that the conspiracy was a fabrication. The Maharana decided to send a delegation of senior Umraos—first-class nobles equivalent to dukes of the realm but limited to sixteen—to bring back the former dewan with honour. When the delegation reached Ajmer, so the story goes, they ran into a huge funeral procession which was that of Ram Singhji himself. His eldest son Zalam Singh was allowed to come back to Udaipur and resume the possession of their old haveli, but the old jagir which had been confiscated was not restored.

There are variants to the story. Some say when the conspiracy was discovered and Ram Singhji was about to be recalled, a ceremonial angharkha—a long traditional court dress—was sent in advance. The angharkha was impregnated with poison, which, when worn with pride as vindication of his loyalty to his master, led to Ram Singhji's death. There is at least some kernel of truth in the banishment and forgiveness of Ram Singhji. Even in exile Ram Singhji received overtures from other rulers of Rajasthan to become dewan, but in abiding loyalty to the House of Sisodia, he said he would prefer to remain in exile.

Ram Singhji was my great-grandfather's grandfather. The family's association with Mewar goes back to Rana Hamir in the thirteenth century. In keeping with the princely tradition, the bride asked that Chiloji, my ancestor, who was young but apparently clever, might be brought along as part of the dowry. Family legend says that this boy, who accompanied the bodyguard, by some strategy, succeeded in ending the occupation of Chittor fort by the subedar who represented the Sultan of Gujarat. Apparently my great-grandfather enjoyed the trust of Maharana Sajjan Singhji, who used to ride with him and who once even spent a night in our haveli. Fact and fiction are mixed, but since Rana Hamir's time, our family has been high-level bonded servants of the House of Mewar. The theme of banishment and rehabilitation recurred in successive generations. The family has seen ups and downs many times, but public service seems to have been written in its destiny.

My father resigns in protest at supersession in 1937

Nearer our time, everybody knew that Maharana Fateh Singhji did not approve of any of his important subjects serving outside Mewar. After all, Mewar had a history of never accepting domination by any foreign conquerors. Fateh Singhji, despite months of persuasion and cajoling and a promise that he would not sit below any other ruling prince, not even the Nizam of Hyderabad or the rulers of Baroda, Gwalior, Travancore, Mysore and Kashmir, was reluctant to attend the Delhi Durbar of King George in 1911. Mewar had prided itself on never having given a daughter in marriage even to the Mughals. Whether it was because—and here legend takes over—the Maharana bribed the king's surgeon or because he inflicted a gash on his own thigh, he was the only Indian prince absent from the Delhi Durbar. This aggravated the simmering dissatisfaction of the political department and in 1921 much of the power of the Maharana was transferred to his polio-inflicted son, Maharaj Kumar Bhopal Singhji. It was then that my uncle, one of the few law graduates in Mewar, was transferred from Kumbhalgarh and appointed Private Secretary to the newly empowered Maharaj Kumar.

The year 1922 was important for our family. As it happens, I was born that year, but that was not the reason. It was the year which is symbolic of traditional notions of feudal loyalty in conflict with the aspirations to democracy—the right to choose, work, and live in comparative freedom. The custom at that time was that anyone connected with the House of Mewar, on the very first morning after arrival, was expected to go to the palace to pay his customary homage. My father duly went to the palace. I used to do the same even as a boy. One of the courtiers prompted the Maharana to ask my father, 'Are you still studying?' As soon as it came out that my father was working outside Mewar, the old Maharana became furious and shouted in Mewari, 'Did I refuse to give you a job that you work for the British?' The result was a crisis in the family as most of our relations were employed under the prevalent feudal dispensation. My mother finally persuaded my father to resign from the Seva Samiti Scout Association and submit himself to an assignment in Mewar. He too, started his career in the state as hakim of Kumbhalgarh, just like his father and elder brother. He was one of the most educated persons in the state and was soon transferred as revenue officer under Chenevix-Trench, an ICS officer from the central province cadre, who had been borrowed to serve as revenue and settlement commissioner of Mewar.

Soon after his arrival, with his background of the nationalistic Seva Samiti Scout Association, my father established the first Boy Scout Troop in old Rajputana. It attracted some middle-class youths of Udaipur, many of whom later attained distinction in the political and educational spheres of the country. Sadiq Ali joined the All India Congress Committee office and went to jail many times but, after Independence, became President of the Indian National Congress, Governor of Tamil Nadu and Maharashtra; Kalu Lalji Srimali, one of the first rovers who obtained an MA, and was appointed headmaster of Vidya Bhawan when it was founded in 1931. Later, he was the first minister from Rajasthan in the central government and ended as an independent minister of state. Shankar Lalji went to Gandhiji's ashram at Wardha. The Boy Scout Troop was the nucleus of volunteerism, adventure hiking, dramatics and social service, and even today, Udaipur has more NGOs than almost any other small town in the country.

My mother was an early victim of tuberculosis and passed away when I was only two. Soon after I was born, my mother had placed me in the lap of my aunt, the wife of my elder uncle, saying, 'Here is your child.' My uncle had no children, and so for many years I was the only child of my generation in our family. Bhabhi, as I called my aunt, was like my mother. She was a very loving mother-in-law to my wife and 'Bada Bhabhi' to my four children.

It was only after my mother died in 1924 that my father decided to go abroad. I suppose he must have been the first person from Udaipur to break the prejudice against voyaging across 'Kalapani' (black water) to study, when he was already over thirty.. He must have worked hard because within two and a half years, he became a barrister of the Middle Temple. At the London School of Economics, he successfully completed his Ph.D. thesis on *Lord Hastings and the Indian States*. But, apart from his double academic pursuits, his weekends were spent with scout troops, particularly at Gilwell Park Scout Masters Training Centre. He also travelled all over Europe and came back full of ideas, particularly about education. He was a regular visitor to the East End settlements and learnt of service with the poor and generally how to mould youth in their commitment to citizenship. Scouting led to Vidya Bhawan and a lifetime's commitment to social service, education and development.

What, if any, was the basis of our family pride?

My son Uday, when he was an undergraduate and spending ten days in Udaipur, used to have breakfast regularly with my father. Uday asked him what, if any, were the running threads of pride in the family. He later summarized the answers to me. My father said that though one is apt to exaggerate, at least until then—this must have been in the early seventies—no one from the family had been tempted by a commercial or profit-oriented career. For all these generations, the family had been associated with administration and had an inclination towards public service. When the family got back from Ajmer, the eldest son of Ram Singhji, namely Zalam Singhji, was made accountant general and discovered that the accusations of corruption made against his father had been false. Zalam Singhji's eldest son Akshay Singhji was made hakim. He was apparently a close friend of Maharana Sajjan Singhji. The prerogatives of the so-called pradhano-ke-ghar—families of ministers—came to mean preferential choice in administration. Jeewan Singh, my grandfather, beginning at the age of fifteen, served as hakim in most districts, including commercially important ones like Bhilwara and Chittor. Before retirement, he was elevated as a member of the Mahendraj Sabha, the highest judicial appellate body of the state.

The belief that one should keep the British carefully away from the administration of Mewar was carefully observed. While the position of dewan in Jaipur and Jodhpur was, at times, entrusted to British officers from the political service, in Udaipur there never was an Englishman in charge. Many dewans were inducted from eminent and educated Kashmiri or Bengali families, but not the British!

The other quality which my father explained to Uday was that our family was a pioneer in stressing the importance of education. Jeewan Singhji was the first to send his sons for schooling to Ajmer in the first decade of the twentieth century. Jaswant Singhji, my grandfather's younger brother, may have been one of the earliest in Udaipur to develop a good command over English. All his life, he regularly subscribed to the *Hindustan Times* from Delhi. He was also a great believer in promoting education in his districts. Hostels in Rajsamand and Bhilwara started by him for poor boys from the rural surroundings still exist.

Commitment to public interest

The third characteristic that my father explained to my son was a feeling of genuine empathy for the people. We were not critical of feudal Mewar, but within those imposed constraints, the family was respected for being fair-minded and averse to inflicting hardship. No one in the family was known to be unjust and callous to the kasthkars (the peasants).

The family always sat together at meals, sitting around one big thali on the floor. My father had a separate thali, partly because he did not like red chillies. I seem to recall that the discussions were fairly intense on administrative matters—revenue laws, problems posed by oppressive jagirdars in relation to khalsa—the state—directly under the Maharana, etc. There were occasional references to personal problems of the family, but the overriding thread was the passion and concern for administrative problems. But we remained bonded slaves of Mewar and its rulers for generations. There was an underlying belief in the divinity of the House of Sisodia, and the Maharanas were our annadatas—the givers of bread.

After the revoked exile of Mehta Ram Singhji, the peak of distinction was reached when my uncle, Tej Singhji—Tej Kaka to me—was appointed as Private Secretary. He remained scrupulously loyal to Bhopal Singhji. Apparently, the old Maharana Fateh Singhji, who was estranged from his son, on his deathbed told him only one thing, 'Keep Tej Singh.' Though the family haveli had been restored, until Tej Kaka came into favour, we had no right to add to the old structure. Maharana Bhopal Singhji gave full licence to my uncle and it was legally changed from baxis—a gift of the Maharana—to the title bikau or ownership. After its reconstruction, the haveli was a massive structure, which even in the thirties cost upward of one lakh rupees. The Maharana approved the cutting down of a 300-year-old mango tree, and carting it from Kumbhalgarh so that a sixteen-foot-high gate could be carved without any joints to enable an elephant, with a seated mahout, to enter the courtyard. The haveli was renamed Akshay Bhawan after my great-great-grandfather. When it was completed, the Maharana agreed to spend a day in it in 1936. I remember that for this 'padravani'—an honourable visit—the first after several decades, rasgullas and other sweets were ordered from Calcutta! Cooks were brought in, and Maharana Bhopal Singh and the elder Maharani Sahiba spent the whole day in the haveli. At the evening durbar, the Maharana conferred the right of 'Tazim' on my uncle, which meant that when he came to the court, the Maharana himself would rise a little from his chair and acknowledge his mujra or salutation, by lifting his hand. Tazim was the hereditary privilege of the first-class nobles but had not been awarded to any local minister except Mehta Sahib Pannalalji several decades earlier. My uncle was so devoted to Mewar and its ruler that until his dying day, even though weak and debilitated by repeated bouts of cerebral malaria, he would not eat his evening meal without a 'durbar ka darshan' or sighting of the ruler. In fact, around his neck, a gold chain carried an engraving of Eklingji or Shiv temple on one side and Bhopal Singhji's image on the other.

In 1935, the Maharana had made Tej Kaka one of the two dewans of Mahakama Khas or State Secretariat. The other dewan was P.C. Chatterji from a Bengali family settled in Udaipur since the nineteenth century. It is widely held that had Tej Kaka remained in good health, he might have ended as Prime Minister of Udaipur. In his heyday, he was certainly considered not only the most loyal but also the most powerful servant of the state. Mewar was hierarchical and vigilant against those demanding democracy. There was a benign side to feudalism, a devotion to heritage which, at least in Udaipur, never discriminated against or was unjust to any subjects, regardless of their religion. The government was transparent and a patron of music, the arts and history. The Dagar brothers, Uday Shankar the dancer, and many painters had the patronage of the palace.

The fourth thing which my father mentioned to Uday was that no member of the family had shirked from resigning in protest rather than compromise on principles. He himself had resigned when a retired deputy commissioner from U.P. had superseded him and been named commissioner for revenue and settlement, succeeding Chenevix-Trench. The then Musahib Ala, a Kashmiri, thought the resignation amounted to insubordination and recommended that Mohan Sinha Mehta be dismissed and his rights and privileges forfeited. Since the Maharana had approved the import of a non-Mewari, he saw no reason to show any harshness to a loyal subject. Later, my father became Chief Minister of Banswara but he returned to Udaipur when Sir T. Vijayraghavachari became Prime Minister and recommended that, because of his deteriorating health, my uncle be retired with a special pension and my father, his younger brother, be invited to join the reconstituted cabinet.

All this background could be egotism but it illustrates the social and administrative story of the family, which provides some sort of DNA to my own upbringing. I was the first in the family never to have served in Mewar but then, it was obvious by 1947 that a new dawn was breaking in India, and even proud Mewar would lose its ancient, fervently defended, separate identity.

2

The Educational Emancipation of a Spoilt Only Son (1928–47)

The whole family came to Bombay to welcome my father when he returned from England in 1928 as a barrister with a Ph.D. The welcoming party included my great-uncle (Jassu Basa), elder uncle (Tej Kaka) and younger uncle (Chandra Kaka). I was dressed in the customary upper-class Rajputana dress: a cap with salma-sitara adornment, a light brocade coat, white silk pyjamas and silk-covered, Mewari half-open shoes or pagarkhias. My father was utterly shocked to see me, and at the first opportunity, took me to a shop and had me dressed in a simple white shirt, blue shorts, blue socks and laced shoes. He then took me to a studio and ordered many copies of my photograph for sending to members of our extended family. The implicit message was that he did not approve of his son being dressed as a minor prince bhanwarji—the deferential designation of an upper-class grandson—and that I was free to run and get dirty like other boys.

As mentioned, I was the only child, especially loved and nurtured by my uncle and aunt from whom I could get anything I wanted. I was their heir with privileges reserved traditionally for the Patvi or the eldest male child. I must have known that I was special—the adopted son of one of the most powerful men in Mewar. The family retainers would not allow me to touch the ground lest I dirty myself. On the other side was my father with his newfangled ideas of moulding youth to genuine egalitarianism. I became dimly aware of the conflict of values of feudal privilege on the one hand and social egalitarianism on the other.

In order to rescue me from this cloying attention, as soon as we got to Udaipur, my father made inquiries and dispatched me to Indore to live with Mrs Gavde, a widow of English origin, married to a Maharashtrian gentleman, who kept some children with her in a kind of dormitory. My being sent away from the protective womb of the family when I was barely six astounded the gentry in town. Though they had anxieties, and my uncle and aunt even shed tears, they did let me go. They had a sneaking admiration for scouting and similar activities for youth promoted by my father.

In 1929, roughly after one year, I was sent from Indore to the Modern School in Delhi, which was then the best known non-missionary educational institution in northern India. Raghuvir Singhji, the son of Lala Sultan Singhji—a rais or a rich landlord—with extensive properties in Kashmiri Gate, had founded the school for the sons of the professionals and the wealthy who were unconnected with officialdom. Modern School was then located in Daryaganj and had attracted the progeny of the independent-minded elite of Delhi. In my class were Daljit, the youngest brother of Khushwant Singh, and son of Sir Sobha Singh (a prominent builder of Delhi), and Ashok Bhadkamkar, the grandson of Sardar Kibe, a minister in the Holkar state, who had followed me from Indore.

The gates of Modern School were opposite the house of Dr Ansari, the leader of the Congress in Delhi. The school had established a semi-nationalistic thrust. I remember Gandhiji coming to the school assembly. The new buildings of the school were under construction on Barakhamba Road, New Delhi, but even before the school moved, I was taken out in 1932 and admitted to Vidya Bhawan, newly opened by my father.

Vidya Bhawan—a toughening boarding school permeated with equality and secularism

Unlike Modern School, Vidya Bhawan was planned not merely for the middle class—its fees were affordable even for the lower-middle class. The tuition fee was Rs 3 and the hostel fee was Rs 12, inclusive of all meals. I must have been the only boy staying in the hostel who belonged to a family in Udaipur. Not only my cousins, but because of fee concessions, even our servants' children attended Vidya Bhawan. The campus was wild, covered with thorny bushes, with some cultivated sugarcane fields nearby. A panther came to the nala (canal) frequently. Vidya Bhawan experimented with many innovations—no one knew who was a Hindu, a Muslim, an untouchable or of Bhil origin; it had a whole-day curriculum with compulsory team games; we washed our own plates and clothes; we bathed in Fateh Sagar which involved a daily trudge of half a mile, and used twigs as toothbrushes. We were never punished in school for not wearing shoes but always had to wear our uniform consisting of a simple shirt and shorts. This was revolutionary at a time when one could not show one's knees or go bareheaded in town. We sat on rough mats; groups of students took turns to serve. Every year we went for a ten-day 'open-air session', stayed in canvas tents, and learnt by relating subjects to our immediate surroundings.

Vidya Bhawan was a toughening process; it was my first introduction to egalitarianism and citizen responsibility, implicit in aiming for independence and democracy. It made me sensitive to the inequities of society. Gandhism acquired a new meaning—not just nationalism but also austerity, simplicity, selfless dedication and respect for nature and the environment.

During the vacations, however, I was back to being spoilt. I accompanied my uncle to the palace. The Maharana often showered me with gifts. In my early teens I would try to take advantage of the duality in values. I would turn to my uncle for a kiddy phone; I was the first teenager in town with a bicycle, but if I wanted books or a Meccano set, I would ask my father. I also saw at close quarters the ethics of hard work and integrity, and the benign side of princely administration in the dispensation of justice and ruthlessness against corruption and exploitation.

Katherine Heilemann who later joined Sevagram in Wardha and became famous in Kumaon as Sarla Behn, was my guardian in Vidya Bhawan. When I was nearing the matriculation examination, I was still under fifteen. My father had been to Europe a second time, visiting innovative educational institutions. He had started exploring the possibility of sending me to an English public school, but an enlightened one.

Leighton Park, Reading, 1937–40

On the advice of C.F. Andrews, a friend of Gandhiji from South Africa, he got me admitted to Leighton Park (LP)—a Quaker school—in Reading. Again Udaipur was shocked that an only son had been sent away to the UK. It was also unusual that my uncle, with a modest income of Rs 400 per month, took a loan of Rs 16,000 to finance my schooling in England. I knew I would have to adjust to a new surrounding and discipline—cold baths, rugger and cricket, and one shilling six pence only as pocket money every week—but LP forbade smoking and corporal punishment. I was the only Indian at the school and was somewhat indulged, especially as a vegetarian, but was otherwise subjected to prefectorial discipline. My father had written to people who were his friends and also friends of India—Henry Polak, who had been with Gandhiji in South Africa; Mme Morin, a friend of the Nehrus; and Agatha Harrison, among others. They took a kind interest in me. Except for the weekly letters—which my father insisted should be in Hindi—for three years, I had no contact with the family. With the minimum help from my housemaster, I had to arrange for four months of vacation each year. I visited English friends, joined school parties, went skiing and stayed with Indians in London. In LP I learnt to be independent and responsible, managing my accounts well. I made just one call in 1940 to tell my family that, despite the war, I was all right. I knew that the family had sacrificed a great deal to send me abroad, paying a fee of sixty guineas per term. With my thrift—it must have cost £300 a year—I was still encouraged to take extras like violin lessons, as well as join in working tours with the unemployed in South Wales.

Kindness exuded from the school, the teachers, and my friends' parents. The three years 1937–40 were the happiest of my youth. In an article, I could make open fun of the non-discrimination towards 'a copper-coloured coolie' for the school magazine!

On the eve of World War II, I was in Zurich trying to learn German. The British Consul told me to get back to England as soon as possible. I can still recall standing on the pavement outside 10 Downing Street when war was declared because Hitler had not accepted the belated British ultimatum given when Poland was attacked. During 1939–40, off and on, we cheerfully spent our nights in the basement because of air-raid warnings. Like my British friends, I was inspired by the monthly broadcasts of Churchill as the first Lord of the Admiralty, and then as Prime Minister when he promised nothing but 'blood, tears, toil and sweat'. The overhang of the Spanish Civil War is little known in India but it had a great impact on progressive idealism in England. Though we were far from the coast, the courage of the sailing boats that evacuated 2,50,000 of the besieged and relentlessly bombed British Expeditionary Forces from Dunkirk evoked great admiration for British character in adversity. The six years of World War II are not for me to describe but I must mention that more boys from my class were killed than from any other class in my school.

After the A-level from Leighton Park, I should have gone to Cambridge where I had been admitted to King's College but the Educational Advisor in India House thought I should return to India. I was therefore booked in a large ship called the *Empress of Britain*. There were hundreds of other Indians going back but, being young, I was assigned the uppermost bunk in a three-tiered converted hold, eight gangways below the boat deck—just where a torpedo from a submarine would hit! Since Italy had joined the war and the Mediterranean was closed, we had to go round the Cape. The crowded ship had a company of troops too, but only one 4.5mm gun on the stern as protection. We started in a convoy escorted by the latest 35,000-ton battleship, the *Prince of Wales* as well as another battle cruiser, *Repulse*, both of which sank later off Singapore. Our ship was taken out of the convoy because of engine trouble and we spent a week in Greenock, off Glasgow, and then our ship set forth alone, zigzagging in the Atlantic for a month in total blackout. The ship's crew did not mix with Indians, but their grim faces told their anxieties. Only after we reached Cape Town did we see lights at night and could walk again on terra firma. We visited the Cape Mountain but the truly unforgettable experience was when a group of us walked into a restaurant and were told 'Sorry, we do not serve coloured visitors.' It was my first encounter with apartheid.

I sent a telegram home, but the dispatch from Cape Town was converted by wartime censorship as 'sans origin'. However, with the help of K.M. Munshi, a well connected lawyer, my father found out that some passenger ships were coming to Bombay. After meeting one or two other passenger ships, my father and younger uncle, Chandra Kaka, with Prem and cousins Ajit and Vijay born during my absence, welcomed me back at Ballard Pier. It had been a long grim voyage. The ship broadcasts had relayed news, at least when we reached the Indian Ocean, of the raging battle, and there was satisfaction over the daring success of the fighter pilots and that the invasion of Britain had been abandoned by Hitler.

Allahabad University, 1940–44

Though it was the middle of the academic year, in November, I was admitted to Allahabad University. I started in the P.C. Banerji hostel which was most frequented by students from Udaipur. Having lost some of my immunity, in February 1941, I fell victim to a serious bout of typhoid and was in bed for two months in the house of Ramooji, Shri Ram Bhartiya, a friend of my father from his Seva Samiti years.

At the beginning of the next academic year, the Vice-Chancellor, Amar Nath Jha, suggested I move to Muir Hostel of which he was the warden—after his death, it was renamed Amar Nath Jha Hostel. Admission to Muir was coveted and restricted to those either from well connected families or with promising academic records. There was a board in the hall carrying the names of the hostellers who had got into the ICS, which included people like Dharma Vira, B.N. Jha, L.P. Singh, L.K. Jha, Govind Narain, etc. The most distinguished of my contemporaries was Harish Chandra, a mathematical genius. I met him subsequently at Cambridge. He was later the pride of the Institute of Advanced Studies in Princeton where he was a colleague of Einstein. But for his premature death, he might have received the Nobel Prize.

The most prestigious club in the university was the Friday Club which met every Saturday. It had a small membership, mostly lecturers from the English department, and some from History and Political Science. About eight or ten students were invited to join. One of the members was the well known Urdu poet Firaq Gorakhpuri who was also one of the English department faculty. It was the only institution in the university where women and men met across a tea table in the staff room of the English department. The regular presence of Amar Nath Jha gave it special prestige.

I was truly grateful that after my English public school experience, I had come back to India. Allahabad, as a residential university founded in the nineteenth century after the Presidency Universities, had a high reputation. The years I spent there, 1940–44, were war years; tensions were evident between Hindus and Muslims, but as secularists and supporters of the Congress, we were in the majority. Most Muslim hostellers were admirers of Jinnah. Among my friends was Nurul Hasan, (the son of Sayyid Abdul Hasan), who was later professor, central education minister, Ambassador to the USSR and Governor of West Bengal; and Zafar, (the son of Syed Ali Zaheer), later Air Vice-Marshal Zaheer. He gave me a false certificate of age to become eligible for joining the air force. He retired as Air Marshal and was

DGCA for a while, but was removed because he dared to warn Sanjay Gandhi not to carry out aerobatics over Delhi. Satish Chandra, a future historian and chairman of the U.G.C., was in my seminar class. Ashok Bhadkamkar had continued at the Modern School until he matriculated. Though we were together again in Muir, I had lost a year by going to England and so was not in his class. But our lives were destined to run parallel as he too, joined the navy and was the only other naval executive branch officer to be chosen for the ICS/Political Service and therefore, appointed to the foreign service. Alas, he died prematurely while he was Ambassador to Egypt.

I was active in various kinds of activities at the university. I played squash for the hostel, but was generally more social than sporting. I joined the University Training Corps (UTC). This involved three parades a week and attending the annual camp. After two years, I became sergeant of my platoon. In the weeklong camp, other universities—Lucknow, Benaras, Aligarh, Agra, etc.—also took part. After the intra-platoon competition, our platoon was judged the best in the battalion and given the privilege of providing the ceremonial guard of honour. My platoon had a truly distinguished band of twenty-seven. It included R.S. Pathak, who became Chief Justice of India; Prakash Narain, Chief Justice of the Delhi High Court; Shanti Bhushan, a future Law Minister who got Mrs Gandhi convicted of transgressing election restraints; J.P. Gupta, Chairman of the Railway Board; Lovraj Kumar, Secretary, Petroleum, who married Dharma Venkatraman; and Bhupi Bhalla, the son of the head of police. In fact, most of the platoon climbed up the professional ladder to reach a post equivalent to the secretary to the government of India. The UTC command structure included distinguished professors like Bhagwat Dayal, a future ambassador (the eldest in a family of civil servants where all the brothers excelled on competitive merit), and my own kinsman Maj. P.S. Mehta, who died prematurely as Military Secretary to Sir Chandu Lal Trivedi, Governor of Punjab. The battalion was commanded by Col. Haider of Aligarh University;

years later, his son Salman was my colleague and one of my successors as Foreign Secretary.

Such social activities took time so I was surprised when in my MA (Final) I got a first class. In the previous four years, the university used to be so strict that even 59.5 per cent, just half a mark short of a first, was not accepted. M.G. Kaul who (like his brother Brahma), got into the ICS before recruitment was suspended because of the war, topped only with a second. Naturally I was thrilled at getting a First. I had intended to join the navy after my MA since doing war service was the only way to compete for the ICS in the second half of the war. The first division elicited a telegram from Professor S.C. Deb, then head of the English department, offering me straightaway a lecturership to teach the B.A. classes and even take some seminars of the MA (Prev). The English department was highly coveted. Harivansh Rai Bachchan, the famous Hindi poet, (and father of the even more famous 'Big B') had been waiting for five years for a lecturership, and was eventually appointed at the same time as I. Some students were older than I and so I started cultivating a moustache in order to look a little more dignified in the classes I was supposed to teach. But I taught only for about six months as the war was coming to an end. During this period, the Friday Club staged *Twelfth Night* and I was cast as Sir Andrew Aguecheek. Bhagwat Dayal was Malvolio, Dr Phiroze Dastoor, the Associate Professor, was Sir Toby Belch. Coral Caleb was the heroine Olivia and Malti Sapru acted as Maria.

The student union was the hub of the political activities in the university. Not infrequently, Jawaharlal Nehruji came to its meetings between his terms of imprisonment. I took active part in the union debates and so stood for the vice-presidentship while still an undergraduate. Prizes in debates helped the door-to-door canvassing as did the support of Daulat Singh Kothari, also from Rajasthan, who was the incumbent president. It was, however, thanks to my cousin Gulab Singhji with his famous hospitality, that I got elected. This was in 1942, coinciding with the historic

'Quit India' resolution of the AICC. The university union led a demonstration in support of the resolution, which ended in a firing where one student was killed. Thereafter, the university was closed for three months. Hemvati Nandan Bahuguna, who was secretary during my term, then launched his political career, which ended in his becoming Chief Minister of U.P. in 1973 and later a minister at the centre in the Janata government. In 1941 he went underground, probably in his Himalayan home, and from 1942–46, he was in jail. N.D. Tiwari was a familiar contemporary, who also became Chief Minister of U.P., and is presently a Governor. The union was truly the nursery for many who subsequently went into political careers, but they were friends in Allahabad.

A commission in the Royal Indian Navy, 1945–46

I resigned as lecturer, sought the approval of my grandfather, uncle and father and, with their consent, got a wartime commission in the Royal Indian Navy in January 1945. I joined *HMIS Feroze*, the training ship located in the commandeered Western India Automobile Association building on Malabar Hill. We practised drill early mornings on the Ridge Road next to the Hanging Gardens. We spent four months on the *Feroze* to attend short courses in seamanship, navigation, etc., then went to *HMIS Talwar* in Colaba for a signals course, thereafter to the anti-submarine school in Versova, then moved to the Electrical Engineering School in Jamnagar and finally to the Gunnery School on Malir Island off Karachi. The South-East Asia Command was then preparing for the invasion of Malaya to evict the Japanese who controlled the mainland. The specialized training centre was located in Coconada, north of Vishakhapatnam.

While we were learning how to manoeuvre landing crafts, on 6 and 9 August 1945, the Americans dropped their atomic bombs on Hiroshima and Nagasaki. The Japanese surrender soon followed and we were given the task of taking the LCAs and LCMs into the Bay of Bengal, putting explosives on them and sinking them. Having cleared our hardware, we were on them sent to an onshore camp outside Karachi and then transferred to *HMIS Hamla* in Malad, north of Bombay. The short naval interlude gave me a little experience of life in uniform but I saw no action except the naval mutiny.

Our *Hamla* establishment came into prominence in February 1946 because the only officer who joined the ratings in the mutiny was Lt Sobani, an Ithnasheri Muslim from Bombay. For a few days, he was in total command of the ship's armoury and transport, and the officers were confined to the mess. Sobani's request to the British commanding officer was to arrange for him to be the spokesman of the protesting ratings. He demanded transport to meet with the flag officer in Bombay, Rear Admiral Rattray. I was only a Sub-Lieutenant (hence junior in rank), but Lt Ranjit and I were told to accompany him, as only we were acceptable to Sobani. When we arrived at Vithal House, the Bombay headquarters of the Indian Navy, the Chief Staff Officer, Captain Nott, told Sobani that he was under arrest. Sobani was furious and cursed perfidious Albion for having lured him away. We were irritated at having been chosen to drive him to the *Feroze* and hand him over into custody.

Because of my rather exceptional record of having come first in every short course, I was offered a permanent commission in the navy. Had I accepted, assuming I did not blot my copybook, I would have been senior to all but six chiefs of naval staff. Meanwhile, I had applied for the ICS, had appeared before the preliminary three-day selection board in Madras, and was called for an interview by the Federal Public Service Commission in Simla. But the results were not yet out. There were 30,000 applicants for sixty-odd unfilled vacancies in the ICS and the Political Service, apart from those for the Indian Police, who would be entitled to covenants from the Secretary of State. One could not be certain of being selected. I knew of many who had a better record. Anyway, I refused the permanent naval commission, as I decided I did not want to spend my life in uniform.

St. John's College, Cambridge

After being 'demobbed', with about Rs 3,500 as gratuity, and again with the approval of the family, I decided to proceed to Cambridge. I had heard that many of my friends in Leighton Park had decided to go to St. John's College and so I switched from King's. I boarded a ship just in time to reach when the Michaelmas term began. Being Indian and allegedly sensitive to the winter cold, I was assigned a second-floor room in Chapel Court which had been completed in 1939 and was the only one with central heating. (My friends had to carry coal for their fireplaces). My room, though small, was single and so I did not have to share it as many others did. Incidentally, Narasimhan, a future Economic Advisor to the Finance Minister, was assigned the same room after me. The bathrooms were still far away across the courtyard but that was part of the Cambridge tradition.

Within a month I heard that the names of those selected for the ICS were released and my own name was fairly high on that list. I was, of course, greatly relieved and only waited for the letter of appointment and the commencement of the civil service training. Meanwhile, in September, the interim government had been formed with Sardar Patel as Home Minister. While accepting the selection made by the British, he decided that the old names, viz. the ICS/Indian Political Service could not continue, but that the selectees would be offered appointments in the successor services—the Indian Administrative Service and the Indian Foreign Service. Thereafter, I really enjoyed my stay at Cambridge doing minimum work. I wrote my weekly essay for my tutor, Claude Guillebaud—the grandnephew of Sir Alfred Marshall, the father of Economics in Cambridge—and, incidentally nine years later, the tutor of S. Manmohan Singh. I also competed for the attention of Chitra Mazumdar and Dharma Venkatraman, the only Indian women at Cambridge at the time. The Majlis at that time at Cambridge was for all South Asians including Ceylonese. The poison of communal passion had not reached Cambridge. I had a grand Christmas holiday driving in the Lake District for a week, two weeks of skiing in Grindelwald with the Leighton Park School party, a week in Italy (Rome, Naples, Venice and Milan), and a few days with a British friend. I had deliberately left no forwarding address as I did not want my holiday interrupted, but I was surprised that no letter of appointment came during my absence. I continued my carefree life at Cambridge. I founded a bow tie club. The qualification was the ability to tie an evenly balanced bow without a mirror! I also remember it was a severe winter and that the Cam burst its banks and flooded the Backs.

Our selection had straddled the transition to Independence but with unresolved political problems. Even if India remained undivided, Jinnah did not want a Delhi-controlled successor to the ICS. The implication was that the Punjabi Muslims amongst the sixty-two would have had to be assigned to Indian provinces like U.P., Bihar, the Central Provinces, Madras, Bombay, etc. An undivided India would have a common foreign policy. As I was born in a princely state, my application for the ICS was undecided. Fortunately, I had also applied for the Political Service and was allocated the Foreign Service, but this meant that I was not summoned in March 1947 when most selectees began their training at Metcalfe House. Meanwhile, after consulting the registry, my tutor found that I had exceptional grounds for residential exemptions. All undergraduates were exempted three terms residence if they had done war service, but I also had a first class MA, which meant an additional three terms. So my tutor was told that I could take the Tripos after only three terms' residence. My tutor, however, hinted that I was not yet intellectually ready for Part II Economics, but since I already had a job and an MA, I decided to take the risk. To this day I am surprised that I passed with a second. I stayed on for the college ball and then flew back to India to see if I would be accepted for the Foreign Service.

Through the circumstances of international politics, my educational experience had been varied and possibly instructive. It straddled schooling in India and in England, and alternated with universities in both the countries. I saw something of the war in Europe and the expectations of Independence in India. As I was flying back home, I asked myself whether I would have the courage to live up to the values, which these institutions claimed to inculcate.

3

Starting Service on the First Floor of South Block (1947–49)

I have repeatedly confessed that it was accidents that brought me good fortune and undeserved opportunities. I had stayed on at Cambridge to finish my degree, while my colleagues had already started training in March 1947 at Metcalfe House. I got back to Delhi at the end of June, and coincidentally, on the same flight, was Sir Cyril Radcliffe who, accompanied by Mr Beaumont of the Political Service, was travelling to India to delineate the boundaries dividing Bengal and the Punjab. The original board who had interviewed my other twelve colleagues had been presided over by Sir Akbar Hydari, with Sir Hugh Weightman (then Foreign Secretary), and K.P.S. Menon as members, but they had all dispersed. Meanwhile, Sir Girija Shankar Bajpai, after returning from Washington, was appointed Secretary General (SG) but only in June. He now headed the high-powered board with H.M. Patel and Sir N.R. Pillai for interviewing the ICS and other service applicants for transfer to the proposed Foreign Service. I was interviewed by this board. The other two candidates were P.N. Thapar, Financial Commissioner in the Punjab, and J.N. Srinagesh, who was also in the commissioner's grade. I was naturally overawed. It was a tough interview. Sir Girija asked me to describe a naval battle in the Mediterranean during World War II; H.M. Patel wanted me to recapitulate any discussion with Sir Dennis Robertson, Head of the Economics department at Cambridge, on problems of the development and the future of the Indian economy. I had to improvise replies to both! Having passed this hurdle, I was scrutinized like the other candidates, by Jawaharlal Nehru, then the Vice-Chairman of the Governor General's Council. Nehru started the exchange on a friendly note asking me why I had preferred St. John's to Trinity. Finally he asked me why I wanted to join the Foreign Service and I replied 'to see the world.' Nehru moved to the edge of his chair in angry amazement. I somehow managed to say, 'If I had said I wanted to serve India abroad, you, Sir, would not have believed me anyway.' He smiled his approval. I waited anxiously for two weeks and I almost regretted having cut short my stay at Cambridge. My father contacted Humphrey Trevelyan (who had been Political Agent in Udaipur and was known to him), at that time, Joint Secretary in the department. He reassured my father that the letter of approval would come soon. At the end of July it did and I was told to join immediately as Private Secretary (PS) to the Secretary General. Despite having waited for so long with the date of 'Transfer of Power' already announced as 15 August, after three weeks, I made an excuse about going home to Udaipur first, and requested to be allowed to defer my joining. I thought I might as well wait until after the Union Jack had come down from the twin towers of the North and the South Blocks. In the post-Independence holidays, I went to revisit my old university in Allahabad and finally joined on 21 August 1947.

Nehru respected the legend that the best room in the Secretariat—in the south-west corner (which gets the sun from two sides in the winter and was cooler in the summer) and nearest to the Viceregal Lodge—was earmarked for the Foreign Secretary. Not wanting to insult the tradition or the British occupant, he took the room at the end of the corridor, presently the Principal Secretary's office. Harishwar Dayal was appointed Deputy Secretary (Political) and Tarlok Singh was Private Secretary for other departments, until he became Director General Rehabilitation after Partition. Harishwar's post was upgraded to that of Principal PS after Nehru became Prime Minister, and H.V.R. Iyengar doubled as Secretary of the Constituent Assembly. Sir Girija was more finicky about prestige, the location and size of his office, and summarily evicted the incumbent, Creighton, the Acting Foreign Secretary after Weightman had retired, to occupy the best room. Creighton was told to move to the adjoining room. He handed over charge on 14 August and so room 151A was vacant and earmarked for me. After Girija Bajpai left to take over as Governor of Bombay, this room (number 152) with its Doric columns, the veranda overlooking the Jaipur column and the forecourt of the Rashtrapati Bhavan, became the office of the Prime Ministers.

My first room has had many distinguished dwarpals or guardians to the PMs—M.O. Mathai with Nehru, N.K. Seshan and R.K. Dhawan with Mrs Gandhi, and V.Y. Tonpe with Morarji Desai, and now young Foreign Service officers.

Being wholly untrained to understand files and secretariat procedures, I turned to the experienced personal assistants—Chellam, a reporter, Subramanyam, a superb stenographer, and others attached to the Secretary General for guidance and insights on elementary secretariat functioning.

Partition seen from my desk in South Block

From the very beginning I saw all incoming and outgoing telegrams, including top secret and personal ones meant for the PM and the SG only. Quite a few pertained to the serious holocaust which had engulfed the Punjab in the weeks after Partition. The emergency alarm led to serious international anxieties. Lord Mountbatten was summoned down from Simla where he had gone after transferring power. I had no transport and had to cycle my way home to a temporary shelter in the house of Hansraj Gupta on Barakhamba Road. Taking pity on me, Ishi Rahman, the only other Foreign Service officer who was then in the Ministry serving as Under Secretary (Europe), offered to share his bachelor room in Western Court. While Ishi came home at about 5.30 p.m. I usually stayed in office till 8 p.m. It was eerie cycling through empty curfew-controlled roads after dark. Groups of Sikhs used to march through Queensway—as Janpath was then called—at night hunting for Muslims, especially in the servants' quarters and then sometimes summarily butchering them. So much has been written about the post-Partition trauma so I will not add to it, but I sensed something of the official anxieties on the terrible situation from my desk. A Muslim bearer slept under the bed of Prof. Sengupta who later headed IIT Kharagpur, but he became such a nervous wreck, it was considered preferable to deliver him to the safety of the Purana Qila camp from where he was transported to Pakistan under escort. When my family heard of conditions in Delhi, they got me a Topolino, the smallest Fiat.

Ishi and I were the junior-most residents of Western Court, but the other occupants were more distinguished, and together, we reflected the transition after the British had left. Sir Usha Nath Sen, one of the founders of the Associated Press of India (now PTI), became the first Indian President of the Imperial Delhi Gymkhana Club. (Now the 'Imperial' has been dropped.) F.C. (Billy) Bhadwar was a member of the Railway Board and, after Mr Bakhle, when the post of the Chief Commissioner was abolished, he became Chairman. There was a joyous interlude when Billy Badhwar got married to Mary in those Western Court years. N.C. Buch and family were occupants of one suite. He was engaged in taking charge of the remnants of the old Political Department and assisting V.P. Menon in the accession and integration of the princely states. This was not easy as it became known that, unlike in external affairs, the conservative Political Secretary Creigh-Cohen had viciously destroyed all confidential records of his department which must have had many historical secrets relating to princely India. Our neighbour was Hugh Davenport, an Englishman married to an Indian who had taken Indian nationality and was engaged in setting up the Employment Exchange system. He became the first secretary of the Delhi Golf Club after the ownership was transferred from the New Delhi Municipal Corporation.

Kashmir question in the UN

I was merely an observer when, in December 1947, the question of referring to the Pakistan-sponsored tribal intrusion into Kashmir was being discussed. This must have been the time that I met Brigadier Sam Manekshaw, who was the first Indian Director of Military Operations, the most important directorate in army headquarters. My contribution was simply being asked by the Secretary General to obtain a copy of the United Nations Charter when the decision-makers were considering whether the reference should be under Chapter VI (Peaceful Resolution of Conflicts) or Chapter VII (which permitted punitive sanctions for violation of the Charter). A high-powered delegation led by Gopalaswami Ayyangar, then Cabinet Minister and former PM of Kashmir, proceeded to New York. The impression created was that Zafarullah Khan, Foreign Minister of Pakistan, in his five-hour intervention, had proved a better advocate than the Indian delegate. Much has already been written about the reference to the UN and, no doubt, will continue to be debated whether it was largely on Mountbatten's persuasion of Nehru. It is alleged that Mountbatten did not want a war between the two new 'dominions' while he was Governor General of one of them. One aspect which has not attracted sufficient comment is that it was a clash of two idealisms. Philip Noel-Baker, who had become Secretary of State of Commonwealth Relations, was a great supporter of the League of Nations as a provider of machinery for the resolution of international disputes by peaceful means. Nehru too, must have been reluctant to appear to be ignoring the spirit of the UN Charter just four months after India's Independence. Noel-Baker was inclined to treat Kashmir in 1948 as a pre-Independence problem, forgetting that paramountcy had lapsed with the British announcement itself, and so the area of the successor dominions was beyond British determination. Once the Standstill Agreement with Kashmir had been superseded by accession to India—ignoring Alistair Lamb's quibbling on the actual timing in his book on Kashmir*—the International Law of sovereign nations carried the right of self-defence. Nehru was under no international legal obligation to offer self-determinatory plebiscite in Kashmir. In other words, the British attitude in the Security Council was not, as it should have been, post-imperialist, but was coloured by the prevailing confidence that Muslim Pakistan, rather than democratic non-aligned India, would be a more lasting friend of the West. It all seems very ironic now.

The proceedings of the Security Council were interrupted by the assassination of Gandhi. When told about it, Nehru was in the committee room next to my own, and I remember him rushing out. John Taylor, a friend from Cambridge, had just been appointed to the British High Commission as Third Secretary. He asked me to come to his office, now the National Defence College, which is located opposite Birla House, to have a grandstand view of the beginning of the funeral procession. But we were forbidden entry by the security guards as there were 'secret' installations, and Indians were debarred from the roof. This prevented me from joining the procession or seeing the massive crowd which accompanied the cortege.

In March when the delegation was due to return to New York, it was strengthened by deputing Sir Girija to go with it and he took me with him. On the way he was invited to meet Clement Attlee, the British PM, in London. Heathrow airport was engulfed by fog and so the Air India plane was diverted to land in Bournemouth on the south coast. There must have been some hurried local improvisations; the stationmaster must have sensed that a VIP from India was landing to see the Prime Minister. A limousine had been hurriedly arranged to draw up to the aircraft, and passport and immigration formalities were waived. Out came a little man, immaculately dressed in a three-piece suit and wearing a homburg hat, accompanied by Brigadier Dileep Choudhary in full uniform (going out as the new Military Attaché in Washington), with me in tow. We motored straight to the railway station under police escort

---

*Alistair Lamb, *Kashmir: A Disputed Legacy* (Roxford Books: 1991).

where the train for London had been held up to take the VIP from India. From the vehicle arriving point, a red carpet had been spread across the platform to the train. The station-master was visibly exhilarated and nervous. As we mounted the awaiting train, he was heard shouting, 'Make way for the Viceroy of India!' Sir Girija had two knighthoods—Knight Commander of the British Empire (KBE) and Knight Commander of the Order of Star of India (KCSI)—and was probably the highest decorated British-Indian civil servant. He may have been inwardly delighted by the stationmaster's gaffe, but as he sat down in his reserved seat, in his Oxford accent he told me, 'Go and tell that flunkey that not only am I not the Viceroy of India but that he is accrediting me to a defunct office.'

Claridges had remained an old-fashioned hotel used by visiting royalty. In my years even at an expensive public school and at Cambridge, I had never stepped into the lobby of a comparable hotel. But to pretend I was not an unworthy PS was difficult as I was wearing a ready-to-wear shiny blue suit acquired from fifty-shilling tailors in a shop in Cambridge! When I entered to register the SG, I had no homburg or bowler hat which was *de rigueur* for diplomats and senior civil servants at the time. But I realized I had to get used to the royal ambience. The reception staff wore red waist-coats and tails, and the room attendants, black uniforms with red piping and buttons with some sort of a crown. Sir Girija must have felt embarrassed to have such a cheaply-dressed PS! One afternoon he said to me, 'Now that you are in the diplomatic service, shall I introduce you to my tailors?' I got the hint and I must have said that I would be grateful, and so we went to Anderson & Sheppard at no. 30, Savile Row. The next morning I went to the premises and ordered my first three-piece suit. Even with the purchase tax exempted, when the parcel was delivered at the airport as an export, it cost twenty-three pounds and ten shillings, which I calculated was exactly equal to my initial salary as an Attaché in the service! Bajpai's introduction meant I was accepted as a client but I was put in category 'C' of the register, which signified payment before delivery! Since then I have had several suits including dinner jackets and, as an extravagance, tails (which I only used once) tailored by them. They were always expensive in comparison with prevailing rates. Over the years I graduated to category 'A', which indicates a reliable, respectable client. They followed my career advancement. At one stage, I was even asked to help realize the outstanding dues from an Indian VIP (I won't mention the name) which, of course, I politely declined. What intrigued me was that there was one man to measure the coat and vest, and another for the trousers! I was also advised that for a proper fall one must not wear a belt, but only braces! The last occasion when, as Foreign Secretary, I went for consultations in 1976, the price of a bespoke suit was 600 pounds.

Sir Girija was a man of extravagance and taste, particular about where he stayed and dined. While the whole delegation went back to Gothams overlooking the Central Park in New York, he insisted on going to his customary base, the old Ritz, which has since been demolished. In New York, he called on the members of the Security Council, notably Sir Alexander Cadogan of the UK, and Senator Austin of the US, but he found the most sympathetic was Ambassador Tsang, who represented Kuomintang, China, now the Republic of China (Taiwan). What surprised and touched me was how devoted he was to his wife, Lady Bajpai. Almost every night he would write to her in Devanagari script using Awadhi. After a few weeks, Sir Girija showed impatience to get home. Almost every single day he would ask me to book the return tickets to Delhi which then had to be cancelled. We were actually in New York for nearly two months. During this period, we paid a visit to Washington, where of course, we stayed with Ambassador Asaf Ali in the official residence in Macomb Street, which overlooks the Rockery Park and which Sir Girija himself had acquired. He had also purchased the Indian Chancery which, though almost on a side street, has the prestigious Massachusetts Avenue address. He incidentally approved the acquisition of Kensington Palace Gardens, the residence in London, the Consulate General in New York and, on a subsequent visit, the ambassador's house in Paris.

The real crisis for me was connected with his proposed return to Delhi. I asked him for his passport, but he assumed that it was with me. I made a frantic search in every drawer and cupboard and finally went down to the hotel laundry and went through hundreds of sheets to see if the passport had been folded with the change of bed linen. While conducting this search of the boss's travel documents, I did not eat the whole day. That evening, Asaf Ali was holding a farewell reception at the Hotel Waldorf-Astoria. On an empty stomach, I gulped down innumerable whiskies. It is probably the only time in my whole career that I got drunk and was virtually carried back in a taxi to the hotel by Dilu Choudhary!

The 21 April Resolution of the Security Council was not to the liking of India or Pakistan but it recognized Sheikh Abdullah in office, and was an improvement on the January version but this too, had to be accepted by the two governments. On 13 August 1948, I remember driving to Maidens Hotel in Old Delhi and delivering our acceptance letter signed by the SG of India to Ambassador Korbel of Czechoslovakia. Later, he wrote *Danger in Kashmir* of which I have a copy with a friendly endorsement by his daughter, Madeleine Albright, while we were both at the Wilson Centre, which is still there in the Castle on the Mall in Washington DC. She later became US Ambassador to the UN and Secretary of State under Clinton, and I suppose the book is more valuable now.

The Ministry, 1947–49

Sir Girija towered over the Ministry. It was at a stage when the old External Affairs had continued its separate identity, but the division of Indian Overseas in the Department of Education, Health and Lands had been transferred and re-designated the Department of Commonwealth Relations (CR) and remained semi-separate. External Affairs itself had no Additional Secretary but had three senior officers at the Joint Secretary level: JS (External) for Political Affairs earlier headed by Humphrey Trevelyan but after the transfer of power, by P.A. Menon, who had been in the Washington Supply Mission during the war; JS (Protocol) of which R.R. Saxena, formerly of the Customs Service (who too, had served abroad, in Canada), was Chief of Protocol and also in charge of the

Consular and Passport Division; and JS (Administration) under S. Ratnam of the Indian Audit and Accounts Service. JS (Ad) supervised over personnel, accounts, supplies and the entire administrative infrastructure. S. Dutt had been called by Bajpai, and was the Commonwealth Secretary (CS). Y.D. Gundevia, who had been Counsellor in the Indian Mission in Rangoon under Ambassador Rauf (of the Congress with a pre-war background of Burma) came back to become Joint Secretary. Crossley, an English member of the ICS and married to an Indian, was Deputy Secretary in the CR Department.

The post of Foreign Secretary had remained vacant after Creighton had left. Sir Girija wrote to K.P.S. Menon in Nanking asking him to take up the post which, for almost a century was the designated head of External Affairs. K.P.S.'s reply showed reluctance and, in his polite style said something to the effect of 'Let us flatter ourselves and take the responsibility in turn'—in other words, he would wait till he replaced Sir Girija himself rather than be his second in command. Thereupon, Sir Girija requested the PM himself to write and finally, K.P.S. overcame his hesitation and joined in April 1948. He was the first Foreign Secretary of independent India and held the post for four years until he was nominated to take over in Moscow from Dr Radhakrishnan who was chosen to be India's first Vice-President after the general elections of 1952. It is interesting that Shivshankar Menon, till recently Foreign Secretary, is the grandson of K.P.S. His uncle (also K.P.S.) was Foreign Secretary, and succeeded A.P. Venkateswaran. Shivshankar's father-in-law, Ram Sathe, took over from me, and his father P.N. Menon too, was in our service, indeed in my batch, and died suddenly when Ambassador to Yugoslavia. There is probably no comparable pedigreed diplomatic family anywhere.

This was, of course, the period when we were expanding our diplomatic network abroad. Asaf Ali had been nominated in February 1947 as Ambassador to the USA; Mrs V.L. Pandit, the PM's sister, went to Moscow in April, and K.P.S., who had been Agent-General succeeding Zafarullah Khan, went back to

China as Ambassador, but all three took up their respective appointments before the formal transfer of power. Krishna Menon was, of course, made High Commissioner in the UK and took over on 15 August from M.K. Vellodi who had been acting since Sir Samuel Runganathan had left. The first full-fledged mission in Western Europe was in Switzerland. The country held special importance for Nehru. It had been neutral during the war and, aside from being the hub of competing allied and axis intelligence, was an island of prosperity. Moreover, it was where Nehru had nursed his wife Kamla, in the last stages of her illness. Dhirubhai Desai (the son of the eminent Congress lawyer Bhulabhai) who, I think, had been to school in Switzerland and was fluent in French, was therefore, an obvious choice for opening the Legation in Bern in March 1948. Later, Sir N.R. Pillai was sent as Commissioner General and Chargé d'Affaires to Paris until H.S. Malik was transferred from Ottawa in mid-1948 as Ambassador.

An insider's view of setting up diplomatic networks in India

This was the time when all kinds of people outside the established civil services, with active or pretended association with Nehru or the Congress, applied for diplomatic assignments. Dewan Chaman Lall of the Punjab Congress, married to the elegant Helen, was an understandable choice for Ankara; Wing Commander Rup Chand from an influential frontier family was selected for Kabul. But there were many aspirants who were political lightweights who wrote to Nehru volunteering for diplomatic appointments. The PM would pass these letters to the SG which landed in my tray. Some aspirants were called to meet with the SG. I remember a delightful epistle from a progressive Muslim who wanted to be sent as Ambassador to France; alternatively, as Ambassador to Australia, but if these were not available, he concluded, he would not mind going as Consul to New Zealand!

All the senior officers, Secretaries and Joint Secretaries gathered in my room before going to the SG's room. All of them sat around the SG's vast table. (Only non-officials were taken to the sofa). In these meetings, incoming telegrams were discussed and directions given for replies. (Now only secretaries meet regularly as there are twenty plus joint secretaries). Sir Girija disclosed even to me his contempt for the ability and drafting facility of most senior officers. I saw no trace of Girija 'toadying' against Indian Independence. The style of the SG and the PM were different, but there was mutual respect for each other's writing skills. Sir Girija had balanced cadences, like Gibbon or Macaulay, which showed he had imbibed the classics. It was a pleasure to hear him dictate; he would specify punctuation marks. Nehru's style was more fluent. The PM invariably came to Sir Girija's room on his way in and out of the Secretariat and seldom summoned him except for meetings. At times, I would be with Sir Girija when the PM walked in. They would exchange drafted replies. More than once I heard the PM say, 'Your draft expresses my thoughts better; let yours go as from the PM to Sir B.N. Rau.' Rau had gone as Ambassador to the UN when India came on the Security Council.

Seniority on interleaving the Foreign Service after initial constitution

The SG became somewhat arbitrary in the recruitment of the overage officers in the Foreign Service. Rao Sahib M.K. Narayanan, working with the new Joint Secretary B.N. Chakravarty and the SG, was involved in the initial constitution of the IFS, interleaving it with the ICS and competitively selected officers like our group. The immediate demands were such that the Foreign Service could not rely on new cadets from the annual examinations, so both the IAS and the IFS had initial overage recruitment. Both Chakravarty and Narayanan used to consult me with various alternatives. Since all of them have passed away, I suppose I am the only one who can throw light on the arbitrariness in the initial seniority pattern and the gratuitous benefits which some got. In the beginning, we took six or seven former maharajas or princes who were selected by V.P. Menon, Secretary and Advisor to the Ministry of States. Since the army headquarters were opposed to former INA officers being embodied in their regiments, political considerations had to find appropriate openings for them in other branches of the civil government. Some, like Shah Nawaz, went straight into politics, and we took a few into the IFS. (Apart from A.H. Safrani, they were Mahboob Ahmed, C.J. Stracey, M.M. Khurana, etc.)

Recruitment and initial seniority of overage selection

The real problem was that we did not—as did the Home Ministry—notify in advance the basis of seniority and so after the selection, the problem of interleaving overage officers arose. For example, an officer born in 1916 was placed as senior to another who was born in 1908 but both would have to retire when they reached fifty-eight. In some cases officers did not have the qualifying university degree. At least one officer was above forty-five, which was contrary to the Cabinet decision; another on V.P. Menon's list of former princes was accepted, but he was nineteen and so, underage. A new categorization of Senior Under Secretary was devised to give ranking equivalent of Deputy Secretary to one with only five years' service—to make the grade one had to have eight or nine years' service. The application of this principle enabled Sunil Roy of our batch who had 1943 seniority to jump several places. Those who had come through competitive selection—whether the ICS or from the Political Service or war service, and were born between 1918–24—had a fixed seniority and a higher ranking than those of the same year of birth. This enabled us to get an advantage over the ones not selected through competitive selection at the normal age.

October 1948: First Commonwealth Conference

In October 1948 the first Commonwealth Conference of PMs after the war was held in London. For the first time Indian diplomatic passports were used. Nehru's was D000001; mine was D000008 and I still have it in my possession as a treasured souvenir. For the first time the Commonwealth had a mixed ethnic complexion. Apart from the white Dominions, there was Nehru from India, Liaquat Ali Khan from Pakistan and Sir John Kotelawala from Ceylon (now Sri Lanka). Nehru was certainly the most handsome and well-dressed person amongst the group and the most dominant personality. I was generally left in Claridges as the archivist and receptionist of telephone messages but I was helped by persons deputed from India House. I did go to Downing Street when Mathai went to look around London! Nehru was assigned the corner suite, number 212 on the second floor of Claridges, and Girija, a smaller sitting room down the corridor. I was in a cubbyhole, overlooking the inner courtyard with a small attached bathroom. I was also the Protocol Officer, Catering-in-charge, and the one to receive and see off VIPs who came to see the PM. I remember Nehru asking me to invite Ernie Bevin, then Foreign Secretary, and to ascertain from the PS what he would like for breakfast. The PS conveyed grateful acceptance and added Mr Bevin would like chicken curry for breakfast! He was already corpulent and Nehru was amused, but asked me to make sure the Claridges cooks knew how to make a curry. 'If not, order it from Veeraswamy or some other Indian restaurant.' I told the Claridges people to do their best and either prepare it with plenty of Indian ingredients or bring it from a restaurant. I did not want to take the responsibility of choosing how spicy it should be to suit Mr Bevin's taste!

Somewhere, I still have a slip from a 10 Downing Street pad from Sir Stafford Cripps inviting Nehru for the weekend to his Yorkshire country home. Nehru wrote back that he was going to Broadlands, the Mountbatten country house in Hampshire. During this three-week stay, I noticed that Nehru went to Broadlands every weekend. Even when invited to Chequers by the British PM for part of the weekend, he drove right across southern England to the Hampshire estate of the Mountbattens. There was really no concealing Nehru's attachment to and regard for Lady

Mountbatten, but to me there was nothing invidious about it. Lord Louis respected Nehru, but between Nehru and Edwina there was a greater mutual trust and special confidence. He went to the theatre on free evenings, sometimes alone with Edwina. He was clearly familiar with the West End shops and frequently went to Hatchards and bought quite a few books.

After three weeks or so, we flew to Paris where the UN General Assembly was having its annual meeting. The PM and Mathai stayed in George Cinq, the best new hotel, but Sir Girija stuck to his old favourite, the Ritz in the Place de la Vendôme and, of course, I was in tow. The Paris Ritz is a famous aristocratic hotel where the wives of the French elite gather for afternoon tea. The suite next to Sir Girija's was occupied by the Duke (formerly King Edward VIII who abdicated) and the Duchess of Windsor. We had already signified our acceptance of the SC Resolution to the United Nations Commission for India and Pakistan (UNCIP) but there were ongoing discussions on the ceasefire, so Sir Girija stayed on in Paris. Mrs Pandit led the delegation; Jam Sahib and Shiv Rao were among the delegates. For me it was fun spending evenings with the junior members of the Indian delegation who were staying in Hotel Royal Monceau off the Etoile. They included P.L. Bhandari, former editor of the *Civil & Military Gazette,* and Senior Public Relations Officer deputed from London, with Subhan who had come from Delhi as his deputy; Baiji Sobhag Kanwar who was fluent in French and German, and with our shared Rajasthani loyalties, became a friend. Mr Ewatt, the Australian Foreign Minister, was President of the General Assembly and hosted the traditional ball which I enjoyed attending with an attractive French girl attached to our Mission.

Dhirubhai Desai was a member of the delegation and, due to his father's friendship, he had special regard for Sir Girija. He used to take the SG to the most expensive restaurants in Paris. I was taken along on several occasions. I remember being taken to La Tour d'Argent, the ultimate in French cuisine. Its specialty was duck, and each diner was given the serial number (running into thousands), of the duck being served, since the end of the nineteenth century when the restaurant was opened. I have never been able to afford to go to La Tour d' Argent or Maxim's since the first year of my career!

April 1949: India stays in the Commonwealth

My work as PS in Delhi was always exciting but I had to get used to the long hours and truncated weekends. The PM and the Secretary (and often, no other officers) came regularly to the Ministry on Saturdays, and even on Sunday mornings and all other holidays. I did, too. One Sunday, just to indicate that it was the weekly holiday, I went to the office in a red shirt and a bow tie—both Cambridge acquisitions. Sir Girija noticed this sartorial audacity and signified his disapproval by politely remarking on my youthful taste. I gingerly mentioned that Sunday had to be different even in the Foreign Office. The PM saw me in the corridors and was amused but unlike my direct boss made no critical comment.

Sir Girija and I also attended the second Commonwealth PMs' Conference in April 1949. This was historically important as, since that meeting, the Commonwealth has remained a multiracial association, and therefore has survived to this day. The specific reason for the 1949 meeting was that India was willing to stay in the Commonwealth but could not repudiate the resolution passed by the Constituent Assembly in December 1946 that India would be a Sovereign Democratic Republic. The Australian PM Menzies and his New Zealand counterpart, Keith Holyoake said that lack of respect to the Crown would not be accommodated in the British Empire or its succession. The Canadians were keen that like Burma, India should not break the British connection established over time. There was a furious debate inside and outside 10 Downing Street. It all finally hinged on finding a string of words which would comply with respect to the King and yet allow association with a republic. Drafts were made with inputs from many, including Nehru himself. Sir Girija intervened one day and quoted from the Statute of Westminster, 'Dominions were to be self-governing, in no way subordinate to each other,' etc. Attlee expressed incredulity and asked, 'Are you sure of this wording?'

Girija pulled himself up to his full height, and in his Oxford accent said, 'Of all around this table, I was the only one there in 1931.' When a copy of the Statute was produced, he quickly turned to the page and identified the relevant paragraph. Everyone was astounded at his memory and expertise. The credit for the final formula must go to Sir Girija and the Canadian Foreign Minister Lester Pearson. The King would be the 'Head of the Commonwealth and the symbol of our association.' Thus King George VI remained the head of the old empire.

After the agreement was announced in the media, I received a telephone call from the PS of Winston Churchill—he had not yet accepted the Knighthood of the Garter—that his chief would like to call on PM Nehru. We were due to leave the next morning and Nehru told me to call the PS and say that there was no question of Churchill's coming to see him; he himself would go on his way to the airport. Churchill's house, if I remember correctly, was on the south side off Hyde Park. Considering Churchill's long and bitter animosity towards India's Independence, this meeting was symbolic of the magnanimity of both statesmen. In the aircraft as we were flying out of Heathrow, Nehru described the meeting. Apparently Churchill said, 'Mr PM, I have done you great wrong. You are like the prodigal whom we thought lost. You have saved the legacy of the empire' or words to that effect.

On a subsequent visit when Churchill was again PM, after a similar Commonwealth meeting, he took Nehru back to Harrow, their old school and joined him in singing old songs. At the banquet in the Hall of Westminster, Churchill in his monosyllabic diction paid his famous tribute, 'Mr PM, you have conquered two great human infirmities. You have conquered fear and you have conquered hate.' Nehru and Churchill developed a great regard for each other. In 1955, Churchill called Nehru the 'Light of Asia'. Nehru would telephone Sir Winston even when passing through London. I have no doubt that had Churchill revisited India, Nehru would have presided over a great public welcome to an old imperialist signifying how both could rise above former animosities.

4

Rama

I met Rama in a chance encounter during a Christmas party treasure hunt in the Delhi Gymkhana Club in 1948 when I disclosed to her that clue number four was behind the picture of poplars in the dining room. A fortnight later, she was assigned to my office in the Ministry of External Affairs for initial training as one of the two newly appointed women Foreign Service officers. An additional desk was put in my room. I had only about a year-and-a-half's experience but was considered senior enough to train incoming overage officers. About the same time, the Nawab of Pataudi, then about 39, was also sent to me to provide him with 'an introduction to diplomacy'. I was Private Secretary to the Secretary General, but had volunteered to work simultaneously as Under Secretary (US). I was made US (AWT) (Arab World and Turkey) so that I had a small area of direct responsibility at the lowest secretariat officer level. The unsolicited training inflicted on me was flattering, but a nuisance. I was distracted by their small talk led by the Nawab Sahib. Rama was also full of charm and used to bring me paan after lunch. I had no alternative but to suppress my irritation.

During the Holi holidays, barely two months after we met, I went to Udaipur and sought the approval of the family of my intention to choose my own bride. I gave plausible arguments. Though not of the same caste, Rama came from a respectable Gujarati family; her father N.C. Mehta was in the U.P. cadre of the ICS and had friends in high places; her brother was soon getting married to Chandralekha, the eldest daughter of Mrs Vijaya Lakshmi

Pandit, the PM's sister, etc. Suggestions for my engagement had, of course, been made practically at every meal since I was ten. By 1949 the family knew there was little hope of finding even a matriculate girl in our caste. Anyway, I was gratified that my grandfather and my uncle approved. I proposed to Rama on my return to Delhi, but Rama gave her consent only two weeks later; in fact, while we were attending the reception for her brother and Chandralekha on the Teen Murti lawns.

My father had been nominated to open the Indian Mission in the Netherlands in 1948. The Dutch were one of the first to establish an embassy and had sent Lamping, a very senior ambassador, to Delhi. In fact, apart from the British High Commission, the only other missions opened before the formal transfer of power were from the US and Kuomintang (KMT) China. Our reciprocal gesture had, however, been postponed until there was indication that the Netherlands was sincere in its intention of transfering power in Indonesia. Our approach became clearer after the New Delhi conference on Indonesia held in February 1949. The American mediatory efforts in April were successful and so our hesitations were set aside. My father was told to proceed to The Hague as quickly as possible. This meant that we had to rush the plans for our marriage. The invitations were posted the day we left so that they would be delivered to people in Delhi including those in the Ministry only after both of us had departed for our respective homes, she for Simla and I for Udaipur. Since Rama was only in the first year of her service, she was not entitled to any earned leave. With ten days' casual leave and weekends added, I went through the shortened, but full traditional ceremonies in Udaipur, and journeyed with a party of twenty-five (numbers were restricted at the time) by train to Simla. I got married on 7 July, attended the reception at Yarrows, the house of my father-in-law, then Chief Commissioner, Himachal, returned to Udaipur for the grahpravesh and more ceremonies, and returning by train, we were both back in Delhi on Monday morning at our respective desks. There was no time for a holiday or so-called honeymoon.

Rama's education

From what I could gather, Rama had excelled both in school and college. She must have done well at the Isabella Thoburn College in Lucknow where she did her first degree and became quite an accomplished bharatanatyam dancer. She came to Delhi and did an MA in philosophy. My granddaughter Megnaa was truly taken aback when, in 2005, she too chose philosophy as one of her subjects for BA at St. Stephen's and found a photograph of her grandmother as one of the early distinguished postgraduates in the subject. In 1946—one year after the end of the war—she went to the US and after an initial stay at Ann Arbor University, moved to Columbia in New York where she did a degree in psychology. For nearly two years she stayed in the International House attached to the university. There were not many Indian boys and even fewer girls then pursuing higher education in America. The UK was still the favoured destination, but the few who did, became industrial magnates like Keshub Mahindra and Ajit Haksar, or managers and great intellectuals like Ravi Matthai. One of Rama's great friends was Valsa Matthai, the daughter of John Matthai, then a director of Tatas, later a minister in the Central Cabinet, and Helen, a pioneer in the incipient movement towards women's emancipation. Valsa committed suicide by jumping into the River Hudson and it left an ineradicable scar on Rama's mind.

Rama returned to India in 1948. It was K.P.S. Menon (Sr), an old friend of the family from Simla, who persuaded Rama to apply for the overage recruitment to the FS, which was then underway. When Rama was selected, she was staying in 22 Curzon Road, the residence of Sir Shri Ram, who was the most eminent public-spirited industrialist in the capital. The Curzon Road residence was a joint family home. While Sir Shri Ram lived simply in a small room in a corner of the front veranda, his sons Bharat and

Charat, with their wives and young children occupied suites on the first floor. Rama was treated as a member of this extended family and it remains so even to this day. Sir Shri Ram was particularly fond of Rama and even suggested that she should get married from his house. Sheila and Arun Bharat Ram (recently Chairman of CII), in fact, travelled to Simla for our marriage. In comparison with Rama's family and those with whom it was associated, I came from a very conservative milieu.

Marriage and Rama's compulsory resignation

It was only thanks to Nehru that Rama was allowed to continue working. He overruled my old boss, the SG who, being socially very conservative, had categorically asserted that in diplomacy a woman's role was that of a hostess.

We were then following the British FS regulation that a woman officer must notify and resign when she intended to get married. Incidentallly, we also had rules that there should be no non-Indian alliances; at least permission had to be sought. Notwithstanding Nehru's intervention, Rama was told she could work only as long as I was serving at headquarters. The rules have since been modified.

The next FS couple after us was Manorama Kochchar and Hardev Bhalla, but that was nine years later. They got six postings together or near each other.

Rama in a purdah household

I confess I was no intellectual match for Rama; I did not have her sensitivity or her insights. I had only superficially described to her how conservative the prevailing atmosphere was in my own family. I remember that the large reception party at the Udaipur railway station was aghast when they saw the bride not only sitting with the groom but wearing a sari with her face uncovered. The maidservants rushed Rama to a corner of the station and dressed her in the traditional Rajasthan ghagra and odhni. Thereafter, she dutifully did whatever she was told by the senior maidservants to observe the traditional rituals, including actually pressing the feet of the many senior in-laws, starting with my grandmother and aunt, Bhabhi. For years thereafter, she kept her face covered and observed modest reticence like any Rajasthani daughter-in-law. We had rigid segregation of men and women in day quarters. She virtually stopped wearing saris during the stay in Udaipur. People did not believe that she was an officer who had broken into a man's preserve in the higher civil service. Rama at once won the approval not only of the ladies but also the senior men for not outraging Udaipur customs. Bhabhi took her to the palace, and the senior Maharani, seeing her purdah-covered docility and dutiful attitude, actually sent for an English newspaper and asked her to read it to prove that she was, in fact, English-educated! Our visits to Udaipur were necessarily short, but she observed the traditional customs. Vijay, our daughter, was born in June 1951 under parental supervision in a Bombay nursing home, but Dhapu, a maidservant had been sent from Udaipur to help before and after the delivery.

Rama in and out of diplomacy

Rama's tenure in the Ministry was brief. After some time she was given independent charge as US (IA) (Iran and Afghanistan) as well as (AMS) (the Americas). When she took over, the most senior Office Superintendent (OS) in the entire government was Rai Sahib Rajaram. He had joined the old External Affairs Department in 1910; in other words, before Sir Henry McMahon became Foreign Secretary. Throughout those thirty-nine years, he had been dealing with the Frontier, Iran and Afghanistan, and was virtually a walking encyclopaedia on the region. He was promoted to Assistant Secretary but, in those days Assistant Secretaries retired at fifty-five while an OS could continue till the age of sixty, so Rai Sahib chose to revert to OS to continue in service. He was utterly shocked to find that his immediate boss was going to be a young girl of barely twenty-six. He complained to Foreign Secretary

K.P.S. Menon. Eventually Rajaram came to respect Rama and even tutored her in the refinements of secretariat practices and procedures.

As Under Secretary for Americas, she must have helped process the first cultural agreement between the US and India. It was signed by Nehru for India, and by Loy Henderson, US Ambassador in 1950. A photograph shows Deputy Secretary I.S. Chopra and Joint Secretary C.S. Jha with Maulana Abul Kalam Azad, the Education Minister, and Dr Tara Chand, Secretary, who represented the Education Ministry.

All her life Rama never stopped teasing me that if she had not been obliged to resign, she would have done better in the Foreign Service than I did! In reality she was primarily a sensitive sociologist. Her strength was in human equations and the ability to forge friendships by showing empathic concern towards those she met, including other diplomats and their wives. She always grudged coming with me to cocktail parties and dinners, but once at a party, while I moved around looking about for others to engage with, she would stay put and others would gravitate towards her. In Bern, she conversed for two hours in French every Thursday with Maria Burgi, a scholar in Indian philosophy, to improve her fluency. Some of my own colleagues in the FS—Salman Haider in Delhi, C.V. Ranganathan, K. Raghunath, Damodarans and Kalyanpurkers in Peking, Wadchu Khanna and Kukoo Sharma in Bonn, Shanti Parthasarthi in Dar es Salaam, Razia Doshi, Kalpana Shashank as young wives, and several others, had independent equations with her. She is also remembered by many of my old PAs, such as Kailash Srivastava, the late Kashi Chakravarty, Om Bhasin (now 95), Thakur Singh and Hella Sarma. Rama took a keen interest in families with children, particularly in small missions like Tanzania. In Peking, she was available to everyone for counsel.

An unusual consular case that came to me was resolved with Rama's help. One day at lunchtime, we got a call from Geneva from Saraswati behn, the wife of Khimjibhai Mehta, a magnate from Uganda. Speaking only in Gujarati, she said that she and her three young children had been abandoned by her husband who had run away with a South American girl. There were many legal complications but Rama, who accompanied me, with her fluency in Gujarati, helped to calm the natural anxieties of Saraswati behn, who developed such trust that she moved to London when we were transferred; she entrusted all her jewellery, worth millions and unlisted, for safe custody to Rama. The friendship lasted a lifetime and included advice on the upbringing of her children. What makes it remarkable is that after fifteen years when Khimjibhai returned home, Saraswati behn, like a patibrata Hindu wife, welcomed him without complaint. But for Rama she might have been shattered, and I learnt how important it was to have compassion in consular cases.

Carol Laise

No story about Rama can be complete without mentioning her lifelong friendship with Carol Laise. Carol was a member of the American Foreign Service and was posted in Delhi in 1956 when we first met her. Thereafter, she adopted our family and we in turn shared her personal concerns. We spent every Christmas, all Indian festivals and many evenings together in her house on 17 Prithviraj Road. Her Austin 1955 vintage car is still with us because she did not want to sell it. Rama, Carol and I visited Kullu, Khajuraho, Mandu, Kashmir, etc. and, of course, Udaipur. When apart, Rama and Carol wrote to each other almost every week.

Rama lived through Carol's period of indecision whether or not to marry Ellsworth Bunker after Harriet, his first wife, passed away in 1963. Ellsworth had been persuaded to become Ambassador to Vietnam when Carol was already Ambassador to Nepal. President Lyndon Johnson promised Ellsworth a jet which could land on the small airstrip in Kathmandu so that they could spend weekends together. It is the only known wedding between two serving ambassadors. Carol and Ellsworth got married in

Kathmandu in January 1967. Rama was on a Fellowship at the Institute of Advanced Studies at Radcliffe (Harvard) so she could not attend. However, except for Ellsworth's younger son Sam, then with the Ford Foundation in Delhi, only the Mehta family was invited to Kathmandu. Vijay, our daughter, was Carol's bridesmaid, and my three sons and I were witnesses. In later years when our children were studying in the US, Ellsworth's house in Brattleboro, Vermont, was a second home for them.

We never tried to conceal this special friendship with Carol from anyone. She rose to be Assistant Secretary and retired as Director-General of the American Foreign Service. Ellsworth, having served eight postwar Presidents, including a spell as Ambassador to India from 1957 to 1961, and in addition entrusted with many special assignments, was in and out of the White House for over thirty years. Accusations were rampant that Carol was a plant from the CIA to ferret secrets from me but we ourselves had no doubt that Carol was both a good American and a great friend of India. In fact, she was befriended by many eminent personalities including Indira Gandhi, Khushwant Singh, Gen. Thimayya, B.K. Nehru, Inder Malhotra, Ms Mukherjee of the AICC, and countless others from most political parties in the Delhi VIP circuit. Carol passed away a few years later, a victim of breast cancer.

Rama's friendship with Carol was a tribute to the strength of two independent characters. It symbolized that, while diplomacy involves political patriotism to one's own country, it does not rule out human relationships. None in our family can think of Rama without the unquestioned affection and generosity of Carol, but there was self-confidence and courage and national loyalties on the part of both Rama and Carol and, if I may say so, on my part as well.

Rama as an intellectual

Rama's sociologically thoughtful perspective was a blend of tradition and modernity. She was a bit of a pioneer in women's emancipation, equal rights and participation, but she believed in preserving the cohesion of the family and allowing it to evolve gradually to modernization. Even so she brought about a one-woman revolution in the traditional homes of Udaipur. Her sociological scholarship became known in the city. University professors and young girls used to flock to Jeewan Niwas to sit with her and seek her guidance. When I was in Delhi, Rama used to go quite frequently to meet Prof. Srinivasan and Prof. Madan at the university. She, in turn, was visited by a succession of foreign academics. She knew how to ask questions. The essence of her approach was that social change cannot be effected with a jolt. There had to be a right to education for girls but the exercise of such rights must not be deliberately provocative.

Rama was a modest person who never boasted of her intellectual achievements, but others discovered her incisive and analytical talents. She was inscribed for a Ph.D on the Bhakti Movement in Delhi University and was invited to international sociological conferences. In the mid-seventies she escorted Rose Jurgensen (née Vincent), the wife of the French Ambassador, around Rajasthan. Rose was an author and wanted to write a book on women in India on the basis of Rama's insights, and call it *Rama*. Rama firmly discouraged the idea. It came out under the title *Mohini*, and was dedicated to Rama but, on Rama's insistence, as a cover-up, many other Indian names were added to the inscription. In the summer of 1975 she lectured at Sorbonne (Paris). She first got a fellowship at the Radcliffe Institute of Independent Study in 1964–65. She must have proved herself because she was again offered a fellowship in 1967–68. I encouraged these sabbaticals and so did the children. Even during her first fellowship, she seems to have made a great impression on the Director, Constance (Connie) Smith.

After Rama passed away, many Harvard and Radcliffe colleagues, as well as Ellsworth Bunker and Carol, Kenneth and Catherine Galbraith, Patrick and Elizabeth Moynihan, and other good friends, endowed the Rama Mehta lectureship at Radcliffe on 'Third World Women's Problems'. It is the only lecture on the subject at Harvard, and possibly any other university. In the last twenty-five years Kenneth and Kitty Galbraith have kept on adding to the corpus, and they make it a point to attend the dinner which follows the lecture. I do not have a full list but, if I recall correctly, amongst the lecturers there have been women leaders from Kenya, South Africa, Jamaica, etc., and also Benazir Bhutto from Pakistan. Geeta Sen, an economist, delivered a lecture, which was presided over and commented upon by Prof. Amartya Sen, who recalled that he had visited us in the mid-fifties. In the year 2006 the lecture was given by Bina Agrawal of the Institute of Economic Growth, Delhi. The last lecture of the 2008–09 series was delivered by Hauwa Ibrahim, a defense lawyer. The title was, 'Stone her to death? Why? Defending women within Sharia Courts.' If the lectureship continues, as I am told Radcliffe hopes, it will be a lasting intellectual memorial to Rama's interest in the emancipation of women.

Rama was a good listener and consistently showed interest in the social problems of the country in which we were stationed. Even in Peking, where I was serving in 1963–66 after the India-China War, when the Indian Embassy was virtually ostracized, she managed to visit Chinese jails in the company of locally resident, foreign-origin communists. In Germany, she became friendly with Frau Dr Karstens, the wife of the then head of the Foreign Office (Auswärtiges Amt) because of a shared interest in social problems. One of Rama's great triumphs was that she attracted the attention of President Julius Nyerere, who ordered and read all her books. He invited Rama to come back and make a sociological study of the problems of women in Tanzania. Unfortunately, she died before she could undertake this assignment.

Similarly, the young King of Bhutan asked Rama to make a study of his country. Only a month before she passed away, guided by and in the company of the Queen Mother, she visited several monasteries and wanted to write an analysis of the evolution of Bhutan with its traditional Tibetan psychology.

Rama's most remarkable achievement was when Shah-Banu Farah, after a dinner conversation in 1977, asked her to come to Iran and make a study of women's problems in the country. The New Delhi Embassy of Iran received instructions from the palace to arrange for 'Mrs Mehta's visit to Tehran'. PM Morarji Desai did not think Rama, the wife of the Foreign Secretary, should avail of such a ticket even though it was transparently non-political. I told her that, since her journey was totally academic and in response to her sociological interest, she could go at her own expense, but she was not wholly convinced and was inclined to decline the opportunity.

Rama as a Sociologist

Between 1956 and 1961, when I was at headquarters, she wrote an article every week for the *Hindustan Times*, and one every fortnight for the *Tribune* in Chandigarh. Her books on sociology were titled *Western Educated Hindu Women* and later, *Hindu Divorced Women*. It may have been one of the earliest studies, after divorce was permitted by the Hindu Reform Act of 1955. Her essay titled 'From Purdah to Modernity' is a compilation of lectures of the Nehru Museum but the title is based on her contribution. All her novels have Udaipur as their backdrop. 'Ramu' is a children's story of how a little boy enjoyed the Haryali Amavasya fair which is held during the monsoon months on the banks of Lake Fateh Sagar. 'Keshav' is the fictionalized story of a young boy who was the son of a chaprasi in Vidya Bhawan. With Kitty Galbraith, she authored *India Now and In Time*. Kitty wanted it to be dedicated to Averell (Harriman), but Rama insisted it should be in the memory of Connie (Smith) (who had been Rama's mentor and friend) as head of Radcliffe (Harvard). We have been remiss in that that a manuscript on *The Hindu Family and Modern Values*, which she completed the day before her heart attack, has not yet been published. Prof. Madan of Delhi University thinks it has great merit and would be as incisive as her earlier sociological works. Unfortunately, Rama had not organized the supporting data on which it was based, but we still hope it can be published sometime. Santha Ram Rao's analysis of Rama's total writing is also a remarkable tribute. It must be published along with a compilation of her hitherto unpublished works.

In 1979 *Inside the Haveli* was chosen by the Sahitya Akademi as the best book of the year by an Indian author in English. Unfortunately, in the meantime, she had passed away. With uncontrolled tears, I received the award on her behalf. It was national recognition of the book as an authentic portrayal of a time when purdah was the prevalent way of life in middle-class homes.

Even after thirty years the last novel continues to have a steady shelf life with an average sale of about 1000 copies every year. It was first published by Arnold Heinemann, reprinted by Women's Press of England, and was eventually brought out as a Penguin classic. The book vividly describes Gita's—a substitute name for Rama herself—experiences with her near and distant relations. It has been translated into French, into Urdu for the Pakistani readership and unofficially also into Hindi.

Rama may have had some premonition that her days were numbered. With the help of my first cousin Pratap Kanwar, she invited all known Udaipuris in Delhi just a week or so before she passed away to emphasize that she now felt Udaipur was her own home. Bim Bissell recalls that Rama insisted that she come for a game of bridge that week. She seems to have made many visits which, in retrospect, appear to have been farewell calls.

Mrs Kaul, at the house of the then Foreign Minister Atal Bihari Vajpayee, saw Rama on various occasions. She felt very anxious about Rama's steady loss of weight and compelled her to go to the Willingdon Hospital—now renamed Dr Ram Manohar Lohia Hospital. But Rama did not allow Mrs Kaul to accompany her during the consultations. I suspect she might have been given a warning by the doctor.

When Rama's dear friend Daisy came to India on a holiday in

May 1978, Rama asked her to come and see her 'immediately'. Apparently Rama disclosed to Daisy that the doctor at Willingdon had shown anxiety about her condition. Daisy was alarmed and said, 'Why don't you tell Jagat to take leave and take you abroad?' Rama swore her to secrecy and said, 'Jagat is busy with too many responsibilities and anxieties. I don't want to be a further burden. The children are also on the threshold of their careers and will be totally distraught.'

Rama had a heart attack the day after Uday came of age

On 4 June 1978, our youngest son Uday turned twenty-one. It is also the birthday of our daughter Vijay, six years older. Rama was happy that her youngest had come of age and she had, as it were, discharged her parental responsibility. I had come down from an MEA consultative conference from Simla that morning. Even though it was a Sunday, since I was leaving the next day on a long and important tour with the PM and the Foreign Minister, I had to spend a few hours in the office. For the rest of the day, the family was together and we were happy to have all four children together after many years. Almost her last private conversation with me was when she showed me the letter of Uday's admission, with full scholarship for his Ph.D from Princeton. He had already done us proud by a double graduation both in philosophy and politics at Swarthmore. Vasu (Vasundhara Raje)—later the Chief Minister of Rajasthan—who was very friendly with our family, was the only other person with us at dinner. After dinner the children left to have coffee in Hotel Taj Mansingh and Rama and I were left alone, but she told me to sleep for a few hours.

I got up to leave at four o'clock to make my way to Palam Airport to board the airplane for Tehran, after which I was to go to Brussels, London and the US. Rama woke up early, which was unusual for her, when I was leaving as if to say goodbye. She knew the first stop was Tehran. Rama told me that on reflection she would follow my advice and go to Iran at her own expense. She knew that the country was facing similar problems in its evolution to modernity from a traditional society. It never transpired because that very evening she had her fatal heart attack.

The PM and the party did stop off in Tehran for a few hours; we flew to the palace by helicopter. I had no chance to convey Rama's consent to travel at her own expense. We then flew to Brussels and had consultations with the European Union. We were staying in the Royal Palace guest house. After the banquet when we were going to our rooms, Vikram rang and told me that 'Bhabhi has had a severe heart attack and was taken to the Willingdon Hospital and then to the ICU of Azad Memorial Hospital.' He also said, 'We had all just come back from dinner with Mrs Bum Suk Lee, the wife of the Korean Ambassador, and Bhabhi was packing to leave for Udaipur the next morning.'

On the morning of 6 June I turned round from London and arrived in Delhi the next day. Rama was unconscious. I would like to believe that she opened her eyes and saw me but she could not talk. On 7 June, in the evening, she passed away. All the children were in the anteroom of the ICU. We had earlier gone to the temple in Chandni Chowk, but our prayers were not answered. The funeral at Nigambodh Ghat was attended by many dignitaries including several ministers and Chandra Shekhar, who was then in the Opposition, but later PM.

After two days we drove to Udaipur for the mourning baithak or condolence meetings. It was here that Foreign Minister Vajpayee telephoned me; they understood the shock, but the delegation would be very ineffective without me and hinted whether I could come for the Washington part of the visit. The PM and party had first gone to the west coast in the US. I decided to rush to Washington and was with the PM and the Foreign Minister at Blair House and during the important talk with President Carter.

Rama had been an escort officer with Rosalynn Carter when the President had visited India in January 1978. She expressed genuine sorrow at the sudden passing away of my wife.

It is now nearly thirty years but the family still feels Rama's absence, as indeed do many relations in Udaipur, and friends in Delhi and all over the world. Her legacy is somewhat intangible. She made the children touch the feet of even the senior servants like Gokulji and be friends with the younger ones.

Ajay and Inder, the son of the faithful retainer Gangaramji, used to go fishing together. To this day Vijay has concern for Sita who, as *Inside the Haveli* indicates, is about the same age and by now is a grandmother. The children were also taught not to be ashamed of Udaipur traditions. They were often criticized in Delhi for not doing namaste but bending down to do mujra. However, they never felt any inhibition at this symbolic gesture associated with feudalism. It was probably this respect for and acceptance of tradition which enabled my daughter Vijay to fit into what may well be the last purdah-observing Muslim family in India. Apparently, Vijay won the trust and affection of Rani Amma, her mother-in-law, the Rani Sahiba of the erstwhile princely state of Mahmudabad.

Since Rama passed away, many friends have confided to me how much they owe to Rama's confidential counsel. Many women have told me that if their marriages have survived, it is largely because of Rama. She was not from Udaipur, but as she said in the dedication in *Inside the Haveli*, Mohan Kaka and Bhabhi gave her a home in Udaipur. She had lived in U.P., Delhi, Simla, studied abroad, gone to Radcliffe in Harvard, travelled with me, but had no shred of doubt that, despite being backward and underdeveloped, Udaipur gave her a feeling of 'roots'. It provided her with the assurance of a support system. She was, of course, accepted not just by my Bhabhi but also by many in the extended family. Rama's affections still remain memorable.

Rama died when she was only fifty-three. I suddenly recalled that the family astrologer had hinted as much by saying that he was not able to read the lines further. I feel guilty that in my preoccupation with work, I had neglected to pay attention to Rama's health. Rama left an imprint not only on her four children but also on a large circle in Udaipur, friends in Delhi and other parts of India and abroad for her exceptional qualities. The walls of Jeewan Niwas and the pages of *Inside the Haveli* evoke both nostalgia and gratitude for the home she created for those of us who knew her, but the grandchildren who came afterwards too, have asked for her photographs in Rajasthani poshak. They seem to have a sense of belonging to Jeewan Niwas because of their grandmother. The Queen Mother of Bhutan lighted 1000 candles in the principal monasteries after Rama's passing.

5

Induction into the Administration (1949–51)

I had been Private Secretary to the Secretary General for two years and was inwardly satisfied that I had belied Baddrudin Tyabji's caution to my father that no one had lasted more than three months with Sir Girija Shankar Bajpai. He had an unmatched reputation of capability, but the trouble was that he knew it and did not suffer fools gladly. I must have managed to conceal my limitations! Just before leaving for my marriage, I had approached Joint Secretary (Ad) S. Ratnam with the hope that he would consider moving me so I could have a little more freedom in determining my leisure. He sympathized with my request, but the problem, he said, was to find a successor. He asked me to help find a volunteer who would have to be approved by the SG himself. Fortunately, Narendra Singh Sarila, having returned after learning French, was tempted by the opportunity and glory of being in the anteroom of the big boss. After I returned from Udaipur, I was assigned as Under Secretary for South-east Asia, but I had barely settled down, when I was summoned to Foreign Secretary K.P.S. Menon's office where Commonwealth Secretary S. Dutt and Joint Secretary S. Ratnam were also present. This made me apprehensive. They started by giving me a pep talk, 'Administration is a difficult job, but Foreign Policy depends on contented staff and efficient administrative implementation. It requires familiarity with rules and attention to mundane details;

it hinges on winning the confidence of personnel at all levels from superintendents down to chaprasis. No Foreign Service officer has yet been tried out in administration, but it is the nerve centre of the Ministry. We want you to take over as O'Meally's successor. He has done over forty-three years of service and has already had nine extensions of varying durations.' They added that 'If you find it too difficult, it will not harm your subsequent career, but success will be widely appreciated and bring you credit. It means you should be willing to carry the responsibility for two years.' O'Meally had joined the External Affairs Department (EAD) in 1906 as a lower division clerk. He was of Anglo-Indian origin; they were thought of as being more reliable in the old British-dominated External and Political Department. K.P.S. had a favourable opinion of him since his own days as Deputy Secretary in EAD. I had no alternative but to acquiesce in the politely communicated and formulated decision which had already been taken.

1949: The domain of the Under Secretary (Ad)

On 25 July 1949 I moved to O'Meally's old room (number 62A). The room had special importance from its long associations. It was the only single room occupied at the Under Secretary (US) level; it was strategically located and had originally served the administration of both External Affairs and the Political departments. It required climbing only one flight of stairs to answer summons from the big bosses on the first floor. (The other Under Secretaries were in distant cubicles or with no separate rooms or PAs). Next door, but around the corner, was the extra-secure cash section with no windows. The cypher bureau, which was in the basement, also had only one entrance and no windows or exit.

The US (Ad) was the hub of the Ministry. I was awed by the reputation of my predecessor. O'Meally had kept senior officers happy as he provided the stenographers and jamadars, and chose persons for non-diplomatic posts abroad. I soon discovered that O'Meally's secret was being prompt on urgent demands from senior officers, but to postpone difficult decisions by locking files in his steel almira. For the next few months, I kept on receiving files from his home in Safdarjang Lane (fifty years later, the same house was occupied by S. Manmohan Singh) but the returning files all carried the date of his retirement—24 July 1949.

I took home all the printed manuals and glanced through them, starting with Fundamental and Supplementary rules, but also accounting procedures, etc.

Administering the lower deck of the Ministry

In the fairly large administrative division, all officers except JS (Ad)—who was from the Indian Audit and Accounts Service—were promoted ones, who really had a limited perspective on Foreign Policy. The US (Ad) was also the disciplinary kingpin of the MEA. There were four sections under the charge of US (Ad); the first section under a senior and experienced superintendent, with handpicked assistants, dealt with postings of non-officer personnel in the EAD. This section was the most powerful as it determined the fate of all subordinates; the second was for supplies and services, meeting with requirements within the Ministry and also the expanding demands of new missions, a section with huge latitude, and so was coveted; the third, the cash section, dispensed salaries, scrutinized and paid bills of all the personnel in the ministry (only officers were entitled to be paid by cheque); the fourth section dealt with pensions, and at that time, was preoccupied with winding up the old British Indian Political Service.

There were able heads of sections and one could generally rely on their experience, familiarity with rules and sound judgement, but one had to be vigilant against sly preferences in the choice of personnel, temptations in bulk purchases, which involved lakhs of

Induction into the Administration 1949–51

rupees. The ultimate responsibility was of the US (Ad), and included false bills, defalcations and abuse of discretion.

The US (Ad) was also in charge of the toshkhana where valuables worth lakhs were kept. One had to be careful with the listing and the custody of the precious items. Beyond specified low limits, all presents received from foreign dignitaries in Delhi or abroad had to be deposited in the toshkhana. The recipient had the first option to buy them but only after market evaluation, and so one had to detect deliberate undervaluations. We were also responsible for the purchase of presents for outgoing visits and for VIPs coming to Delhi. The discretion of purchase was often entrusted to some lady of 'taste and high position' but it required tact to keep the selection within moderate financial limits. The toshkhana gave more headaches with the wives than even the officers. I often waged a losing battle against extravagance for what was justified as 'prestige of India'.

I soon learnt that the secret of good administration lay in not shirking the courage of being clean and transparent. I made spot checks, which, at times, could be unpleasant. Without prior notice, I used to walk around the offices, almost every week; some offices on the second floor were dingy and dirty; most wartime huts south of the main secretariat building were worse. I had to sign the monthly salary bill for several hundred persons amounting to lakhs of rupees, more or less blindly, but I knew I could trust S. Mela Singh, the chief cashier. For new recruitments, I started written tests and thus replaced my own inherited discretion. All those concerned became a little more alert about obvious favouritism and inducting close relations. I had to resist being unfair, yet at all times be seen as transparently sympathetic to genuine hardship. All through my career, I was served by Kundan Singh as my peon. He always came back to me in all my subsequent postings, but I had a second one, also a Garhwali, who, in fact, was caught forging my signature and withdrawing money from my bank accounts with Grindlays. Administration required blending not only fairness with objectivity but also constant vigilance.

Finding suitable personnel for our rapidly expanding diplomatic network was not easy. I discovered that there were plenty of volunteers as long as the postings were in America or in Europe, but there was reluctance when it came to finding nominees for postings in new missions in Asia and Africa.

Constitution of Foreign Service 'B'

Under Central Secretariat rules, no one was obliged to serve outside India. I soon realized the need of having an infrastructure of personnel, or a Foreign Service 'B', underpinning the separate Indian Foreign Service, who were obligated to go wherever sent, including to places with harsh climate, no schools and perhaps, hostile people like in Pakistan. But creating a new service by separating it from the existing Central Secretariat Services was difficult and complex. It meant laying down new rules for recruitment with new conditions of service. One had to ascertain the size of families and non-orthodox habits. We had to integrate unsuitable ones in equivalent posts in other ministries, etc. Moreover, we had to keep a kernel of experienced hands at headquarters when quite a few wanted to go to New York! The Foreign Service then had about 120 officers, but I was dealing with several hundreds, perhaps thousands. A new service required a gradual general post, accommodating individual problems as well as ensuring service efficiency. There was a special problem in the expansion of the cypher bureau, which was then dominated by Anglo-Indians under the direct control of Mr Courtney, also an Anglo-Indian. I wanted it more democratized with new criteria of reliability. One of the subsidiary problems was to give the option to embody some of the Indians belonging to India House in London, who were locally recruited and governed by the Whitehall Establishment Code with high salaries and promotion expectations, but no obligation to go out of the UK. Some of them merited a higher rank but only if they were prepared to go wherever they were sent. In fact, we only took three or four, but it included people like R. Axel Khan who rose to be a very successful ambassador in the Gulf. We had to gradually delink the Whitehall rules and provide for more India-based personnel, especially in dealing with confidential papers. In other words, bifurcating an existing cadre was far more complex than creating a new IFS after embodying a handful of Indians already in the Political Service.

The scheme for an IFS 'B' was my brainchild but I realized how much detailed work it entailed. I received the cooperation and invaluable guidance of Deputy Establishment Officer R.C. Dutt from the Bengal ICS cadre. B.N. Chakravarty, also from the Bengal cadre, who had been Counsellor in China and then headed our Mission in Tokyo, replaced S. Ratnam as JS (Ad). I have seldom come across a person of greater integrity and uprightness. But for his support in laying down principles which had transparency, and which minimized disaffection, I would have given up the ghost. After a lot of work, I managed to create the framework for an IFS 'B', but I could not begin implementing its provisions.

I was overdue for a foreign posting. In four years my colleagues had done two postings and some were on to the third. But again I had to find a successor for this non-glamorous job. Eventually I managed to lure Abid Hasan Safrani—an ex-INA nominee, who had travelled with Netaji Subhas Chandra Bose in the submarine from Germany to Japan—to take up as US (Ad). He had just come back from having been First Secretary in Cairo. He was from a Hyderabadi aristocratic lineage, had a straightforward outlook and was above flattery; but, while he coped with day-to-day work, he left the IFS 'B' scheme alone! The entire scheme of the IFS 'B' could only be taken up when Y.K. Puri, ICS, became JS (Ad) five years later. Some element of objectivity and transparency was modified when the original outline was brought into force in 1956–57.

A Foreign Service Board, presided over by the Foreign Secretary, with the Commerce Secretary and other secretaries as members, and the JS (Ad) as its Secretary, to decide on postings and promotions of Foreign Service officers had started, I think, in 1949 itself. The Board was actually serviced by Rao Sahib M.K. Narayanan, who in 1947–52 was US (FSP) or Foreign Service Personnel. Prior to transfer to EAD—that was before Independence—he was Administrative Officer of the Intelligence Bureau. He had exceptional experience in the secretariat; rules and precedents were at his Tamil Brahminical fingertips. With Mr Chakravarty's approval, I proposed that we also constitute a junior IFS 'B' board to be presided over by the most senior Deputy Secretary in the Administration, with other Deputy Secretaries as members and US (Ad) as Secretary. Postings, transfers and promotions of non-diplomatic personnel could then be collectively decided. In effect, I was again volunteering to surrender the discretion, which earlier had been the prerogative of US (Ad) and the Administration branch, with only an occasional suggestion from the Deputy Secretary (Establishment). O'Meally could thus oblige senior officers in the choice of their registrars, private secretaries and assistants when proceeding abroad. My innovation, of course, curbed my ability to fall in line with the pressure from unreasonable bosses or the recommendations from other ministries. Recommendations or sifarish were frequent and could not always be refused. While every posting was discretionary, I thought collective decision would be fairer. Mr Chakravarty, a man of exemplary rectitude, got the Foreign Secretary to endorse the idea of a junior board. It may have been refined but, ever since, has been institutionalized.

Categorization of posts to ensure rotational fairness

I was also the first one to categorize all our posts into A, B and C, and C^x for extra hard stations. Each official was expected to rotate between the categories, preferably starting with a tough post in category C. This enabled us to entice volunteers or insist on acceptance of hard stations so that they could earn a coveted one, with English language schools for their children. In other words,

Induction into the Administration 1949–51

to get nominated to New York, Washington, London, Paris, one should have done Peking or at least Prague or Dar es Salaam! This was not generally popular, but when a hard posting was made mandatory for improving future prospects, it was not resisted. It was a better shield against external influences. This categorization of posts for IFS 'B' was eventually adopted by the senior board too. Though exceptions have been made, and to this day complaints are many that the Secretaries tend to overlook enforcement of the rotational principle, categorization did make administration smoother and, more transparent, and provided a justifiable basis of representation.

Dispensing pensions to senior Political Service officers presented few problems since the section was headed by P.C. Sen, a very knowledgeable and meticulous officer. But a hundred-odd Indian Political Service officers (IPS), some very senior ones, would make exacting demands and complain of delay if the service records had gaps or inaccuracies. Occasionally I had to correspond with officers who had retired with a knighthood or were former agents to the Governor General (AGGs), when they accused us of mistakes. But if I remember correctly, all pensions of the IPS officers were authorized by 1951. Anyway, the section gave me no serious headaches.

Working as US (Ad) was very taxing but I was at least master of my own time. It was part of my job as US (Ad) to react to diverse complaints by senior officers—of blowers in the room not working, PAs or peons being absent without leave, electricity failures, etc. They all insisted on quick repair or improvisation even if the demands were unreasonable and petty.

As part of the duty of providing supplies and equipment to our missions, I remember going to Junagarh which had come under Indian control, because the Nawab had acceded to Pakistan and had fled to Karachi. I went there to select carpets from the old palaces which I thought we could send to embellish our new missions.

The South Block quadrilateral at the western edge also housed the PM's office, which was then very small in comparison to those of the Ministry of External Affairs and the Ministry of States, the successor to the Political Department. The former had overall responsibility of gate six and the main staircase which were used by the PM and VIP visitors. What I remember is how few the demands from Nehru himself were. He used the toilet marked 'Officers' some distance from his own room. An exclusive bathroom was built only when Mrs Gandhi became PM.

The experience and learning process as US (Ad) gave me insights into administration which I have never regretted. By 1951 my reputation was reasonably well established. I was nominated by the Foreign Service Board for a posting as First Secretary in Bonn where I would be second in command in the newly opened diplomatic mission. An officer when first appointed to the so-called military mission was given the rank of brigadier. I remember Khubchand of 1935 seniority awkwardly practising the military salute. When the diplomatic mission was opened in Bonn, the Second Secretary remained in Berlin, with ten servants on occupation costs, but had little more than consular work. The political game had shifted to Bonn. I looked forward to the posting, but my nomination was changed at the very last minute.

6

Bern and Vienna: Nehru in Burgenstock (1951–54)

In the 1950s, Panditji in his capacity as Foreign Minister used to attend the National Day receptions of most countries. Queen Wilhelmina's birthday on 30 April is still observed as the National Day in the Netherlands. Unlike the King of the Belgians, Queen Wilhelmina had refused to compromise with Nazi Germany and had spent the war years in London and so, on her return, she had the affection and respect of the Dutch. On the afternoon of 30 April 1951, I had handed over charge as US (Ad). For some weeks, I had been helping in packing and labelling the heavy luggage for shipping to Bonn. Incidentally, the Netherlands Embassy is the corner house at the crossing of Queensway (now Janpath) and Aurangzeb Road and was one of the earliest diplomatic purchases. It had belonged to Quaid-e-Azam M.A. Jinnah and, though the domed drawing room was added later, the study where historic discussions must have taken place remains unchanged. When Panditji saw me amongst lesser diplomats at the reception, he took me out of earshot of the other guests, and told me that my posting had been changed. I was to go to Bern and to get there as soon as possible. Panditji added that I was to relieve all officers, including Nambiar, the Chargé d'Affaires, and 'clean up the place'. I was baffled but dared not mention to him that I had some real personal difficulties.

For those who are not 'midnight's adults', a little background behind this peremptory decision at the highest level affecting a junior official may be useful. As I have mentioned in the previous chapter, Bern was the first diplomatic mission opened on the continent of Europe with Dhirubhai Desai as Minister. For historical reasons, except the Nuncio and France in 1951, all missions were legations headed by ministers harking back to old days when only 'great powers' could have embassies entitling them to have direct access to monarchs and heads of states. Our Mission was uniquely unorthodox. Many Indians who had spent the war years in Hitler-dominated Europe had gravitated to our Mission in Switzerland. A.C.N. Nambiar, who had served with Netaji Subhas Chandra Bose in Germany, was designated Counsellor and number two. While we have had political appointees as heads— Dhirubhai was one of them—we have never had non-career subordinates. Notable amongst these wartime 'European' Indians were Dr Tarachand Roy, an academic caught by the war in a German university; Krish Sarma (married to Hella, an Austrian) who was studying chemistry in Vienna, and Chowdhury who was doing some business in Hamburg. Dhirubhai's entourage on the other hand was composed of Bombay residents. Soli Batlivala was Private Secretary but, in fact, ran the entire mission. There were clerks, waiters, etc. from the Willingdon Club, Bombay, who had been appointed as drivers or messengers. Initially, there was only one India-based officer, V.H. Coelho. He, and the trained clerical staff from Central Services, were often bypassed. Within a year Coelho returned to Delhi and became PS to the PM, succeeding Tarlok Singh. Coelho was replaced by my brother-in-law Ashok Mehta, who had married Chandralekha, Mrs Pandit's eldest daughter, but after only six months, had got himself moved to Paris. He was succeeded by Avtar Dar, who came from Washington as First Secretary, but he too, was marginalized from the very beginning.

Dhirubhai Desai himself had impeccable credentials. He spoke French, and was very energetic—commercially, socially and culturally. He had a substantial personal flow of funds from the wealth of his distinguished lawyer father, Bhulabhai Desai. His personal car was an Alfa Romeo, and he was quite capable of going to Zurich in the morning, 150 kilometres away, and coming back to fulfil engagements in Bern in the afternoon. The contract with Oerlikans helped India to pioneer indigenizing our defence capabilities. On the advice of his cultured wife, Madhuri behn, the Mission produced a map of India with photographs of our famous historical sites. It was exported to our missions. Her right-hand man was Soli Batlivala, who was dynamic, but no respecter of bureaucratic and administrative constraints. In fact, the Mission was split into two groups—those loyal to Dhirubhai, and the others who were remnants of Indians who had been trapped or stayed back in Europe through the war; they were progressive and well educated but unused to an official dog-collar, and chafing at comparatively low-level jobs.

A.C.N. Nambiar was a gentleman to the core but unable to adjust to Soli's unorthodox domination. He had quietly resigned to go back to his friends and disappear in the Europe he knew so well. He left no clue to where he was going. When Dhirubhai died suddenly, just two days before Easter 1951, a crisis erupted between the two factions. The Foreign Secretary, K.P.S. Menon, ordered that Nambiar should take over but he could not be traced. When located, he was reluctant to come back to the Mission, but on the plea of K.P.S., agreed to take over. Soli Batlivala made public his protest and apparently even threatened that if Nambiar were present at Dhirubhai's funeral, he would humiliate him in front of the Swiss dignitaries and would beat him with his own shoes! This altercation became public and grossly embarrassed the Indian diplomatic representation. This entire story was front-paged in the *Blitz*, a Bombay weekly, edited by the influential Rusi Karanjia. The story attracted the attention of the Foreign Affairs Committee of the Cabinet in New Delhi. Rajagopalachari, who demitted office as Governor General after the new Constitution came into force on 26 January 1950, had joined the Cabinet as Home Minister and was a member of the Committee. He argued for quick surgical action to end this embarrassing crisis of factionalism in our Mission.

The Mission had been wrong in not showing appropriate courtesy to Madhuri behn in her bereavement. According to the *Blitz* report, the official car was summarily withdrawn and no help volunteered in winding up the household. It was alleged that the head of Chancery showed insensitivity towards Madhuri behn; anyway, Soli was not restrained in his accusations. It was this event that led to my last-minute diversion from Bonn to Bern.

When Panditji told me of the change, I could not express the reasons for my reservations. The next morning, I went to Joint Secretary (Ad) B.N. Chakravarty, and reminded him that I had not taken any earned leave in four years, and that he himself had sanctioned me two months. He knew Rama had taken maternity leave and that we were expecting the first addition to our family in late May or early June. Chakravarty showed understanding, but he confirmed the orders and advised that I should cut short my leave. After all, it was a mark of special confidence and there should be no hesitation in compliance. After two weeks in Udaipur, I proceeded to Bombay and I was rebooked on a boat sailing on 1 June for Naples. I heard about the birth of Vijay, our daughter, on 4 June, when the ship was approaching Aden and saw her only after six months.

Geneva was still the symbol of internationalism with its Palais des Nations, the headquarters of the International Red Cross, and the International Labour Organization. The reason for this change in my posting was the first major administrative crisis in the working of India's diplomatic network.

Cleaning the Augean stables in Bern

Although he had been in The Hague only two years, at about the same time, my father too, received intimation to move to Karachi as High Commissioner to Pakistan. I went to The Hague directly for a few days and joined in some farewell dinners, and reached

Bern by the end of June. My carte-blanche brief, from no less a person than the PM himself, was known not only in the Ministry but had spread to the Mission and enhanced my authority. But it was not easy for one officer to relieve five incumbents and keep the Mission running, especially in the busy summer months. I had no difficulty in taking over from Nambiar who was the Chargé d'Affaires. Avtar Dar, a senior colleague and Head of the Chancery, was incoherent in giving me the background of what transpired. He was probably guilty of allowing matters to get out of hand. M.A. Vellodi, who was the Commercial Secretary, was in a sanatorium for suspected tubercolosis. An officer called Agrawal was deputizing for Vellodi. The registrar, S. Krishnaswamy, had played politics between the two factions. The cash book was in a mess. Although there were no suspicions of defalcations, advances were unaccounted for and nobody had dared to ask for receipts. The registrar and accountant should not have allowed further advances without signed proof of proper use of previous withdrawals, but the rules had been ignored.

The one person who posed a problem and refused cooperation was Satya Narain Sinha, designated First Secretary. He travelled where and when he wished and no one knew to whom he reported. He claimed he was covering Europe. One story was that he had served in the Imperial Guard of the Emperor of Ethiopia, another, that he was in the court of the Russian Czar. When he was requested to hand over charge, he refused and went underground. Confident of the authority bestowed on me, I told him that I would refuse to pay his travelling allowance bills or his salary unless, within a reasonable period, he vacated the rented house and allowed us to redeploy government-owned furniture. I denied him the right to use the official channels of communication and eventually brought him to compliance.

At my request, S. Krishnaswamy was replaced by another registrar sent from Delhi. As it happened, it was another Krishnaswamy (K.R.), also of the Central Secretariat Services. I do not recall all the details but over the next year I faced a real problem tracing the funds that had been spent lavishly. Exercising my plenipotentiary powers, I recommended writing off a total sum of about 400,000 Swiss Francs, which could not be accounted for by proper receipts.

The real problem was to bridge the in-house tensions between the India-based staff and the 'locally assembled' Indians, who were recruited on merit. Some of the Indians were scholars with command over 'hoch Deutsch' (high German), many with expertise on Europe and fluency in French, and also Czech. I was very careful to be seen as being above rancour and the persisting bitterness between the factions. N.V. Agate, a Foreign Service officer who had come as Second Secretary from Tokyo, was of little use as he had a drinking problem. I needed effective support but had no help except from the newly-arrived registrar, K.R. Krishnaswamy, and my carefully chosen stenographer-personal assistant K.N. Chakravarty. After nearly one year of sorting out the mess, I thought we were on an even keel. Frankly, I have never enjoyed such discretionary latitude in financial matters during the rest of my career, not even as Foreign Secretary.

After a gap of some weeks, the new Ambassador, Nedyam Raghavan, arrived on transfer from Brussels. He was an eminent lawyer, who had been practising earlier in Singapore. He had been made Finance Minister of the INA under Netaji, and with such credentials, before Brussels, he had been the first Consul General of India in Indonesia. I could not help noticing he was all too conscious of the dignity of his diplomatic rank; he expected honour, not only from the government and the citizens of the country of posting, but even within the Embassy. I met him in Basel with the staff car; he insisted on not covering the car pennant which, technically, should have been delayed until after he had presented his credentials to the Swiss President. He wanted the staff and his own children to refer to him as 'His Excellency' instead of simply 'Ambassador'. Having been in Delhi for four years, I felt this did not quite correspond with Nehru's notions of conduct within our own establishment. Raghavan also had a penchant for secrecy, and not just telegraphic communication with the Ministry, but all letters, including on routine administrative matters, had to be authorized or shown in circulation. He insisted that all incoming bags from Delhi, even the non-secret ones which generally contained newspapers and publicity material, were to be opened in his presence by the First Secretary (myself) and the registrar. After some time, I thought that all this suspicion and secrecy was unnecessary and told the Ambassador that I would leave it to him to see who was corresponding with the Ministry.

In the autumn of 1951, Sir Girija Bajpai called me to Paris when the General Assembly was again being held in the French capital, but that was just out of courtesy for having served with him. At that time we did not even have a Consul much less a Permanent Representative at the European headquarters in Geneva. So, quite frequently, I had to go to Geneva, especially as it was the customary stop of Air India constellations. Moreover, there were committees of the WHO and the ILO which did not warrant a representative coming from Delhi. I got to know quite a few international diplomats. For the first and the only time, I was offered a post in P-5 as a representative of the UN High Commissioner for Refugees for the whole of Asia. I was not yet thirty and this was a pretty high grade. But the Ministry said I could not be spared and that was the end of my prospects as an international civil servant. Had I not kicked the ladder I might have climbed quite high in the UN system but I am glad I remained tethered to national diplomacy which, though poorly paid in comparison, gave unique opportunities and responsibilities.

Ambassador Raghavan returned from home leave in early March, but we heard soon afterwards that he was being transferred to take over as Ambassador in China succeeding K.M. Panikkar who had served 'Two Chinas'. We were asked to obtain an 'agreement' for Asaf Ali as his successor. In February 1947, Asaf Ali was our first Ambassador to the US but he stayed only for a year and then returned to be Minister of Transport in the central government in New Delhi. He was one of those early-generation Congressmen who, like Nehru, was elegant, well educated, with

Anglicized style and taste, yet with unquestionable commitment to Independence. I think he also had some lingering nostalgia for what he felt was Western diplomacy. He arrived soon after Raghavan left.

Asaf Ali was very different from his predecessor. He enjoyed an old friendship with Nehru as both shared occidental refinements. He loved good food, well cooked in the Mughlai style. He disliked eating alone and frequently expected Rama and me to dine with him. Instead of secrecy and suspicion, he bestowed great trust and left the responsibility of running the Embassy to me. Asaf Ali did not even want to see the draft of the periodic reports, but I took care to keep him informed. Politically, Switzerland was stable; there was little of interest to India. As a lark, I sent the 1951 annual report when the 1952 report was due and nobody noticed it until I myself sent the current report and drew the attention of the concerned officer! Eisenhower's envoy arrived in 1953—he had been the Protocol Chief of New York City—and he found it ignominious to be called a Minister when he represented the mighty USA. Therefore his and other missions were given the option of upgrading themselves to the ambassadorial level.

The stream of summer visitors was unending. In 1952 we had Dr Radhakrishnan, a delegation to work with the UNCIP led by Gopalaswami Ayyangar, and including D.P. Dhar, General Thimmaya and V. Shankar to discuss Kashmir. For me, considering her anger when departing, the most gratifying was Madhuri behn accompanying Soli Batlivala back on a visit, which went off amicably.

Early in January 1953, Asaf Ali wrote to 'Jawaharbhai' that after attending the coronation of Queen Elizabeth II scheduled for early June, on his way back, he should come to Switzerland and hold a meeting of the heads of Indian missions in Europe, as he had in Paris in 1951. The Prime Minister, with his old love for Switzerland and the Ministry, readily agreed to the suggestion.

The sudden death of Asaf Ali

By early January 1953, the administrative problems which had preoccupied me were nearly sorted out and the mission's functioning, morale and unity were restored. Since the load of work had somewhat eased, I sought the Ambassador's permission to take one month's earned leave and, on the concurring approval of the Ministry, arranged to spend it at Grenoble in the French Alps where there were arrangements for foreigners to improve their French. I went by car, leaving Rama behind with the children. As previously arranged, Rama came down by train at the end of the month and both of us proceeded to the south of France to have a quick look at the famous playground of European aristocracy. I had left my contact number in my lodgings in Grenoble.

While I was in Nice, I was told to call the Embassy urgently. When I got through, I was told that Ambassador Asaf Ali had suddenly passed away. Rama had left him hale and hearty two days earlier and thought he seemed excited that Mrs Asaf Ali was at last joining him nearly a year after he had taken over. I could only react to the shock by saying that I would come back immediately cutting short a few days of the proposed drive along the French coast. I learnt later that the French and the Swiss broadcasting systems were repeating every few minutes, 'Jagat S. Mehta driving black Chevrolet no. BE 25103 should be stopped and Mr Mehta told to ring up the Indian Embassy in Bern immediately.' My Chevrolet did not have a radio, and when we were finally stopped, we were already on the way back. I did not realize that Bern was about 1200 kilometres away and that it meant driving over the French Alps, mostly at night. Leaving Nice at midday, Rama and I drove nonstop, over several high passes, where, in April, the snow had not yet fully melted. I told Rama to keep talking, to prevent me from sleeping. We must have reached Geneva after dawn. From there I rang up the embassy and asked the registrar, K.R. Krishnaswamy, to meet me at Lausanne in a staff car so that we could drive back together and he could brief me on what had transpired and what decisions awaited my return.

Asaf Ali was a member of the Congress Working Committee, representing Delhi. After consulting Maulana Azad, Foreign Secretary R.K. Nehru had instructed the Mission that the body should be sent back as soon as possible to Delhi where a public procession and ceremonial honour were being prepared. It would be met by the PM, the Cabinet and Delhi dignitaries.

K.R. Krishnaswamy reported that the long Easter weekend had complicated matters such as obtaining the death certificate, finding suitable undertakers for a coffin and getting the necessary permission to send the body to India, etc. (We were aware that according to Muslim custom, burial would not brook delay). Judging from the repeated calls from the Foreign Secretary and Maulana Azad's secretary, there was also the anxiety of unintended discourtesy to Mrs Asaf Ali. The Embassy was cautioned that there should not be a repetition of what had happened after Dhirubhai Desai had passed away exactly two years earlier. This was heightened as I was away from Bern.

Asaf Ali had died in the same room in which Dhirubhai had passed away, on the first floor usually used as the study, and also on the Wednesday before Good Friday. Two days earlier, Mrs Asaf Ali had arrived in Zurich and the Ambassador himself had received her. She was more grieved by the calamity because she had not come earlier. She obviously went back with her husband's coffin. As may be recalled, Aruna Asaf Ali had broken away from the official Congress and become part of the Leftist faction under the leadership of Jaiprakash Narain and Ram Manohar Lohia which, after the Quit India Resolution, had rejected the Gandhian non-violent sacrificial method and had decided to go underground and actively sabotage the British regime in India. Though politically divergent, as far as one knows, husband and wife had remained devoted to each other.

A catastrophe averted

Before I reached Bern, the Ambassador's body had been laid inside the coffin and Mrs Asaf Ali had paid her last homage in private. On arrival, Rama and I went up and offered over condolences to her. Neither of us had met her before. (In subsequent meetings she showed great affection for us). The coffin lay in state in what is called the winter garden. Swiss dignitaries and diplomatic colleagues came to pay their last respects. In rotation the Embassy officers stood in solemn dignity around it. We had been in touch with Air India to coordinate the exact timing when the body was to be driven to Geneva for the flight to Delhi. I had succeeded in reaching the Chief of Protocol at his home so he could join the long drive to Geneva. Our Military Attaché Brigadier Chopra, who was based in Paris, had been summoned to Bern.

On a hunch, I rang up Nari Dastur, the Station Manager of Air India in Geneva, to inquire if there were any restrictions on the size of the coffin to be carried by Air India. Nari did not know and had to contact Bombay. He gave the maximum size which could be carried in the aircraft. To my horror, I found that the ceremonial coffin, in which the body had already been laid, was too big to be manoeuvered into a Constellation.

I asked most of the officials to go home and put on black sherwanis instead of dark suits so that only three or four were witness to the rather sacrilegious transfer. Very quietly we removed the large outer coffin and got another of the specified capacity. It was highly embarrassing to remove the original coffin and replace it with a less decorative one. Mrs Asaf Ali was not informed of this operation.

With Mrs Asaf Ali sitting in the van and, with her consent, accompanied by Rama, escorted by a police car and followed by the mission cars, we reached at exactly the right time when the plane which was conveniently parked, ready for take-off. We saluted our departing chief. Rama and I had developed a deep respect for the Ambassador and he, in turn, had shown us genuine affection. I have often had nightmares since that, if the idea of asking for measurements for the coffin had not come to mind, we would have been grossly embarrassed on the tarmac and, quite deservedly, it would have been an unforgivable blot on my career!

A legend grew that there was a ghost in the residence, which took toll around Easter, especially of alternate occupants. As it happened, the next but one Ambassador was my own father. As far as I know, he spent Easter of 1955 in the house, but the suspicion of a ghost haunting the Indian Ambassador's residence is still not completely buried.

The conference to be held in Switzerland had already been notified and now there were only five weeks left to go before the notified dates. The responsibility of going ahead with arrangements for the conference fell on my shoulders. New Delhi was in a frantic search for a successor ambassador, who had to be in position before the PM's arrival on his second official visit to Switzerland. Yezdi Gundevia, who was the Minister in Moscow, was selected and told to pack up and take charge of the post. Like a good scout he wound up hurriedly and arrived just three weeks before the PM was due. We managed to arrange the presentation of his credentials to the Federal President and he rushed through some of his protocol calls. The Queen's coronation in London was fortunately followed by somewhat extended festivities. Mrs Gundevia had to settle the house in Bern to make it fit for Panditji's visit, however brief.

Burgenstock: the PM's visit and the Heads of Missions Conference

The responsibility of fixing a venue, making arrangements for the stay of all the ambassadors, many of whom were coming by car from different European capitals, some by air, reaching different parts of Switzerland, and coordinating it all with only one staff car fell on us in the Chancery with the ultimate decision on me. To find twenty-five rooms and suites in an appropriate place at the height of the season was not easy. It occurred to us that the ideal spot would be an isolated five-star hotel, which had not yet opened for the summer. Hella Sarma arranged for me to call on the proprietor in Zurich of the Burgenstock Hotel which overlooked Lake Lucerne. He was persuaded to reopen his spectacular hotel a week ahead of the normal summer schedule. For him it was obviously good publicity to have the PM of India and all the ambassadors in his hotel. As it transpired, we had this huge and conveniently located hotel for the PM and the Indian envoys, entirely to themselves. Panditji, but no one else, had been to Burgenstock before and the venue gave us a head start.

Panditji, accompanied by the SG of the Ministry, Sir N. R. Pillai, landed on the small airfield in Bern, made a brief call on the President in Palais Fédéral, came to the Ambassador's residence for rest and a brief talk, met the families assembled on the lawn, visited the Chancery, agreed to have a group photograph with all the staff and drove off to Burgenstock some seventy kilometres away, all in three hours! Fourteen ambassadors, most of them from the ICS, came individually and had to be escorted. B.G. Kher, the former CM of undivided Bombay Presidency and then High Commissioner in London, and G.L. Mehta, Ambassador in Washington, were the two non-career heads. For the first time, Kewal Singh, Chargé d'Affaires in Lisbon, was seen without a beard and a turban. The only non-head of mission was P.N. Haksar, who accompanied B.G. Kher. K.S. Bajpai, who had just joined the service was working as PS to the SG. On the periphery—not in the Conference—were A.C.N. Nambiar, an old friend of the Nehrus, who was living in Zurich as a private resident, and M.O. Mathai, accompanying the PM.

On the way to London, Mrs Indira Gandhi had left her sons Rajiv, nine, and Sanjay, six, in Switzerland. I had met the Air India flight in Geneva and driven them to the Odenwald School run by Paul Geheeb in a small valley in the Bernese Oberland. This was an unusual school where learning was combined with adventure and exploring of nature. Geheeb had first established the school in the Black Forest, but as a protest against Hitler's National Socialism he had moved the school to this obscure village in Switzerland. (The Duke of Edinburgh and later, Prince Charles went to Gordonstoun in Scotland, which was based on the Odenwald School). I dare say few in India except Panditji and Indira Gandhi had heard about the school. Fortunately, I had come across some information on arrival in Bern and had invited Paul Geheeb to our flat in Switzerland in 1951 and so, when I brought the PM's grandsons for a few weeks' stay, I was not a complete stranger.

Mrs Gandhi went straight from Bern to Paul Geheeb's school, stayed two days, and then brought her sons to Burgenstock after the Conference concluded. The hotel was in a spectacular location with Engelberg peak and cows with their large dangling bells at pasture just behind, and Lake Lucerne in front. It facilitated informal consultations between the PM and his ambassadors on the sunny terrace. The conference hall with its Gobelin tapestries on the wall had a wonderful view of the mountains. It was one of the most successful and enjoyable meetings.

Visit of Austrian Foreign Minister to see Nehru

Three notable events coincided with the Conference in Burgenstock. The workers in East Germany rose in protest in what must have been the first expression of dissatisfaction with the imposed Communist regime; Nasser in Cairo took over from Neguib; what was politically more significant was that, in consultation with Delhi, we had agreed to Dr Gruber, the Foreign Minister of Austria, coming to Lucerne to call on the PM of India. Stalin had died in March 1953, and Gruber requested Nehru—who then had a commanding position in the world—to urge the Soviet Union to end the four-power occupation of Austria, which after all had been only a reluctant partner of Nazi Germany. Panditji expressed sympathy, and instructed K.P.S. Menon, the Ambassador to USSR, to plead with Molotov to consider the idea constructively. It is widely believed in Vienna that it was Panditji's plea which led to the State Treaty being signed in 1955 and culminating in Austria regaining its complete independence. On the last day, we had arranged for a boat ride on the lake, going past the Schiller's Rock and living through the Swiss Cantonal story of enlarging their freedom.

The PM with Indira Gandhi, her sons and Nambiar, stayed on for two days after the envoys had left. Only Mr and Mrs Gundevia and Rama were in attendance. After all this conferencing and sightseeing, when only the family remained, we arranged for the PM to go up to the Engelberg Peak. This involved a boat ride across a small lake and then by chairlift above the snowline. I have a photograph of Panditji having a snowball fight with his grandsons. On top of Engelberg Peak, in the café, we all had the traditional hot chocolate drink. Gundevia and I took pictures of three prime ministers, present and future, in a row—Panditji, Indira Gandhi and Rajiv Gandhi with Sanjay's back to the camera.

Charlie Chaplin calls on Nehru

In accordance with what I had arranged with the approval of the PM's Secretariat, on the last afternoon, I met Charlie Chaplin at the Lucerne railway station and brought him by boat and then up the funicular to Burgenstock. Charlie Chaplin spent the evening talking with Panditji and we listened before and through dinner. (Earlier I had overheard Panditji telling his grandchildren about Charlie Chaplin having been exiled from the USA for his alleged political leanings, which in the then prevalent McCarthyism condemned him as a suspected Communist). Here, in fact, were two truly great men, both famous the world over for their deep social concerns. Charlie Chaplin obviously felt honoured to be called to meet Panditji. I still recall his expressive face supported by his agile hands and fingers. The only part of the conversation I remember is when Charlie Chaplin said to Panditji that he liked everything about him that he had read except that he did not drink! Panditji reacted in his friendly way, 'If that is all you have against me, I'll have a sherry.'

The evening was such a success that, instead of returning by train the next morning, Charlie Chaplin invited the PM to have lunch with him in his villa on Lake Leman (Geneva) near Vevey. This meant Chaplin would drive back with the PM and have a long talk. I showed Panditji and Mrs Gandhi a shortcut across the mountain but this involved travelling by a narrow road. A Swiss photographer took this shot for the cover page of a pictorial magazine—a First Secretary showing the way to the great man and his daughter—but what you cannot tell from the photograph is that it was only across Switzerland!

Mrs Gandhi and the boys, as well as Nambiar and Mathai, went separately; Rokshi Gundevia and Rama returned to Bern. Only Gundevia and I remained on duty with the PM. There was no police escort and, while the PM and Charlie Chaplin went in the Ambassador's car, Gundevia and I travelled in my personal Chevrolet across the narrow road over the Bernese Oberland. At Charlie Chaplin's beautiful villa with its manicured lawns overlooking Lake Geneva, we met Claire Bloom, who was then married to Charlie Chaplin and expecting a baby. We had lunch in the portico with overhanging rose creepers.

Panditji remembered that Sir B.N. Rau, the former Constitutional Advisor and Ambassador to the UN, was in a sanatorium near Vevey. He was suffering with TB. The PM had asked me earlier to find out if Sir B.N. could come to see him at the villa. Sir B.N. readily agreed and so I went to fetch him. That was the last meeting between Panditji and Sir B.N., and probably the last time that the latter went out. He died soon afterwards.

In the afternoon, Gundevia and I accompanied Panditji to Geneva from where he took off for India. Panditji, in his parting words thanked me rather affectionately, and said that I drove too fast! This was with reference to my nearly hitting the Cadillac carrying Panditji and Charlie Chaplin when Petrov, their driver, had to break suddenly to avoid an incoming car on a narrow road! The Ambassador and I breathed a sigh of relief that the heavy responsibility of looking after the PM, the many ambassadors, and even the improvisations had gone off without a major catastrophe. We drove back to Bern where, with Rokshi and Rama, we had a drink to celebrate that our burdens and revels had both ended.

Tenzing in Bern

After the coronation, another VIP visit followed, but it gave no headaches. Tenzing Norgay and Edmund Hillary, after their triumph in reaching the summit of Mount Everest, had been invited by Sir John Hunt to London, along with their families.

On his way back, Tenzing came to Switzerland. Rama and I became great friends with him and Ang Lahmu, his wife, and their two daughters, Pem Pem and Nima. Tenzing was hosted by the Swiss Foundation of Alpine Research. Ernst and Maria Feuz were the chaperons. Ernst had earlier been the world downhill ski champion. Tenzing was taken to the Swiss Training School and did some rock climbing with the students. Throughout, Tenzing insisted on being accompanied by Lambert, a Swiss national, who had been his companion in the near-success in an Everest expedition the previous year (1952). One of my treasured mementos is a signed photograph of Tenzing Norgay on top of Mount Everest— a copy of one taken by Edmund Hillary.

Skiing with J.R.D. Tata

I truly enjoyed the winter of 1953–54. I was a mediocre skier, but also the only diplomat from Asia and Africa who indulged in the sport. I drove to different ski resorts almost every weekend. I nearly had one or two major accidents because my car did not have snow tyres but, fortunately, I crashed on the hillside and did not fall into the deep valley. Skiing helped me make lasting friendships. I skied with J.R.D. Tata and Gianni Bertoli (J.R.D's brother-in-law), the regional manager of Air India for continental Europe. J.R.D. took great care to be fit for winter sports. He was a beautiful skier, who came every year during the skiing season.

My skiing escapades made me famous in the Bern diplomatic corps as 'that mad Indian' who was a mediocre skier but refused to acknowledge his limitations. I broke my ankle in Saanenmöser in the 1952–53 season. After my school and Cambridge antecedents had been checked, I was accepted as a candidate member of the Kandahar Club, named after Lord Roberts for his forced march during the Second Afghan War (1878). 21 February 1954 was the annual meeting of the Kandahar Club, which Field Marshal Montgomery, then Deputy Commander-in-Chief of NATO, used to attend every year. I could not resist going too; it was a foolish thing to go to Murren for the Kandahar meet. Fortunately, I came back in the evening, but soon afterwards Rama told me that she had to go to the hospital because Ajay was on the way. I dread to think what might have happened if Ajay had decided to come into the world a day earlier.

It was more foolhardy to ski down from Jungfraujoch with short skis. I broke my ankle again. I had to be pulled back up to the mountain and the next day it was put into plaster. There were hundreds of signatures and some friendly sarcastic remarks on my plaster.

Orders had come for my transfer to London. I had been expecting to stay till July when my home leave would be due. I could not expect the same understanding in London as I had received from Ambassador Gundevia. My posting to Bern was initially distasteful but it had proved unexpectedly eventful. I started on my first post as a First Secretary and Chargé d'Affaires and in less than three years I had had three ambassadors, wholly different in their personalities. Being with Yezdi and Rokshi was too good to last! But we had enjoyed being with them in Austria and the Vatican.

7

London and the Suez (1954–56)

It must have been at the Burgenstock Conference that B.G. Kher, then High Commissioner (HC) in the United Kingdom, asked Prime Minister Nehru to transfer me as his Principal Private Secretary (PPS) to London. Panditji was obviously not inclined to rebuff a senior Congress colleague who, in 1952, had been requested to take on Krishna Menon's controversial mantle. By 1953, the administrative crisis in Bern was all but resolved and an experienced administrator like Gundevia was in position as Ambassador; therefore, the ministry must have approved my transfer. The last few months with Yezdi Gundevia were free of anxieties and tensions. The Bern posting was based on a prime ministerial decision and could not be questioned, nor was this one. The trouble was that it went against my own rotational principle. London, then, was a mission of 1300 with most ministers having their own representatives. I could not very well arrive with a plaster around my broken leg.

Even before completing two years as High Commissioner, B.G. Kher had asked to return to India, and M.J. Desai had been ordered to leave Stockholm, where he was Ambassador, to take over as acting HC. I found an old Victorian house with six bedrooms just off Kensington Church Street, which was conveniently near the HC's residence and had a direct pathway to the Kensington children's park. Vijay and Vikram, our two elder children, had been sent away with my father to Karachi. Rama came with Ajay by air once we had a large enough house with room for an Indian nanny.

Relishing diplomacy in London

London is on the crossroads to Europe and America. The summer months had the usual frequency of visitors and respected dignitaries like Kamladevi Chattopadhyay and Pupul Jayakar, many of whom expected a bed or meals. Even so, we enjoyed the summer months. With the help of the Commonwealth Relations Office (CRO), I managed to get tickets to Wimbledon, seats for Trooping the Colours and the theatre and entry to the special enclosure at Ascot. In a black tie, and with a British friend, we even indulged in the extravagance of an evening at the Glyndebourne Opera where, in the interval, it was *de rigueur* to have a picnic hamper with champagne!

After three months, M.J. Desai left as he was nominated Chairman of the International Control Commission for Vietnam, the biggest of the three commissions constituted by the Geneva Conference on Indo–China to wind up the French attempt to reestablish the old colonial hold. M.J. was to be replaced by B.N. Chakravarty, my former boss in Delhi. He came from The Hague where he had succeeded my father as Ambassador. Rama respected Mrs Chakravarty (as she had like Rokshi Gundevia) for her affectionate guidance. But only a few days after Mr and Mrs Chakravarty arrived, Rama and I left on home leave by steamer. (It was only in 1962 that the Government of India made it a rule that all personnel on transfer or leave must travel by Air India and not even avail of cheaper foreign-owned surface transport, because it involved foreign exchange outlay. This rule ended the luxury of weeks of travel in first class, and still have it considered as being on duty!) We visited Karachi, and after a week's stay with my father, took back our elder two children to spend some time in Udaipur and Delhi. We returned to London by December. Meanwhile Mrs V.L. Pandit had been appointed HC and had presented her credentials to the Queen in the traditional ceremony of going to the palace in a horse-drawn coach with an entourage of senior officers.

Being in London as PPS with Mrs Pandit was an unusual experience. Along with Eleanor Roosevelt, Mrs Pandit was possibly the best known female political figure in the world.

London instantly recognized that India had honoured the country by nominating her to be HC. It was, of course, also known that she was the Indian PM's sister but she had established an independent identity for herself. She had been Ambassador to both the USSR and the USA and, to crown it all, she was the first woman to be elected to preside over the United Nations General Assembly. She was a frequent visitor to the palace as well as to Windsor Castle for weekends.

The result of such distinction was that literally thousands of letters of welcome were received and as PPS, I had to cope with this personal and institutional fan mail. Using three stenographers for three months I must have dictated some fifty or sixty individual acknowledgements every day. The trouble was that, while spontaneously exuding charm and readily accepting invitations, she made far more commitments than was humanly possible for her to discharge. We had Maharaja Madan Singh of Kutch (with the unique designation of Minister 'Social', without salary but with diplomatic immunity) who was happy to deputize for the HC at national day functions, receptions and other formal events, where heads of missions were expected to be present. The extravagant individual promise of her personal presence made it almost my daily duty to telephone the hosts that the HC regretfully would have to cancel the committed engagement, frequently causing great embarrassment.

Sometimes the last-minute inability gave me an undeserved opportunity. I remember the unveiling of a statue of Churchill, sculptured in a sitting position by Rodin, in Mansion House in the City, which the great man himself had agreed to grace. Only the PM, Anthony Eden, the Lord Chancellor, senior cabinet ministers and the HCs were invited—and in 1955, there were only a few. Churchill was pleased with the statue and walked down the line of VIPs thanking each one individually. Seeing me wearing a sherwani (all the others were in morning coat) he must have guessed I was from the old Empire. Believe it or not, Churchill specially bent down at the waist, thanked me profusely for being present and added, 'You have done me great honour, Sir.' Sadly, I never got a still photograph as a memento! He seemed to remember me, no doubt because of my sherwani, at the Buckingham Palace annual garden party and so wound his way to shake my hand when I was milling around with lesser guests.

After having been PPS for nearly six months, when P.N. Haksar was transferred to Delhi, I was made Head of the External Department. In our entire diplomatic network, at least then, this was the only First Secretary's position which had exclusively political responsibilities. I had done administration, unravelled accounting confusion and also done periodic political reporting in my last post. I handed over private secretary-ship quite readily to Surendra Alirajpur who was socially more suitable for the job. Yezdi Gundevia had come as Deputy HC, and V.C. Trivedi was Counsellor but I was let loose for political contact-making. I went frequently to the galleries of the House of Commons and the House of Lords to listen to debates related to foreign affairs. I made many high-level contacts in Parliament and in the Foreign and Commonwealth Relations offices. India's attitude was important to Europe and world diplomacy. For example, Frank Roberts and Joe Garner, both of whom had been Deputy HCs in Delhi, were in very high positions, but received me or joined us for drinks or dinner. Much lower in the hierarchy but with a great intellectual future as a Sovietologist was Robert Conquest. He ended up in the Rand Corporation.

Tikhvinsky, designated Counsellor of the Soviet Embassy, was the first Russian to come to lunch without an interpreter. The next was Ambassador Vorontsov twenty years later!

Outside office hours, I got to know three of the resident clerks, actually unmarried officers, who took turns to be on twenty-four-hour duty to scrutinize incoming telegrams. One of them, Philip de Zulueta, remained attached to Harold Macmillan, when he became PM. He did not revert to the Foreign Office but instead, was knighted and went to the City. An old colleague telegraphed him 'I never liked early (k)nights!'.

Aide to Mrs V.L. Pandit

Mrs Pandit, of course, had all doors open to her including those of many ex-India hands. She took me to lunch with Lord Hailey who, as Sir Malcolm Hailey, had been Governor of UP when she was a Minister in the 1937 Congress government. (Hailey had been the Chief Commissioner of Delhi during Lord Hardinge's Viceroyalty in 1910. The two had galloped over scrubland and, overruling all other suggestions, decided that Raisina Hill was the best place for the future Viceregal Lodge around which stands the present Lutyens' New Delhi). After a lifetime in the ICS, Lord Hailey in 1955 was busy compiling details on the tribes of Africa which came out as a masterly volume entitled *African Survey*. Mrs Pandit was one of the few diplomats who cultivated persons prominent on stage and in cinema, apart from those in the political life of the country. Thanks to her, I met Sir George Catlin, the father of Shirley Williams. We became friends with Shirley and her husband Prof Bernard Williams who held a chair in philosophy, both at Oxford and Cambridge. Shirley helped us to get our children into the Chelsea Nursery School which had been her own school, famous for combining education with intellectual stimulus.

I made useful contacts with high-powered journalists: John Freeman, who was assistant editor to Kingsley Martin of the *New Statesman*, and who later became HC to India and Ambassador in Washington; Anthony Hartley, editor of the *Spectator*; Gould-Adams, who wrote for the *Observer*; Richard Harris, the China expert for the *Times*, and Arthur Gavshon, an expert on South Africa. There were others also: Mulgaonkar of the *Hindustan Times*; K.S. Shelvankar, the correspondent of the *Hindu* and G.K. Reddy of the *Times of India*.

The most useful were the contacts with the leaders of the Opposition. Kenneth Younger had been a deputy to Ernie Bevin, the Foreign Secretary. He later became the Head of Chatham House. Their children, Sam and Lucy, were the same age as Vijay and Vikram. (Sam today is the nearest equivalent in the UK to our Chief Election Commissioner.) It was in Kenneth's house that

I first met Tony Wedgwood Benn, son of Lord William Stansgate, the first Viscount Stansgate, who was one of the earliest protagonists of India's Independence. At a dinner at the HC's residence, as small talk, I happened to say that while most of the houses in Kensington Palace Gardens were embassy residences, one house belonged to a Labour Member of Parliament. My dinner companion said, 'It is I.' George Strauss was the former Minister of Transport. I was greatly embarrassed, but we became great friends and we spent many weekends in their Tudor country house. His wife was a Director of the Old Vic.

I was delighted by the visit of Mr Chenevix-Trench, ex-ICS. His son got a first in Classics, took a commission in an Indian army regiment to maintain the Indian connection, was taken prisoner in Singapore and spent three years in a Japanese camp. He was such an intellectual that he translated Homer's Odyssey from Greek into Urdu! Another Udaipur hand who ascended fast up the British diplomatic ladder after retiring from the Political Service was Lord Trevelyan. After serving as Ambassador to the Soviet Union, he became Governor of Aden, then a Keeper at the British Museum and was one of the few to get the Knighthood of the Garter—the highest British order, but limited to twenty-four, mostly of the royal family.

Mrs Pandit's nightmare in London was the uninvited and unexpected arrival of Krishna Menon who then wanted to get in touch directly with his old cronies of the Labour Party. Often I would be directly asked by him to make his appointments. I would, of course, inform the HC but I was not unaware that she did not like being bypassed. Mrs Pandit was very close to her brother, the PM, but even she did not quite comprehend why her brother was so indulgent towards Krishna Menon, who was spoiling India's image in the UN and the western world.

Holiday in Spain with Dinesh and Kaka Brajesh

In an extended ten days' leave, in two Volkswagens, we—including Sardarni H.S. Malik and Dinesh, then Private Secretary in Paris—

went on a holiday touring Spain. The soul of the group was Brajesh, the left-leaning uncle of Dinesh. He later married Svetlana, the only daughter of Marshal Stalin. Following Brajesh's death in Moscow, Svetlana came to India, ostensibly to scatter her husband's ashes in the Ganges, but defected to America. Rama was at Radcliffe in 1967 and may have recalled the holiday. I received a lucrative offer in New Delhi for my photographs of the Spanish holiday which, of course, I declined!

In Dublin with the High Commissioner

Mrs Pandit made headline news with photographs in the Irish papers throughout her stay in Dublin. The Irish felt a special sense of affinity with India, both having been victims of British imperialism. I can never forget one bit of conversation after the presentation of credentials. The Irish President said to Mrs Pandit, 'We have great respect for India and personal admiration for your brother.' But he added, 'We cannot understand how India stopped hating the British.' That remark summarizes the uniqueness of Gandhi's India.

For me the intellectual and political exhilaration of being in London came to an unexpected sudden end. One evening at a reception, Lady Mountbatten came and told me that she was sorry that I was leaving London. I was horrified as we thought we still had another year to go. Next morning I went in a complaining mood to Mrs Pandit and asked why I was being transferred prematurely. On questioning I told her the source of my information. She shot back that there was no question of my being moved. 'Bhai would have told me or even consulted me.' She added that she wanted me to accompany her when she presented her credentials in Dublin. I was greatly relieved, but three days later when our diplomatic bag arrived, it contained the official orders of my immediate transfer to Delhi. Lady Mountbatten's warning is my private proof that the PM managed to write to her more frequently than our official bags. The reason for my transfer to Delhi was because there was indication that the Kashmir question was going to be brought up in the Security Council in early 1957. I was one of the few who had been even marginally connected with the discussions in 1948, but before I got back to take charge, B.L. Sharma, after retiring from the Commonwealth office in Colombo, had surfaced in Delhi. He had been the Public Relations Officer with the Gopalaswami Ayyangar delegation and was familiar with the Kashmir question. He was an able, scholarly man, better suited to assembling the relevant documents and not liable to be moved around like a Foreign Service Officer. He was made Officer on Special Duty (OSD) Kashmir. It was too late to cancel my transfer and so I had to be fitted into another Deputy Secretary slot.

For some time it had been felt that recruitment to the Foreign Service was going on in an ad hoc manner. There had been no planned cadre review as to what should be the eventual size and structure of the service and, in that light, to regulate the annual intake. Having done some administration and service planning, I was made Deputy Secretary (Personnel) and charged to make a cadre appraisal of the long-term requirements of the Foreign Service.

Doubling up as Private Secretary to Krishna Menon

Just about this time, following the spectacular improvement in the relations with China, a large cultural delegation was being assembled under the leadership of Anil Chanda. An Indian troupe was to spend three months performing in different cities. Romesh Bhandari had got himself attached to Krishna Menon since the New York days and had been appointed as his Private Secretary when he became Minister without Portfolio in the central government. Romesh was eager to go with the delegation to China and apparently I was selected by Krishna Menon to temporarily deputize for Romesh and at the same time continue as DS (Ad-P). Krishna Menon had been assigned the large corner room at the end of the corridor to the PM's room. He moved next door to what used to be the waiting room for the Maharajas, about one-fifth its size, but he ordered a five-ton air conditioner so that any one but the occupant froze in a few minutes. Panditji, in a similar-sized room, had no air conditioner whatsoever. He told me to move into his big room and so I found myself in the old Political Secretary's office. (It was alleged to have had a secret safe where the dubious wills of Maharajas were kept!).

Suez nationalization: Users' Conference

It was quite a trying experience to work with Krishna Menon. He worked incessantly but seemed to live on just innumerable cups of tea, occasionaly with biscuits. I saw from close quarters how he manoeuvered his indispensability. For example, he would telephone a chosen ambassador, such as Ali Yawar Jung in Cairo, to send a message that the Egyptians wanted to consult him. It was during his term in 1956 that Nasser decided to nationalize the Suez Canal. Much of the Canal permitted only one-way passage of ships; 110 m. tons passed through the Canal during one year. There was alarm among all the European and most East-Asian Users at Nasser's decision. The right of nationalization of an international company was to be challenged at an eighteen-nation Users' Conference called in London. Krishna Menon was designated the leader and I was nominated the Secretary of the Indian delegation. We were briefed by Prime Minister Nehru and I remember he was horrified at the conservative attitude of most Canal users. 'What has happened to liberal approaches?' he asked rhetorically. The US was represented by Secretary of State John Foster Dulles, and Australia by Prime Minister Menzies himself. Krishna Menon consulted Ali Sabry before his own intervention—the last to do so—in which he made clear that India was, of course, vitally dependent on the use of the Suez but that we not question the sovereignty over Egyptian territory, unless its use was obstructed. India's attitude was consistent with the post-colonial era but India was in a minority. (We did not attend any of the subsequent Users' Committees in which Australia took an aggressive attitude.) Krishna Menon's presentation was well argued from the point of view of international law, but he personally got a very bad press.

Contrary to widespread fears of the Users, there was no inefficiency in the operation of the Canal. The ongoing proposal to widen and deepen the Canal continued.

The sequel to the nationalization of the Suez was the Anglo-French and Israeli conspiracy to re-take the Canal area militarily, which was an abysmal failure. India was prophetically right on the Canal but not so on Hungary where, at about the same time, a revolt against Stalinist imposition took place and nationalism was brutally suppressed. It raised doubts whether our non-alignment meant an unprincipled tilt in favour of communist governments.

Suez led to a painful military debacle. Any attempt to frustrate nationalism and reestablish hegemony over world communications was bound to fail. But the British and the French were under the illusion that they had the right and the military capacity to protect their perceived interests. It was significant for another reason. While the superpowers remained vigilant against each other, both separately condemned the Anglo-French action in the Canal Zone. The US restraint in Hungary also signified that, unless there was a threat to their homelands, neither superpower was prepared to risk nuclear war. Suez also ended the illusion that the Commonwealth was a sort of successor to the empire. It was only after 1956 that the British government started examining its residual commitments 'East of Suez.' It ended in the dismantling of all military establishments including the major base in Singapore. Hong Kong alone was left as an outpost of the old empire.

The residents of all old colonies continued to be entitled to British citizenship which, in turn, facilitated substantial migration into the UK until it was restricted in the sixties. The old common citizenship concept brought economic gain but also racial tensions. The Commonwealth ballast was the principal reason why the UK stood aloof when six European countries signed the Treaty of Rome in 1957. Britain was slow to recognize that its own overriding interest was in being integrated with Europe.

Suez accelerated the decolonization process. Malaya and Ghana became independent in 1957. By the 1960s the 'winds of change' as Macmillan defined it, led to freedom for Nigeria, then East Africa and other British colonies. When de Gaulle came to power, France was ready to abandon Algeria, but after Suez, Belgium too, began to see the writing on the wall. The era which started with India in 1947, got its fulfilment in 1956.

Nehru recognized the end of European hegemony. I personally wish that immediately after Suez, seeing the parallel interest of superpowers in supporting nationalism, Nehru had started crusading for détente and disarmament based on non-aligned ideological agnosticism. In Belgrade in 1961, he openly disagreed with Sukarno that neo-colonialism was still strong. Nehru's focus was on the end of nuclear testing with the priority shifting to indigenous development. He thought there was insufficient recognition that this was primarily a national responsibility to be pragmatically evolved by each country. People's empowerment had begun; it would lead to a horizontal bipolarity between the rich and the poor. A centrifugal force with a hundred liberated new countries was the reality of the twentieth century. Suez was the last gasp of western empires but, sadly, instead of showing a greater sense of responsibility, the Third World itself became more dependent on dole-outs and the centripetal force of the Cold War.

The immediate consequence of the Suez fiasco was the resignation of Antony Eden as Prime Minister of the United Kingdom. The developing countries forgot that with the demand for freedom and self-determination, we had also promised our people austerity and moral rectitude.

8

The North-Eastern Limitrophe: bogged down by the India–China Boundary Question (1956–61)

I was pitchforked into dealing with China and I have remained its hostage for much of my career since then and, even after retirement, I am considered an 'expert' on Sino-Indian relations. It best illustrates happenstance.

The rationale for my posting to the Eastern Division: IFAS and Tribal NEFA

I was moved from Deputy Secretary (Pers) to Deputy Secretary (East) at the end of 1956 only because I had some experience in administration and in conceptualizing a new service. Our Ministry had inherited the responsibility for North-East Frontier Agency (NEFA) and Nagaland. Nehru brought a constructive attitude towards the tribal belt to be implemented by a newly constituted Indian Frontier Administrative Service (IFAS). The British-Indian policy had been to quarantine the 'primitive' tribals, away from political contamination. Prime Minister Nehru desired to introduce a controlled development of NEFA, as well as to protect the tribals from commercialization and exploitation, which was likely by the duplication of civil administration as practised in the plains districts. Non-tribals were still not allowed to enter and settle beyond the 'inner line' which ran along the edge of the hills.

The first problem I encountered when I was moved to the Eastern Division was that we had about ninety Koreans behind barbed wire in the Delhi Cantonment. The reason for their imprisonment was only that they did not want to go back to North Korea or to Taiwan but to stay in a neutral country like India. The Korean Repatriation Commission, of which India was Chairman, was entrusted to sort out individual preferences. These neutralists had been incarcerated for four years and were virtually forgotten by the External Affairs and the Defence Ministries. I decided to reopen the case and give all of them the option to migrate, if accepted, to any country of their choice or be gainfully occupied in India. Many went to Brazil, but nine were left in India. One became a watch repairer—his former profession—and we provided him with a loan to open a shop; another was a photographer and so we gave him the wherewithal to buy a camera. The person I became interested in was called Peter. (His Korean name was Nwang Ji.) He wanted to start a chicken farm and so we managed to get him a small piece of land in Okhla that belonged to a church and provided him with funds to buy some hens and a cock and a stock of feed. He lived in a tent with a kerosene lantern right through the summer and winter for a year or two. He carefully tended his chickens, gave them a clean habitat and the right mix of feed. Very soon, limousines from the diplomatic corps residences started going to his farm to buy quality eggs and chicken! The long and short of it is that, after making a profit from the chicken hatchery, Peter started collecting long tresses of widows' hair, generally from the South, where widows shaved their heads after their husbands died. Peter took the trouble of grading the hair by length, colour and quality, and then exported the classified hair to South Korea where they were turned into wigs for export to US at enormous profit at every stage of the transaction.

Thereafter, Peter went into the garment export business and subsequently, started screening people for suitability for employment in Saudi Arabia and the Gulf. The recipient nations were grateful to have a reliable intermediary. In twenty years' time, he was a multimillionaire, with a large house in Friends Colony (East). He always remembered with gratitude what India had done for him.

Peter became a friend, and I went to visit him from time to time. He also became a great golfer and used to play regularly with Bharat Ram. The family is a permanent resident of India but keeps up a thriving trading relationship with the Republic of Korea.

I used to take my young children, when they were between four and eight, to visit Peter in his tent with his kerosene lamp and cleanly-nested chickens. I held him up as an example of firm determination to make good.

NEFA remained outside the domain of the Assam administration and its legislature. My distant cousin and much closer friend, K.L. Mehta, was ADGA (Advisor to the Governor of Assam). Verrier Elwin, a distinguished anthropologist, who had worked with tribals in the Central Provinces, and had married a Gondal, had been appointed Tribal Advisor for NEFA. His counsel was to establish an administration, respecting local customs. The IFAS was composed of a handful of specially chosen mid-level officers, mostly from the army, who were likely to be compassionately inclined to study the distinct individuality of the tribals, and be prepared to live for many years in the austere NEFA conditions. I was to implement this so-called single-line administration at the Secretariat end. T.N. Kaul, Joint Secretary (East), and in charge of the Division, told me 'Forget Europe, look East.' He had no crystal ball for the crisis with China, which I would have to handle with an approach very different from his own during the 1954 negotiations for the Agreement on Tibet.

The Foreign Secretary, Subimal Dutt, was rather conservative in attitude towards travel but even so I was allowed to visit the area in order to familiarize myself with my new parish. After talking to the ADGA and his deputy, Yusuf Ali, and Verrier Elwin in Shillong, I went to some divisional (district) headquarters. By 1957, we had small airstrips where Dakotas could land; a few roads were under construction but generally, civil supplies including food-grain bags had to be brought in by air over a vast area. I also went on airdropping missions and, since it meant skillful banking between high ranges on either side, it was quite dangerous and so, each time I was required to sign a declaration that I was doing so voluntarily in order to exempt the contracted company from contingent liability. But it was a great experience to be associated in understanding different customs, helping to fashion a sympathetic administration and consolidating control over what, we had no doubt, was part of India but had been left in tribal primitivism by British imperialism.

There were sections other than NEFA under my charge. East Asia (EA), covering Japan, China, Mongolia and the Koreas, was nearest to normal 'foreign' countries. I realized that, as Alistair Lamb* in his monumental work describes it, there was a running conflict between Tibet as seen by Calcutta, Simla and New Delhi, and as perceived by Whitehall. The shadow of the majestic Himalayas straddled my other two sections: Bhutan, Sikkim and Tibet (BST) and Nepal. Each section had a separate Under Secretary, but the ethnicity, culture and history were different and so was their politics. The unity and link came from the high mountain chain.

My first encounter with two approaches to civil services ethics

The conventional practice was that, at the Deputy Secretary level, the working responsibility was confined to marshalling facts and ensuring implementation, while policy was decided by the head of divisions. My personal view has been that a good professional Foreign Service officer should always have a long-distance vision. The Deputy Secretary's task is limited to what is decreed from above. I remember one small incident. Bandhopadhyay, a young Foreign Service officer (who later resigned, became an author and a distinguished professor in Calcutta), was subsequently attached to the Eastern Division for training. After talking to him, I gave him

---

*Alistair Lamb, *Tibet, China and India—A History of Imperial Diplomacy 1914–50*, (Oxford Books: 1989).

the nearest 'top secret' file on my desk to study and write a 'policy note' on a separate paper as an exercise in analysis. Two weeks later, he made a courtesy call on the Joint Secretary. Apparently he was told, 'Understand this, young man, that at this stage of your career, your business is not to think on policy but to make sure that the facts are summarized.' Young Bandhopadhyay surreptitiously shared the contradiction between the approach of the Deputy Secretary and that of the Joint Secretary. When I eventually heard about it, I advised him that he should go by the senior advice. My view, however, remains that the Foreign Service approach to obedience should be different from that of the military. As in the Charge of the Light Brigade, we should be prepared to 'do or to die'. We should have the courage of thought, exercise the right of dissent at the advisory stage, and have no hesitation in implementing clear decisions. I knew the Joint Secretary often put up files to the Foreign Secretary and, after recording his own minutes, ended with the submission 'For orders'. I have never done that. Unless one has independent views on major problems, and keeps correcting the approach with experience, one may be stumped suddenly at the policy level and fumble in constructive diplomacy. Anyway in 1956–57, I was not in the loop of actual policy-making, but occasionally, I was a proximate observer.

In the spring of 1957, after the celebration of 2500 years of Lord Buddha's birth, T.N. Kaul, in charge, Eastern Division (who had brought me to the Division), was engaged in persuading the Dalai Lama to return to Lhasa and not to complicate the friendship with China. He was, of course, reflecting the PM's own inclination. But he left on transfer to Tehran. Later, in 1958, bilateral talks were held in Delhi on the issue of the Bara Hoti plain and were led by B.K. Acharya, Kaul's successor. This is a high-altitude pasture beyond a steep mountain on the Indian side, which was traditionally used as a grazing ground in summer both by Indians from the south and the Tibetans from the north. There had been competition and even clashes between the two parties but the Bara Hoti pasture lay south of the watershed divide. I was only an observer during the talks but at the time we did not publicize them. The talks ended inconclusively.

The Division was subject to different policy impulses caused by trying to interpret Nehru's mind, but doubts, if they existed, were never articulated. Nehru's dominant thought seems to have been that China, though it had not been occupied, had been humiliated even more than India, and so was delayed in its aspirations for development and, therefore, should be helped to face the Containment policies of the West. Containment in this part of the world meant South-East Asia Treaty Organization (SEATO)—of which Pakistan, Thailand and the Philippines were members—whereas our policy of non-alignment implied non-hostility. India exerted itself to be China's spokesman with Burma and Nepal at the Afro-Asian meeting in Bandung (1955). Nobody told Nehru, at the time, that proud China would deem it as patronizing.

The Himalayas: strategic barrier or bridge of friendship

Nehru himself did not wholly ignore the evidence of China being guilty of unilaterally smothering the innocent, peaceful people of Tibet and of not fulfilling the seventeen-point internal Agreement of 1951 with the Dalai Lama's government, or the 1954 Agreement with India where we had readily surrendered many advantages inherited from British India. Traditionally, the Himalayas were deemed sacred not only in Hinduism but also in Buddhism and were considered an impregnable barrier militarily. There was the beginning of a suspicion that 'south of the Himalayas' was not accepted in China as part of India's outer strategic and cultural frontier. For the sake of promoting a climate of peace, it was considered prudent not to raise these controversial questions, which could dilute the solidarity of anti-imperialism. India was inclined to be indulgent and suppress the differences. The dominant credo was that non-alignment must assuage fears aroused by Containment. Thus, while India was firmly democratic at home, it did not endorse the anti-communist rhetoric of Western democracies or even of some leaders of Ceylon like Sir John Kotlewala. But the economic pull of the West could not be denied, at least in the North Block; in the South Block, however, it was believed that we could presume our political inclination was to the East. Anyway, there were problems in relation within BST (Bhutan, Sikkim and Tibet) and Nepal where, following India, nationalism was asserting itself with the winds of decolonization.

Sikkim and Bhutan

Nehru respected the cultural identities of Sikkim and Bhutan. These two principalities bordered India, but like Nepal, lay south of the Himalayan watershed. This brought out Nehru's empathy for their distinctness. Sardar Patel, a more strategic pragmatist, drew the policy for post-imperial India. In addition to being Home Minister, Sardar Patel was successor to the Political Department with V.P. Menon as the Secretary and, later, Advisor. Sardar Patel's policy led to the integration of 550-odd princely states even before our Constitution was adopted in 1950. Sikkim was a member of the Chamber of the Princes and its head, like that of other states, was titled Maharaja and, on arrival in Delhi, was given a fifteen-gun salute calibrated to its medium size. (The Deb Raja of Bhutan was also eventually called 'Maharaja,' but he had no connection with the Chamber of Princes and was more akin to Nepal, a 'foreign' country.) The Political Officer in Gangtok was like the Political Agent in the princely states but he was also the supervisory officer over the Consulate General in Lhasa and the Trade Agencies in Tibet. I believe that, had the location of the Political Officer been Kalimpong (in Bengal) instead of Gangtok, Sikkim, like the other gun-salute states and following the standard policy, might have fallen in line with post-Independence policy, and been persuaded to accede to the Union of India in 1948–49. The Political Officer in Gangtok came under External Affairs rather than the Political Department because of its supervisory responsibilities in Tibet and Kashgar and the semi-diplomatic position of Bhutan and Nepal. The ruling family of Sikkim was of Tibetan origin. By 1947, the majority of the resident population in Sikkim were, in fact, immigrants from Nepal, but a sizeable number, especially in posts of higher responsibilities, traced their links to Tibet. Nehru inherited External Affairs, and his approach was different from that of Sardar Patel. He wanted to respect the distinct cultural personality of Sikkim in much the same way as Nepal. In my own view, Nehru's approach to Sikkim, Bhutan and Nepal was consistent with their non-Indianness and decolonization. Unlike China vis-à-vis Tibet, he did not want to impose subordination and obliterate their identity. In fact, there is still revulsion for China in Tibet; indeed the basis of their nationalism, as that of Mongolia, Korea and Vietnam, is fear of China; despite half a century of ideology and propaganda, China has failed to win their hearts and minds.

Nehru knew that, notwithstanding their separate identities, Nepal, Bhutan and Sikkim were equally important strategically because they lay south of the Himalayan water shed, and were within India's outer defence parameter. He believed that by giving them sustained friendship, he could make them not merely depend on India but identify with it. Nehru did not fully recognize, and the Ministry failed to advise him, that in the twentieth century nothing was as difficult as diplomacy between unequal neighbours. The spread of communications was bound to sharpen the sensibilities of their separate identities. Most of us, having been schooled in European history, had imbibed the old notion that the ultimate trump card of national destiny is military power. Not even Nehru made allowance for the suspicions—sometimes justified, at other times not—of crediting giant India with hegemonic propensities, which would virtually landlock these limitrophe neighbours.

Sikkim, Bhutan and Nepal illustrate the oscillation between anti-Imperialism and modern nationalism. Harishwar Dayal was appointed the first Indian Political Officer in 1949. He negotiated the treaty with Bhutan in 1949, repeating the exact words of the

1910 Treaty that 'Bhutan will seek advice of the government of India in its external relations.' This inevitably raised the question whether Bhutan was obliged to act according to India's advice or merely to seek its counsel. Bhutan's reservations came to surface in 1950.

Under the treaty with Sikkim, concluded in 1950, it was declared a protectorate, which was no doubt a pseudo-imperialistic phrase, but even so, less undignified than integration. (After the lapse of paramountcy this theoretically meant the return of the right of independence.) Under the treaty the Indian army could be deployed wherever it was considered militarily necessary from the security viewpoint. The astute diplomacy of the Maharaj Kumar, supported by the beauty and charm of his two sisters—Coola and Cuckoola—slowly but systematically managed to erode the provisions of the treaty. For example, the Dewan in Sikkim was to be nominated by India, but the Sikkimese government got India's consent to choose one outside the treaty. Most political officers would swing between initial admiration and support for enlarging Sikkim's autonomy, avoiding treating it as a 'protectorate,' and a harsher attitude reflecting deep suspicions of the intentions of the royal family, before completing their tenures. For example, the Maharaj Kumar, who succeeded his father, appropriated the title of Chogyal (meaning King in Tibetan). He married Hope Cooke, an American, and we in India began to suspect that she was a stalking horse of the CIA. We would have been justified in taking Sikkim into the Indian Union when our Constitution was being drafted, but when the actual integration took place in 1973–75, it laid us open to the charge that even India with all its principles, 'annexed' beyond its own declared frontiers. It did not add one whit to our national security but it did violate Nehru's instinct for respecting Sikkim's separate identity and relying on diplomacy to preserve the strategic interdependence. We were forced by the Maharaj Kumar (Chogyal), and the royal family into contributing to the erosion of Sikkim's defined autonomy, which ended in connived integration, and made India guilty of violating the principles of International Law. I, for one, am not critical of Prime Minister Nehru's respecting Sikkim's historical identity. I am unhappy that we deliberately abandoned our principles. The story of Bhutan is different because there, Nehru's consummate diplomacy earned a lasting friendship.

Nepal: India wavers between hegemonic instincts and benign development

Initially in Nepal, after the defanging of the Rana regime, democratic India was held up as a model and Nehru accepted as a reliable friend and leader. The treaty with Nepal was signed with the oligarchic Rana regime, but our diplomacy did not go so far as to respect a small country's sensitivity and its rights as a landlocked country.* Kosi and Gandak flood control projects were designed to give maximum advantage to Bihar but ignored the resultant increased submergence of the Nepal terai. Our officials and engineers did not live up to the spirit of Nehru's approach in foreign policy. I visited Kathmandu in 1958 when Bhagwan Sahay was ambassador. It was his masterly diplomacy that persuaded King Mahendra to approve the democratic constitution. After Bhagwan Sahay left, while B.P. Koirala did not want to alienate India, Nepalese nationalism was inclined to be neutral between India and China, and this provoked anger in India. By 1959, the hatred of the overlordship of India had become part of rising Nepalese nationalism. Earlier incidents, like ambassdor C.P.N. Singh choosing M.P. Koirala instead of the more respected B.P. Koirala as head of the first post-Rana government, and even asking the Nepalese Cabinet to meet in the Indian Embassy were recalled. Nehru's reaction in 1961, openly expressing regret when the democratic government was overthrown by King Mahendra contradicted his own declared adherence to the principles of non-interference in the internal affairs of another country including the USSR. The fact remains

*Ibid Chapter VIII

that no two countries in the world had such a natural and irreversible interdependence as India and Nepal but looking back, it is perhaps the biggest diplomatic failure in history.

Accompanying Nehru on an election tour, 1957

I must have evoked the envy of my colleagues and even senior officers when, in February 1957, I was told, presumably with the PM's approval, to accompany him on a ten-day election tour. This was probably because Kashmir was being discussed in New York. It was the first time that the PM was to travel in an IL-14 aircraft presented by the Soviet Union. After flying from Delhi, we went directly in a motorcade tour of Panditji's constituency (Phulpur) adjoining Allahabad. Thereafter, the pattern was three stops every day when he would address public meetings and, without rest, go back to the aircraft and on to the next destination, staying overnight in a major township. We visited Nagpur, Vijayawada, Hyderabad, Bangalore, etc., and then went on a three-day tour by car and rail along the Kerala coast ending in Mangalore. This was the only election that Panditji did not win. On the last but one day when we were flying to Jabalpur, the port engine of the aircraft caught fire and we had to make a landing on the nearest unkempt airstrip, in Raipur. The automatic built-in firefighting mechanism in the IL-14 worked in the nick of time. A national calamity and the loss of our beloved PM was averted. In the rear cabin, Panditji was reading Krishna Menon's nine-hour speech on Kashmir. What remains engraved in my memory, is the immediate recognition of Panditji by a passing cattle herdsman from an obscure village.

Accompanying the Vice-President to South-east Asia, China and Mongolia

I was also asked to accompany Dr S. Radhakrishnan, who deputized for the President on many state visits covering Kampuchea, Laos, North and South Vietnam, China and Mongolia. They started with a mishap on the very first day in Kampuchea, when an ADC banged the door of the huge sedan shut on the little finger of the Vice-President and fractured it. The Vice-President overruled the idea of cancelling the trip.

The most memorable part was in Hanoi, where Ho Chi Minh played host. When he appeared in public and took off his coat because of the heat, it was found that he was wearing only a vest under it!

The most crucial of these visits was, of course, to China. Within the country, we used a Chinese air force plane. The Vice-President and I were put up in the house called Chrysanthemum Fragrance next to Mao Zedong's own library in Chang-Nan-Hai. (I am going by the diagram contained in the biography titled *The Private Life of Chairman Mao* by his personal doctor Li Zhisui*).

Until I met Lord Chris Patten, former Governor of Hong Kong, I did not know of any other VIP having been put up in this vast Chinese garden next to the Forbidden City, with residences reserved for the members of the Politburo. Mao himself made immediate arrangements for the treatment of the Vice-President's fractured finger by calling his own specialist. This was more effective than the bandages that had been used on the earlier stops.

The Chinese knew that the Vice-President was a vegetarian. Every meal followed an elaborate menu which was relished by the invitees and the guests. At the first formal banquet, one of the dishes was described as 'The dragon and the tiger'. In fact, it was a slow-cooked cat and a decapitated serpent! It shocked Mrs R.K. Nehru, the wife of the Indian Ambassador, but it was obviously part of the special culinary dishes prepared to celebrate the occasion of the Indian Vice President's visit! Dr Radhakrishnan was usually done after the first course and would lit bored during the next twenty-three items on the menu!

The discussions were conducted mostly by Chairman Mao himself, but to underline their significance, the entire Politburo

---

*Li Zhisui, *The Private Life of Chairman Mao*, (Random House: 1994)

was in attendance, including Liu Shao-ch'i, Marshal Zhu De, Zhou Enlai, etc. I have a prized photograph of the Chairman with members of the Chinese hierarchy on either side of Mao and Dr Radhakrishnan. I am standing behind Mao himself with Natwar Singh, then Third Secretary, next to me.

The Chinese had obviously made detailed preparations for the Vice-President's visit. Kalidas's *Shakuntalam* had been translated from Sanskrit and was performed for Dr Radhakrishnan. But the ultimate honour was inviting him to address the National People's Congress. We had heard that the experiment to 'let a hundred flowers bloom and a hundred schools of thoughts contend'—a licence for allowing the expression of dissent through big-character wall posters—had evoked such criticism instead of giving a feeling of freedom and participation, that it was summarily withdrawn. Dr Radhakrishnan, in his address, felicitated the People's Republic and, while not criticizing the one-party communist government, he made bold to add that people must be allowed a sense of democratic participation. Ambassador R.K. Nehru was opposed to such frank expression as it might cause needless offence to the hosts, but Dr Radhakrishnan wanted to be true to his own conscience. After paying tribute to the arduous and protracted Long March of the P.L.A. under Chairman Mao, he hinted that if the people felt frustrated, then 'with raw courage' they could challenge the government. It was clear that Dr Radhakrishan himself commanded great respect as a philosopher-statesman. Though he went against the Ambassador's advice, his open criticism of the National People's Congress seemed to have no adverse effect. Mao continued to preside over the other functions in his honour. After a few days in the capital, we went to Shanghai and Hangchow.

Thereafter, we flew to Ulan Bator, the capital of the Mongolian People's Republic. It was September but I remember that when we landed about midday it was snowing. At night it was bitterly cold; there were only a few stone buildings but tents with double covers were visible everywhere. The modernization of the Mongolian

People's Republic had not yet got underway. I recall seeing Molotov, who had long been a fixture as Stalin's Foreign Minister, but now banished as Soviet Ambassador to Mongolia, the least important Socialist country, by Khrushchev!

It was immediately after Dr Radhakrishan's visit that the *China Pictorial*, an official magazine, carried a map of the Sinkiang highway clearly cutting across Aksai Chin which, as notified in our official map of 1954, was part of India. One wondered whether this had been deliberately delayed in order not to complicate the Vice-President's visit, but no one had raised the boundary question during the discussions in Peking. To me this reflected the national self-confidence of China, but it also proved that, while China secretly harboured notions of its extended limits, in 1957 it saw an advantage in maintaining friendly relations with India. No one in the Chinese hierarchy understood the working of a Parliamentary democracy. What followed thereafter is related in my book, *Negotiating for India*. There was deep concern in India over the Kongka Pass incident in 1958 where nine from an Indian party were killed. It was at this stage in December that Nehru wrote to Zhou Enlai, but he still hoped that China would be frank, and his ideas of non-alignment would not be exposed as hollow and wishful. It should have been clear that both sides were on different wavelengths and neither understood the other.

With the PM on a trek to Bhutan

The third special tour in which I was involved (fuller details given in my book*) was Panditji's visit in September 1958 to Bhutan. It emanated from my spontaneous and, perhaps unthinking suggestion, in a one-to-one conversation with the PM, to use part of the three weeks blocked in his calendar for going to Lhasa to visit Bhutan too. I still remember the dressing-down I received

---

*Jagat S. Mehta, *Negotiating for India* (Manohar: 2006) Chapter II.

from the Foreign Secretary the next morning. He asked me who had authorized me to make the suggestion. I went back to my room, locking the door from the inside and almost crying, thinking what would happen if, on one of the high-altitude passes, Panditji were to get an angina attack, as had R.K. Nehru, the previous Foreign Secretary. Panditji, however, could not be persuaded to cancel the visit however hazardous. As it happened, once again, although merely a Deputy Secretary, I was asked to accompany the PM.

The Bhutan visit was perhaps Nehru's longest-lasting diplomatic achievement. Had Nehru not gone when he did, no prime ministerial visit might ever have taken place. Without a road connection with India, Bhutan might have suffered the same fate as Tibet. The Chinese must be cursing themselves that they did not issue the promised permit to Nehru to go to Lhasa where, like any present-day tourist, he would have gone around the 1000-room Potala Palace. While in Lhasa, Nehru was unlikely to play the Tibet card with China, and the Dalai Lama might even have prevaricated before seeking refuge in India.

We have to be grateful for China's unintended mistake which enabled Nehru to go to Bhutan* on horseback, riding on yaks and on foot, transitting through the Tibetan Chumbi valley, finally reaching Paro, the westernmost Djong. Nehru had friendly discussions with the old King and allayed any psychological hesitations about India's intentions. By selling surplus electric power, Bhutan has augmented its own resources for development, and even graduated to greater democratization. The important point is that Bhutan, lying south of the Himalayas, with all its rivers merging with the Brahmaputra, seems to recognize that its strategic identity is linked with India's progress. Bhutan resisted resorting to non-alignment as blackmail between two large neighbours, as was done by Nepal. By supporting Bhutan's

---

*Jagat S. Mehta, *Negotiating for India*: (Manohar 2006) Chapter II.

membership of the UN, and by not objecting when, using its sovereign discretion in voting, Bhutan demonstrated its independence, India's friendship with Bhutan was not damaged.

Dalai Lama's escape triggers the India–China crisis

Even after Nehru's letter of December 1958, we did not expect a sharp deterioration in our relations with the People's Republic. My bit of proof about this is that, at the end of January, I was allowed to go with a small group on a ten-day skiing holiday to Gulmarg, and the PM asked us to take his grandson Rajiv, who was on vacation from Doon School. The simmering anxiety about relations with China increased only after the Dalai Lama arrived on the first India–Tibet border on 31 March 1959. When it became known that he had fled in disguise from Norbulinka Palace, it was publicized as the greatest escape of the century. When the Dalai Lama narrated how the Tibetan civilization was being trampled on, in his heart of hearts, Nehru, like the ordinary people of India and the world and certainly our Parliament, had sympathy for the fate of Tibet. By giving refuge to 1,00,000 fleeing Tibetans, authorizing Tibetan language schools financed by the central government, and permitting Tibetan monasteries for monks, Nehru may have actually saved the remnants of a peaceful civilization. The Chinese insensitivity to and disregard of Indian territorial integrity, as publicly notified, came only in September 1959. Nehru's chief concern was still not to get deflected from non-alignment, but due to being generally misled, or even deliberately deceived, he was put on the defensive in Parliament. Without prior consultations, he committed himself to the release of all correspondence and notes exchanged with China since 1954 in 'White' papers.

My own conviction is that the turning point was the article in the *Peking Review* titled 'The Revolt in Tibet and Nehru's Philosophy.' It was probably authored by Chairman Mao himself.

There is a curious non-professional switching from the third person to the second person, which could not have happened if it had been drafted in the Waijabu (Foreign Office). In my view, Nehru's being denounced personally left no latitude for negotiations when Zhou Enlai came to Delhi in April 1960. The Chinese leaders who had never worked a democracy probably failed to understand this. One can understand their misjudgement since Nehru himself had given the clarion call of 'Hindi–Chini Bhai Bhai' (Indians and Chinese are brothers). The Chinese must have thought that Nehru could mould public opinion in India as they could in a communist state.

Leading the Indian team: defending our frontiers

Being required to lead the delegation and furnish detailed evidence to confirm that 50,000 square miles claimed by China was traditionally Indian, *after* it had been declared as such by our PM himself, was not only an onerous responsibility, but it was also largely one of diplomatic advocacy. Following the conversations between the two Prime Ministers, when the joint communiqué was issued, I knew it had been hurriedly conceived. On careful scrutiny, we had an impossible brief in a deadlocked situation. I myself was surprised by the extent to which we were successful as advocates of national territorial integrity. We handled an anxiety-riddled, irksome and difficult burden tolerably well. No fresh violent incidents occurred. Throughout there was bonhomie between the delegations. During the Delhi session, the Chinese came to dinner in my flat; such a visit had never before taken place. There were even a few light moments when I discovered that Chang Wen-chin knew English because he alone understood my stupid parody of Heine's *Watch on the Rhine* in German:

'Zum Lein:
Zum Indishe Lein
Fest steht und treu
Die wacht McMahon Lein.'

'To the line:
The Indian line
Faithful and vigilant stands
The watch on the McMahon Line.'

As a matter of interest for my grandchildren—there are not many who interest for have had the privilege that I have had of signing a map certifying the 'frontiers of India.'

My greatest satisfaction, however, was Panditji's approval of the concluding chapter of the draft where I tactfully accused China of betraying the five principles of good relations between independent states. Chang immediately saw its frightening implications but we parted as friends.

All our discussions were held during the grey period of India–China relations; friendship had proved only skin-deep, but nobody anticipated that, after two years, there would be an India–China war. I feel it may have been precipitated by the misjudgement behind our Forward Policy. Panditji was mentally not prepared for the massive scale of the attack that took place in 1962. It proved a fatal setback to Nehru's vision and Foreign Policy, and could have shortened his longevity.

The six-month-long talks with China and the meetings every other day without any hope of substantive progress (and not simply reiteration of propaganda), were the longest sustained negotiations in Chinese or Indian history. The exercise was certainly nerve-wracking, but I learnt that, for a democracy, diplomacy is necessarily more difficult, and there are penalties for naïvety in timely anticipation. However, in the twenty-first century perspective, I remain convinced that Nehru was prophetic in his faith in interdependence. We professionals must share the blame for there being not a single word of dissenting caution.

The India–China report was signed in December; it was printed hurriedly and presented to Parliament mid-February. I have a precious copy signed by Jawaharlal Nehru. Many years later, China published its own report and Chang Wen-chin sent me a signed copy. The report, in a single cover, contains both the Indian and the Chinese summaries. It dominated the discussions on the President's annual address. There was generally a favourable view of the case as argued by the Indian officials. Though we had made a better positive case than the Chinese, there has been no progress since in the negotiated resolution despite the meetings of many committees and officials. Of course, it should never have come to this. In retrospect, it was proof of diplomatic failure on both sides. If Zhou had been more straightforward, Nehru might have piloted an exchange of NEFA with Aksai Chin in 1957, but it was no longer possible in 1960.

In my book on the negotiations, I have briefly mentioned the Herculean task of four stenographers who, within one week, flawlessly typed two original sets of nearly 600 printed pages of the Indian and the Chinese reports. I urged Panditji, and he readily obliged by coming on Christmas Day 1960 so that we could reward each of them with a photograph posing with the PM in his South Block office.

Working on relations with China was not always without spasms of anxiety. As a precaution, I had had all my PAs cleared by Intelligence Bureau (IB). For a month I slept in my office rather than take top-secret files home. The PAs took turns working till late in the night but, after a long day, some would go out to relax. One of my stenographers was arrested because he went to a dance party and was caught talking to an Assamese, who looked Chinese! I had to intervene to certify his reliability.

The Queen's visit

After being the chief guest at our Republic Day parade, the Queen made short trips to different parts of India and Pakistan. Considering that this was the first visit after the transfer of power, the British wanted the reception for their monarch to match the one given to President Eisenhower in 1959. Udaipur, which was famous for its historic dislike of foreign conquerors was included in the itinerary. The royal party came after visiting the Taj Mahal in Agra, but protocol demanded the stay be low-key as 30 January was the anniversary of Gandhiji's assassination. Rama and I were brought along because it was known to be my hometown.

Much of the day was spent in Jag Niwas, now Lake Palace Hotel. The host, Maharana Bhagwat Singhji, must have mentioned that he had been feeding a huge crocodile for this visit. Notwithstanding the advice of MEA, Prince Philip could not resist the temptation to shoot the creature. Surreptitiously, accompained by only a few persons, he sneaked out to the little island on a rowboat and, sure enough, the crocodile was sunning itself on the rock where its food had been thrown for months. Never having fired a shot from a rowboat, Philip missed but the shot was heard by all on the mainland. It was only because of the lavish flow of Scotch whisky, etc., superintended by Rashid Baig and myself, that the multihued journalists did not advertise the incident; otherwise the Queen's visit might have been summarily terminated. *Tehelka*, or its likes, would certainly have leaked the attempted outrage. In Ahmedabad, the next stop, the crowds broke the bamboo barricades and tried to touch the Queen's hat; the security people were alarmed but the photographers got a shot which made it comparable to the welcome accorded to Eisenhower.

By May 1961 I had been in Delhi for five years and was overdue for an overseas posting. At the end of the Parliamentary session, I left on transfer. Tyabji had just come back from Germany and was Secretary-in-Charge of Administration. He changed my posting from Ambassador elsewhere to go as second-in-command Germany. I was a distant, but anxious, observer of the Forward Policy started in the second half of 1961 which had led to the India–China War of 1962.

9

Divided Germany: 'Ich bin ein Berliner'; Franco–German Reconciliation (1961–63)

I arrived in Bonn in July 1961 and took over from Avtar Singh as Minister Political and number two in the Mission. Tari, as he was fondly called, lived in a largish manor house in Wesseling on the left bank of the Rhine, and from our garden, we could see the constant stream of barges going up and down the European waterway. Wesseling was a semi-industrial township with a warbuilt refinery where Hitler's Germany had converted brown coal into oil. The trouble was that, on a warm sunny day when the wind blew from the south, it was impossible to escape the smell from the refinery. I wished for a house in Bad Godesberg, but I did not want to go through the chore of finding new accommodation so I moved into the house even though it was not ideally located. However, it had large sitting and dining rooms and was suitable for entertainment.

We put Vijay, our daughter, and Uday, our youngest son, in the local Volks schule, and after only three months, Vijay qualified for the Hersel Gymnasium, where all instructions, including Latin and Greek, was given in German. On the advice of our friend, Anne Money-Coutts, who had a large house in Hampshire, Vikram, then aged nine, had been put into a preparatory boarding school. Anne had ups and downs in her marriage. Her son Crispin became manager of the Coutts Bank, the Queen's bank, and Vikram has remained Anne's adopted son. Ajay, I think mistakenly, was put in the English language British Army School in Cologne; otherwise his German too, would have been well grounded. I had to travel seventeen kilometres every day to the Chancery in Bonn in the south, and Ajay was driven to school about eighteen kilometers to the north; so we were obliged to have two cars—one large Mercedes for Ajay and the entire family for weekends, and a Beetle Volkswagen for me to go to the office.

Germany had performed a miraculous recovery from wartime devastation and had become the most important economy in Western Europe, and India had benefitted from it. Germany was one of our biggest and least troublesome aid donors. It was with the initiative of Krupps that Rourkela Steel Plant with a capacity of one million tonnes of high grade steel was proposed. Durgapur was British-aided, and Bhilai which was Soviet-supported, came later. When I arrived, we were negotiating aid to enhance Rourkela's capacity to 1.8 million tonnes.

P.A. Menon was Ambassador, and in accordance with ICS tenures of thirty-five years, Bonn was to be his last posting. His residence was in Cologne; he came to office only in the mornings. He was intelligent and had extensive experience at home and abroad, but was not too interested either in developing Indo-German economic potential or following too closely the nuances of the surrounding political crisis. He placed full trust in me to superintend a fairly large embassy with active responsibilities in the economic, commercial, educational and military sections, and coordination links for purchases for Indian Railways. In addition, we had fairly active Consulates General in Frankfurt am Main, Hamburg and Berlin (the last no longer paid for as part of British occupation costs). Frankfurt had become the civil aviation hub of continental Europe so we were frequently obliged to hold courtesy receptions for transiting VIPs. I was given full licence to travel and often represented the Ambassador at functions all over Germany.

Our most active contact was with the Ministry of Economic Development and its subordinate, the Kreditanstalt fuer

Wiederaufbau (KFW), with headquarters in Frankfurt, which had the responsibility of enforcing conditions for dispensing aid to the developing countries of Asia, Africa and Latin America.

Soon after I arrived, in fact, on 13 August 1961, the Soviet Union and the Government of Deutsche Democratische Republik (East Germany) tried to stop East Berliners from crossing over to the West by building a massive wall right across Berlin city. Despite sixteen years of imposed ideological reorientation, die Mauer (The Wall) always remained a symbol of the failure of the communist system. Desperate attempts to get across to West Berlin continued; several escaped before the division became watertight; some jumped from the high windows of divided houses, others tried innovative means for crossing over to freedom.

To see for myself, I went to Berlin soon after 'The Wall' was built. I heard the agonizing stories of those who had escaped. I can never forget the sight of a middle-aged woman who had managed to come through, lying on top of the hot engine of a big truck, with the result that, on the entire front of her body she had third degree burns, but she was happy to have escaped the rigour of imposed communism.

There was worldwide moral condemnation, but it also heightened anxiety for the survival of this island of democracy in a city surrounded by the Democratic Republic which, at any time, could smother the symbolic Western presence. It survived the blockade in 1948 because of a non-stop airlift of food, coal and essential supplies from the West until finally, Stalin declared that canal 'locks' had been repaired, and lifted the ground stranglehold. When I arrived in 1961, our Consul General in Berlin was Mahboob Ahmed, who was ex-INA. He and his wife had become very friendly with Willy Brandt, who was the Oberbürgermeister, and was destined to become Chancellor and make a breakthrough on East–West relations with his Ostpolitik. But the shining light of this prosperous enclave in the midst of communist austerity was highlighted by television pictures of life in West Berlin which could not but show the contrast between the two blocs.

While paying verbal homage to reunification, the paradox was that France and the UK, and many Rhinelanders—who were mostly Catholic while East Germany was Lutheran and Protestant—who had experienced two world wars in a quarter century, were inwardly happy that Germany had got emasculated. Germany had posed a problem of clash of national economic interests and our approach as regards Foreign Policy. The Hallstein Doctrine, named after Walter Hallstein, the West German President of the Commission of the European Economic Community (EEC), had made it clear that any recognition of East Germany would forfeit aid from the Federal Republic. The Soviet Union's anxiety was different but quite obvious. The outer parameter provided by the Warsaw Pact covering Eastern Europe was the security shield of the Soviet Union. Our chief political problem was a negative one—not offending the Soviet Union but also not recognizing the division of the country as permanent. Our positive task was to harness Federal Germany's economic assistance for our Second and Third Five-Year Plans. We knew, but could not affirm, West Berlin as a symbol of freedom and a functioning democracy. It was a difficult international problem which many thought could mean war or peace. It provided sufficient material to fill up the periodic reports to the Ministry, but we had to put the political problem of re-unification (Wiedervereinigung) on the back burner. The political work was interesting but not exacting for us, and I tagged along in the economic negotiations.

K.B. Lall, as Ambassador to Belgium, concurrently accredited to the EEC, had a kind of supervisory role in all Europe–India aid negotiations. In this role he was a frequent visitor to Bonn and KfW in Frankfurt but, on minor issues, I negotiated on my own in the development ministry. K.B. Lall was generally accompanied by R. Venkateswaran, his specially chosen counsellor.

'Der Alte', as Chancellor Adenauer was known, was eighty-five or thereabouts when I was in Bonn, and had dominated German politics since the War. He had in fact retired before the Nazi period and cultivated roses in his Rhineland home, but he came into his own after the German defeat. He shaped the independence of the Federal Republic. Success was symbolized when, in 1955, the Federal Republic was admitted as a full member of the NATO.

The culmination of this period was the visit by President John Kennedy in 1963 when I was serving in Bonn. In the jet age, VIP visits are frequent and generally leave no lasting significance except for textbook historians. Kennedy's visit to Berlin, however, was an exception. Facing The Wall, more or less opposite the Brandenburg Gate, from a high platform, President Kennedy made the famous speech of which extracts are worth quoting: 'Two thousand years ago the proudest boast was "civis Romanus sum". Today, in the world of freedom, the proudest boast is "Ich bin ein Berliner" (I am a Berliner).' We only saw this on television, but it brought about a tumultuous fifteen-minute ovation from the assembled crowd. It was interpreted to mean that the US considered Berlin as a part of it. The entire German nation was reassured that the US would not abandon Europe, particularly vulnerable Federal Germany, to any aggression by the Soviet Union. This is the only occasion I can think of where a lasting political impact was made by a single public declaration. As Ted Sorensen's autobiography* reveals, in German the grammatically correct wording is 'I am Berliner', but it has become famous as 'I am a Berliner'.

On his way from Berlin, Kennedy also visited the Dom (Cathedral) in Cologne. Max Adenauer, the son of the Chancellor, was Oberbürgermeister (Chief Mayor). Kennedy spoke just a one-liner from the steps of the Cathedral. In his Bostonian twang, he said, 'In Massachusetts they say there are too many Kennedys in politics. I have never heard anyone say that there are too many Adenauers in Cologne.' With that one sentence, he won the city. The high point of Kennedy's visit was a long, prepared speech in Paulskirche (St. Paul's Church) in Frankfurt. After reiterating permanent

---

*Ted Sorensen, *Counselor: A Life at the Edge of History*, (Harper Collins: 2008).

American commitment to the defence of Europe, he explicitly said, 'We will risk our cities to save yours.' Sorensen, the probable author of the speech, was obviously an intellectual. He was able to succinctly convey an idea in a few words in a speech. Though he does not have the analytical depth of Schlesinger's *A Thousand Days: John F. Kennedy in the White House*, his insights on Kennedy have a vivid recall. We in India have some memorable phrases from Panditji's extempore speeches (for example, *Tryst with Destiny*) but it is one of our professional failings that, since Nehru did not ask, we seldom volunteered drafts for him and so indiscretions crept in. Sorensen's speeches made Kennedy's visit unforgettable in politics and transformed US–German relations.

The other memorable political event of my stay in Bonn was the visit of President de Gaulle. These two large countries of Europe—Germany and France—have a record of several hundred years of dislike and conflicts. Provinces like Alsace and Lorraine and indeed, the control of the Rhine itself, had changed hands several times between the two countries. Millions from both had perished in the two great wars and all but destroyed their respective heritages. After de Gaulle's visit, France and Germany were at last partners in Europe. The burial of old hatreds and the process of friendship started with the Schuman–Mollet Plan, but the embrace of Adenauer and de Gaulle was the symbol of a historic reconciliation. Thousands from each country now go to visit the other in organized programmes to consolidate the growing mutual confidence. Our German neighbour, who was a veteran of the War, was in tears when he saw de Gaulle on television laying a wreath on the grave of an unknown German soldier. He asked rhetorically in German, 'Why did this not happen fifty years ago?' Both Kennedy's and de Gaulle's visits were of great political importance and, to my mind, left a hope that some day geography and technology would prevail and India too, would have constructive functional relations with all its neighbours.

It was also on the sidelines when J.R.D. Tata was firming up the deal for the assembly of Mercedes-Benz trucks. We managed to combine it with watching part of the Wagner opera series in Nuremberg.

It is not worthwhile recapitulating the detailed negotiations regarding the extension of the Rourkela Steel Plant, but being in Germany was an exhilarating experience. There was great anxiety during the thirteen days of the Cuban missile crisis, which coincided with the Chinese attack on India. In my view, the timing was accidental and not causally linked. The West did not realize that although the Sino-Soviet Treaty had remained in force on paper for thirty years, since 1958–60 and after the summary withdrawal of Soviet technicians, there was deep, hidden antagonism in their foreign policies. While the Cuban missile crisis was unresolved, the USSR temporarily moved away from its neutralist posture between 'fraternal China' and 'friendly India' to the old communist solidarity. But the USSR corrected its bias and negotiated the MIG 21 deal, but wanted to keep the sale confidential.

Even if India was not politically important in Germany, there were frequent VIP visits in both directions. The German President Luebke went to Delhi; our Finance Minister, Morarji Desai, came to Bonn with L.K. Jha and his Private Secretary Tonpe. Rather mischievously, I almost got Morarji to sign the wine list in a wayside luxury restaurant on the Rhine. It would have been a prize souvenir since he was so strongly against alcoholic beverages!

We had made some good friends in Germany. Alfred Horton was a Christian Democratic Union member of the Bundestag who introduced us to Vice-Chancellor Erhard. He must have heard of my involvement in the negotiations with his ministry. I have a prized autographed book signed by Erhard on the day he took over from Adenauer as Chancellor.

This interlude in Germany was too good to last. In October, when I had done just over two years and was really enjoying fraternizing with other diplomats and many Germans, I received orders of transfer to take over as head of our Embassy in Peking. There were regrets all around—or so I would like to believe— within the Embassy, the German Foreign Office and the Ministry for Economic Development. But I was not altogether surprised as I knew China was in my horoscope. I did not protest. I was informed privately that the decision to send me to China was taken by Prime Minister Nehru himself.

I returned to India at the end of October 1963. I had my usual briefing from the Foreign Secretary and the officials within the Ministry and also by the Chief of the Army Staff, the intelligence organizations, etc. I made trips to Ladakh, NEFA, Sikkim and all the sensitive points where conflict had taken place during the previous year. The Delhi consensus was that the Chinese were bent on attacking again in 1964. One Cabinet minister almost gave me a date when it would happen. I did not agree, but at that stage, I was at the listening end.

While normally an outgoing Head of Mission is given one opportunity to call on the PM, I must have been summoned five times. Panditji asked me to stay on until Mrs Indira Gandhi, accompanied by Dinesh Singh, returned on 30 December after attending the transfer of power in Kenya. Shaken out of his certainty, Panditji was a picture of baffled despondency. I got a sense of Panditji's worry and hope. He still thought China would see the wisdom of peaceful cooperation with non-hostile India. He was obviously physically weak and mentally troubled. I did not know that his kidneys were already damaged. During my conversations, he used to doze off and one did not know whether to withdraw or to wait till he woke up. It was sad to see that the old lion had lost his self-confidence, but it never crossed my mind that this would be the last time I would see Panditji.

Having received an undeserved share of affection, as well as occasional scolding from Panditji, on the last occasion, I made bold to request him to give me a souvenir which could sustain me in my mission. He got up and took me down the corridor to his bedroom and said, 'Take whatever you want.' That baffled me and I stuttered, 'Sir, give me a couple of your handkerchiefs or one of the dandas.' He pulled out two handkerchiefs with J.N. emboidered on them. Then he went to his cupboard and brought out a fairly sturdy walking stick with steel ends. I said that I would like to have something which had been used and he handed over the danda which he was carrying. 'Take this. Only yesterday I gave away one which had my initials on it.' These two souvenirs I have bequeathed to my son Ajay as the wand of a great statesman and patriot.

10

Enjoying the Peking 'doghouse'; observing the Sino–Soviet Rift and receiving an Ultimatum threatening War (1963–66)

After a brief halt in Hong Kong I arrived in Peking in January 1964. Peking was notorious for non-availability even of essentials. Even though our Embassy in Peking ran a provisions shop for day-to-day necessities, one had been advised to stock up personal requirements, refurbish one's wardrobe and buy leisure items like cassettes and long-playing records. Hong Kong was then a shopper's paradise and we tended to buy more than we needed. The formal briefing with the Indian Commissioner, the former ruler of Kotda-Sangani, was a farce. He was one of the former princes nominated to facilitate the integration of the States. He was married to the sister of the Maharaja of Mysore; she was an accomplished pianist and a greater public relations asset than her husband. Kotda may not have been great as a professional diplomat but he was a very affectionate host. He started the day with a glass of what looked like water but which, one discovered by accident, was undiluted gin!

After the India–China War, I knew Peking was going to be a difficult post, but intellectually, it was my most exhilarating assignment. The residence in Peking was not imposing but comfortable. Our son Uday was six and too young for a boarding-school in India. He was with us, but we had taken an Indian helper to supplement the competent Chinese staff. R.K. Nehru, after having been Foreign Secretary, had chosen to go to China in 1956, and the house still had marks of tasteful refurnishing done by Mrs Rajan Nehru, specially the ladies' toilet, which had a silk-covered sofa! G. Parthasarathi, his successor, had been recalled in 1961 after relations deteriorated. P.K. Banerjee, the counsellor, was left in charge and had to handle the critical period of 1962.

The Legation Street: the monuments of Imperial Peking

In Sun Yat-sen's time, the capital had been moved to Nanking, but after the Japanese brutally overran the city in 1937, for the duration of the Japanese War, it was moved to Chungking, upstream of the Yangtze. The People's Republic of China (PRC), however, decided to come back to Peking, which had been the capital for several dynasties and had monuments of China's old glory. I was able to get hold of Arlington and Lewisham's book, published in 1935, titled *In Search of Old Peking,* which had drawings, charts, maps, plans and illustrations of the old city. The first chapter in the book is about the Legation quarter which, for the Chinese, symbolized the ultimate humiliation inflicted by the imperialists. The old city was dotted with temples and palaces, each with picturesque and poetic names in Chinese such as Hsien-An-Lin (the Palace of Perfect Peace); Qianging Gong (the Palace of Heavenly Purity); Kun Ning Gong (the Palace of Earthly Tranquillity) and, of course, Tiananmen (the Gate of Heavenly Peace). They were reminders of a 4000-year-old distinct civilization which—not wholly unjustifiably—carried the illusion of a mandate from Heaven. The Europeans had come to China with the arrogance of Western technological superiority which communism was determined to erase, not just politically but also physically. Diplomats were restricted to Peking, the adjoining western hills and a few cities. Foreigners (and diplomats) were not allowed to enter any private house. The focus of the old pride was the Forbidden City with a succession of pavilions with roofs of golden-coloured tiles, each engraved with the five-clawed dragon—the imperial dragon has five, the others have only four claws. Although I had stayed in the adjoining Chang-Nan-Hai when I accompanied Vice-President Dr Radhakrishnan, in nearly three years in Peking, I had never even peeped inside those massive red gates. For the tenth anniversary of the People's Republic of China, ten massive buildings were built, including the National People's Hall, the Revolutionary Museum, the Peking railway station and a guest house complex. Thereafter, President Liu Shao-ch'i, Premier Zhou Enlai and even Chairman Mao Zedong, who had residences in Chang-Nan-Hai, met visiting foreign VIPs in the National People's Hall. Generally, no one else stayed where Dr Radhakrishnan and I had.

The final victory against the Boxers was by a contingent of the Indian Army, mostly Sikhs, which landed in Tientsin and then marched up to Peking. As we all know, they destroyed the belief that the armbands of the Boxers made them invincible against firearms. After the Treaty of 1900 and the Protocol of 1901, all Legations were grouped together; some were rebuilt but all the 'foreign devils' were kept out of sight of the Chinese people.

India had bought the vacated Hong Kong Shanghai Bank from the People's Republic of China on Legation Street. Even so eventually, we too, were evicted from the street, but that was after my time. No trace now remains of the old diplomatic quarter. I still have a board of the Hong Kong Shanghai Bank as a souvenir. In glass letters, it states 'This way for deposits.' After assiduous research, I came to the conclusion that in 1900, the defence of the legation quarters against the Boxers was planned out in what was the dining room of my residence. A tailor's shop continued to be near us at street level. I was told this shop used to make suits for Mao and the top communist hierarchy. I therefore got myself a two-piece suit stitched which, on the inside pocket, carries the label of the tailor. I wear it not more than once or twice every winter. After forty-four years, I treasure it as a sartorial reminder of Chairman Mao.

All the old European countries had missions on Legation Street. They wanted to ensure that diplomatic missions could better defend their locality if ever there was a repetition of anti-foreign insurrection in the future. Understandably, the biggest compound, with a nine-hole golf course and barracks for several companies of troops, was the British Legation. I was told the compound had seven big houses built in the Chinese style. It was no surprise that resurgent China evicted the British in 1957 and, in due course, all foreigners were banished to a less pretentious ghetto so that the 'barbarians' could not be seen from the main road. In 1964, however, Legation Street still reminded one of the last days of the Manchus.

In our acquired property, there was a separate building for the Ambassador or Chargé d'Affaires and adjoining it was the Chancery. The boundary wall was shared with the old German Legation which, in my time, was occupied by the German Democratic Republic (East Germany).

When I arrived, some missions were still in their old legations but, following the US, others had no resident representation. The Dutch Legation, which was headed by a Chargé, was a replica of a mansion in the Netherlands. The Austro-Hungarian Empire had built two identical diplomatic missions resembling Central European palaces: one was in Constantinople and the other in Peking. After World War I, when the Austro-Hungarian Empire was splintered, the building in Constantinople went to Austria and the one in Peking to Hungary. The Burmese were in occupation of what used to be the Belgian Legation, possibly because 'B' could also stand for Burma. The Portuguese Legation remained unoccupied. Czarist Russia also had a legation on the street, which at one time had barracks to house 1000 troops. After the Sino-Soviet friendship treaty signed in 1950, even the old legation with barracks was considered too small and so the Soviet mission moved to a new compound in the northern part of the city. The Russians built the Chinese Embassy in Moscow and, in turn, China constructed the building in Peking on the Russian pattern with big chandeliers and halls. I heard a story that when Premier Zhou Enlai inaugurated the new Soviet Embassy in Peking, in his speech, he said that the friendship between China and Soviet Union would be as indestructible as the marble behind him. Mochulski, the Russian number two, who related it to me, with a twinkle in his eyes, volunteered that the marble was artificial!

I had a suspicion that my office was bugged but, despite many requests, the Ministry would not send anybody to dispel or confirm my suspicions. In fact, except Mrs Helb, the wife of the one-time Dutch Ambassador in Delhi, we had no houseguests in Peking. We knew that all diplomatic telephones were tapped but discovered this could be of advantage as well. By prior arrangement, I complained bitterly to a diplomatic colleague that 'this great country with ambitions of being a superpower can not even repair the plumbing; they might as well allow direct access to an approved list of sanitary fittings shops. Weeks have gone by; even requests for minor repairs are not attended to by the Foreign Mission Bureau.' The next day, a plumber came and put the toilet right!

De Gaulle's recognition: exhilaration and disappointment

Nehru was put up in the old French Legation in Peking. It was also the venue for the talks in 1960 on the India–China boundary. When President de Gaulle announced the recognition of the PRC in January 1964, the Diplomatic Corps thought that the PRC may have even promised that the French would be allowed to go back to their old mission. Leading the advance party of the recognition was Claude Chayet. (Claude's father had been 'Minister' to China and Claude remembered playing in the compound.) But one day, the diplomatic missions received a note from the Foreign Office that from the coming Monday, a part of the Waijabu (Chinese Foreign Office) would move to a specified address. When we located the place, we found that the address was the old French Legation! Breakthrough or not, the Chinese were determined to obliterate any remaining symbols of the Boxer defeat and the legation quarters.

The social life of the Diplomatic Corps in Peking

I commanded particular interest from many heads of mission because I had the experience of six-month-long talks on the India–China boundary question. The Diplomatic Corps was small: no Americans, Japanese or Australians, but those accredited were sympathetic to the achievements of communist China. The British, Dutch, Yugoslavs and I were permanent Chargés. Terence Garvey, Hobson's predecessor, and his wife Rose Marie, displayed their admiration for China, yet could not be sure of any special indulgence. He had a crew of very able Chinese-speaking colleagues, who climbed high in their subsequent careers. David Wilson, then a Second Secretary, became editor of the *China Quarterly*, ended as Lord David Wilson and the last but one Governor of Hong Kong. He not only knew Chinese, but had also studied old maps of the city. Almost every Sunday, David would conduct walks around the western hills. He knew the surroundings well enough to avoid noticeboards forbidding diplomats to go beyond them! Hobson, who succeeded him, had done a full term as Ambassador in Laos.

Unlike these days, there were not many visitors then from the non-communist world. Among the exceptions was Field Marshal Montgomery, who was shown very special honour. The most notable visitor from western countries was André Malraux, then Minister of Culture in de Gaulle's government. Malraux, of course, had followed China for decades and written about it in *La Condition Humaine*. He was in Nanking in 1927 when the Soviet Communist Party sided with KMT against the Chinese communists. Malraux's great regret was that he had missed the Long March defying Chiang Kai-shek's army. Malraux had come to make amends and pay tribute to Chairman Mao who was then the dominant figure in the communist world.

The figure in the Diplomatic Corps everybody talked about was General Raza, the Ambassador of Pakistan. He was in his second tenure in Peking. He received me with gracious charm and mentioned that in the mid-fifties, he had been ostracized the way he supposed I must be at present. General Raza had an elegantly furnished residence; his lifestyle reflected his Sandhurst background and incurred everyone's envy. The cushion covers were made out of the safas of his ceremonial regimental uniform (I think Rajputana Rifles); his Chinese servants were dressed like mess orderlies with cutaway monkey jackets and bow ties. In the Diplomatic Corps, it was well known that General Raza could make any demand and it would be met to consolidate the newly formed friendship between China and Pakistan. For example, the Foreign Office traced the 'amah' who had looked after their daughter in the '50s even though she was 'lost' amongst the billion Chinese, and she was brought back to serve Mrs Raza.

Although relations were tepid, there were amusing sides to diplomatic life in Peking. David Wilson and Kishan Rana alone possessed Spitfire sports cars, the only open cars in the city. Kishan, a dashing, popular bachelor, would park his red Spitfire in Tiananmen Square, and then stroll around the square and watch the Chinese who had never seen a fancy sports car, crowd around it, intrigued by this capitalist curiosity.

A frequent pastime in diplomatic drawing rooms was to plan a special tie for those who were serving in Peking under the prevailing harsh restraints. I suggested having a spot tie with the huge Tiananmen Square gates closed!

Entertainment was lavish. The informal social life in the non-communist community was non-hierarchical. Blond stenographers of the Scandinavian Missions were designated Third Secretaries so that they enjoyed diplomatic status and were cultivated not just by their equals in age and rank but by Ambassadors whose wives were often absent on long furloughs! We all had access to the Peking Club where tennis players could relax in the summer. In winter, many of us ice-skated on the Summer Palace Lake or the moat around the Forbidden City. When not entertaining each other and whiling away dull evenings with no cinemas and few distractions, many diplomats became bridge addicts.

One could still detect traces of xenophobia. Once there was an unusual snowstorm and the city roofs and pavilions looked even more beautiful. With Uday and our Chinese driver, we went to take photographs in a public garden. We found some children—aged between four and seven—who were playing with snowballs. I asked our driver to make inquiries if I could photograph them. At this request, they went into a huddle. Suddenly they scattered and ran away shouting, 'You are foreigners'.

We in the Indian Mission knew that we were under special observation. One of our officers was deliberately involved in an accident; we believed he had been falsely accused of being in the wrong lane. We had brought a puppy for Uday but we had to be careful during weekend excursions to the city environs. *No Dogs in China* was the title of a book but it was almost literally true; if our pet went astray, it would provide soup and dinner for a local family. On the file I found a letter, written some months before 1962, with a specific warning that the Chinese were planning an attack on the Indian frontier. I felt this was explosive and so I removed it from the file and took it with me when I went home for consultation in 1964 and showed it to Foreign Secretary Gundevia. He recognized that it could be dynamite in its implications, as it should have been transmitted to Delhi. Without much ado, he promptly tore it into shreds!

Periodically, anonymous letters were thrown into the Embassy (perhaps with the knowledge of the Chinese Security guards), suggesting a surreptitious meeting in some obscure hutung (street) or restaurant. We knew there were non-official intelligence representatives on every street; even ordinary citizens were asked to report any foreigner behaving suspiciously. I warned my colleagues never to photograph any old woman who had had her feet bound and who could walk only with small steps. The practice of binding women's feet had been abolished after the People's Republic was established, but old women continued the habit as undoing the bandages after a lifetime was very painful.

The missionary school for the Diplomatic Corps

In 1964 my wife was given a fellowship at the Radcliffe Institute for Independent Studies at Harvard. Our three elder children were in boarding-schools in India but as Uday was too young we had put him in the only mission school in Peking. I was told that, when the People's Republic was established, it ordered the closing down of all missionary establishments. Apparently the Diplomatic Corps went in a group to Zhou Enlai and pleaded that some arrangement had to be made to enable their children to continue with their education, otherwise, in Peking, there would be either Ambassadors who were seventy or Envoys who were just married and inexperienced. After considering the matter, Zhou Enlai said that the PRC would make a concession in the case of the Belgian Benedictine School but on some conditions. No Chinese children would be admitted; the nuns would not be allowed to leave the compound even for shopping (instead, approved Chinese servants could be employed); the nuns would not be permitted to go home on furlough and, if they did, they would not be permitted to return. (Most missionaries had been in Peking since the Japanese invasion began in 1937, and had not visited their homes for at least twenty-five years.) If any foreign member of the staff died, she could not be replaced. Zhou Enlai may have expected that with such harsh conditions, the school would voluntarily decide to wind up. To the surprise of the Chinese and the gratification of the Diplomatic Corps, the nuns accepted the conditions, even though some were already around seventy. So schooling for the diplomats' children continued, preparing boys and girls ranging between six and seventeen years of age, for the national school-leaving exams.

Our son Uday was greatly touched by the affection he received from these elderly devout Christians. He was driven to the school by our Chinese driver (Lau Ma) who, incidentally, used this daily journey to teach him Chinese. Lau Ma had tears in his eyes when we left finally. Subsequently we learnt that in fact he had been assigned the duty to report periodically on the activities of the Indian Chargé and Embassy. For me this school remains the most memorable example of missionary dedication. During the Cultural Revolution, the Red Guards summarily closed down the school and evicted the surviving but virtually imprisoned nuns, some of whom were then over eighty and who had undergone such a long exile. I believe one died on the journey home.

Using bag couriers for morale and national advantage

After our relations deteriorated, we alone amongst the developing countries sent a courier to Hong Kong every week to exchange our outgoing and incoming diplomatic bags. This allowed officers and staff to escape briefly into comparative freedom. It was also a morale booster for our confined Embassy staff as it enabled them to buy stuff for their home postings. But politically, it was a means of obliging diplomatic colleagues who were paid in non-convertible currency such as roubles or yuans. We would make purchases for them which could be paid for only in convertible currency, get repaid in yuans, and place the ideological adversaries under a psychological sense of obligation. If the courier went by train—which took forty-eight hours—he could lay hands on local papers at intermediate stations, which could be sold at twenty times the price in Hong Kong dollars. These provincial papers were subsequently analysed by the China-watching think tanks in the island colony.

I myself went to Hong Kong once in three months and was met by many diplomats who were part of the 'embassies-in-waiting' notably, the American Consulate General. I was greeted as if I were privy to the darkest secrets of China. There were also eminent journalists who watched China and shuttled between

Hong Kong and Vietnam where the war was escalating in intensity and frustration. I first met many future star journalists and eminent diplomats on my Hong Kong courier trips. China-watching for many was a shared intellectual preoccupation and the bag services proved a political advantage.

Sharpening the Indian diplomatic expertise

The Indian Mission had an exceptionally capable team. We always had two or three Hong Kong-trained people who spoke Chinese. Among them were Kishan Rana, Bhupat Oza, Raghunath and later, C.V. Ranganathan. A. Damodaran, the First Secretary and my deputy when I arrived, spoke Russian and was of a very high intellectual calibre. He had also been with me in Germany. Vinod Khanna, Ranjeet Sethi, Shivshankar Menon (later Foreign Secretary), Nalini Suri, and Nirupama Rao (now Foreign Secretary), came later, but they continued the tradition, and our China language-speakers have been the pride of the Indian Foreign Service. In my time, there was also Thampi Srinivasan as Press Attaché. Each one was fired by an intellectual zest to understand the vast closed shop which was Mao's China. Rana and Srinivasan, both bachelors, shared a house. Both were passionately fond of Chinese snuff bottles and spent their leisure hours finding fresh specimens to add to their impressive collections. I have no doubt that my colleagues could match China language experts as well as political observers of any other foreign mission serving in Peking. The irony was that the quality of their Mandarin vocabulary deteriorated after coming to China as they could not speak to anyone except the Foreign Affairs Bureau and the domestic servants sent by it. Comprehending China and trying to keep up their professional zest against these odds was a challenge which could not be overcome by the known lure of convertible currency and electronic goods.

Of course we all scanned through the daily dose of propaganda carried by the official New China News Agency (Xinhua). The Embassy subscribed to two newspapers from London, the *Times* and the *Guardian*, and two from Hong Kong, the *Japan Times* and the *Paris Herald Tribune*. In addition, I would go through half a dozen Indian newspapers which came by the bag in a collective bundle, and every Thursday, I spent half the night going through them. I glanced through all these newspapers to know what was being said about China outside. It took enormous effort to piece together some small bits of relevant information and deepen our understanding while sitting in Peking. They did not often tally with what we could observe around us, but China-watching was an international industry, which engaged, but at times, also deceived us. For real insights on China, this was not always enough.

I felt that we had to find some other method to sharpen the professionalism of our 'China boys' and make sure that they did not regret choosing China and Chinese as their area of specialization. The main handicap was that we in the Indian Embassy were deprived of all briefing beyond what was published in the *People's Daily* and the English translations carried by Xinhua. There were some one-to-one meetings between Indian diplomats and their counterparts in other missions where information was shared, but there were no serious students of China beyond what concerned their own country. At public functions, diplomats of other missions shied away from being seen with the Indians. The Europeans were more forthcoming but among the Asians, the Nepalese and the Sri Lankans were friendly in private, but did not want to be seen 'conspiring' with the Indians while the Chinese were watching. Yunus, the number two from Pakistan, was more self-confident and fraternized with my junior colleagues since they all liked curry and pulau!

I felt that we had to work harder to get immediate and long-term insights. I decided to assign to every officer a subject for careful study and to prepare a self-contained dispatch, using published literature to supplement local observations. Each assignment was typically allowed a month or even more but I promised my colleagues, including those in the junior scale, that I would forward their dispatch signed by them with a covering letter signed by me, probably with a comment, to the Foreign Secretary himself. Thus they would be spurred to analyse a problem in depth. I made it clear that they could list important reference books at the end of their dispatch so that no one would accuse them of plagiarism. I undertook to write such dispatches myself, for example, on Sino-Soviet relations, and before sending them I requested my colleagues to refine them. I then showed some of these scholarly studies, pointedly marked 'secret', to other serious missions, adding verbally that since we had limited methods of checking our facts and analyses, I would be grateful if they could confidentially share their criticism of our dispatches with us.

The result was that every officer became more scholarly and something of an expert on a particular aspect of China. Their work also became an instrument of professional exchange. The dispatches we shared had little to do with Sino-Indian relations. Incidentally, I found that the intelligence officers, who hypothetically had greater latitude, really had no insights and so, benefitted from this kind of pooled analysis.

I remember asking Bhupat Oza, who had a background in Economics and Statistics, to work on a dispatch projecting the likely growth of population in China using different parameters. I showed it to the French Ambassador who asked me whether he could borrow it for further study. I knew he would copy it but, in return, we built up a confidential friendship with each other. Since the French were particularly close to the Chinese, I got secondhand benefit of Sino-French confidence on some inner political manoeuvering.

One advantage of such dispatch writings was that they went beyond the usual 'cut-and-paste' monthly reports, which we were required to do as a uniform exercise. I wished we had adopted a variant of the British practice of having regular self-contained dispatches from heads of missions so that the author could study a problem more deeply than in the periodical reports. Thus there would be a document with a full background and pros and cons on future projections in our archives.

Visit to DPR Korea

After getting permission from headquarters, in 1964 I visited Pyongyang, the capital of the Democratic People's Republic of Korea (DPRK) for a few days. Looking out of the window, the train journey through Manchuria, especially crossing the famous Yalu Bridge, was quite interesting. Once in the capital, it was quite evident that it was a communist state entirely under the control of the Party. There was some appreciation that an Indian diplomat had come at least for a visit. I had taken a colleague with me and we knew we were under constant surveillance. We could not go unescorted even for a walk around the guesthouse. Indeed one had to be careful about asking questions. Like all communist countries, there was a huge square dominated by the Flying Horse with portraits of Kim Il-sung and smaller-sized ones of Marx, Engels, Lenin and Stalin. Here, there was still personality cult, which outdid the one when Stalin had been around.

During the visit, I was taken to a steel factory. Success in productivity was attributed to the 'expert' advice (even in steelmaking) of Comrade Kim Il-sung!

What struck me was the choice of theme for a cultural performance. They would select a historical anecdote, which showed how Korean nationalism had defied the Chinese-imposed tributary system. It only confirmed that, while the contiguous countries (Vietnam, Korea and Mongolia) derived their culture and language from China, their political identity or the seed of nationalism was anti-Chinese. Despite all the constraints, the visit was instructive. I may have been the first to report on DPRK as it was years before we opened a mission in Pyongyang.

Diplomatic Tours

(i) Szechuan and the Yangtze

There were some events during my posting which are worth recalling. Although I was in the Chinese 'doghouse' and not allowed to travel outside the open cities such as Shanghai, Tientsin, Nanking, Canton, Hangchow, etc., I was not excluded from functions for heads of missions. In April 1964 the heads, accompanied by a large number of protocol officials, were taken on a two-week diplomatic tour by a special train. This was the first such tour of 'showing off of China' after the People's Republic was established. The first stop was Chengtu, the capital of Szechuan, a prosperous province and one of the most ancient centres of Chinese culture, agriculture and irrigation system. From there, we were taken to Chungking, the wartime capital. What I particularly recall was the steamer voyage from Chungking, lasting three days, on the Yangtze River where no foreigner had been since the Japanese invasion. We went through the famous gorge, where the world's largest (50,000 MV) hydel project is now under construction. As far as I know, it was then not even on the drawing board. Being in the heart of China was a thrill, not just for us but also for our accompanying Chinese protocol officers. We passed ancient temples, saw well-cultivated fields and a continually changing but beautiful landscape. The spot where the river narrows, is described in Chinese literature as 'The Galloping Horses.' It was a photographer's dream shot but sadly, it was a day of cloudy skies. All of us enjoyed the trip and it certainly served to reflect China's growing self-confidence.

(ii) Manchuria

There was another diplomatic tour while I was in China. This time we were taken to Manchuria which, during the Japanese occupation, had provided the industrial backup for the invading army. We passed through at the point where the Great Wall touches the China Sea and then goes up to Harbin, the famous Chinese port. The informal contacts with the protocol officers were particularly welcome, but I wished I had had a smattering of Chinese, instead of French and German.

Notwithstanding all our observations and intellectual curiosity, China, like the USSR to Churchill in 1939, was 'a riddle, wrapped in mystery, inside an enigma'. I felt that the Diplomatic Corps engaged in China-watching, had only a superficial insight into the working of the PRC, but the serious effort gave the Mission greater purpose. Sometimes we guessed right, at other times we didn't.

Mao: a detached national icon or an active party boss?
Pre-Cultural Revolution

The main problem in comprehending China was the internal politics which revolved around Chairman Mao's role and power still being wielded by him. He was unquestionably the national hero and unchallengeable icon. *The Thoughts of Mao Zedong* were made public in millions of copies to be compulsorily carried, even more so than the Bible for orthodox Christians. Even when he ceased to be President of China, everybody in the government and the party still swore by Mao Chusi (Chairman Mao), but was he simply 'reigning' over China, detached from actual management? The campaign around a young enthusiast—a possibly fictitious Lei Feng who was prepared to risk life and limb for the Party and even help old women across the road—had the stamp of Mao, the activist. Perhaps the Lei Feng heroics were the forerunner of the Cultural Revolution.

A Xinhua bulletin announced that two giants, Mao and Liu Shao-ch'i had swum in the Ming Tombs Lake. This, the diplomatic chanceries interpreted to mean that Liu Shao-ch'i had been chosen as the successor. We did not know that the story may have been inspired by Party headquarters without Mao's approval. The elegant sartorial style of Liu's wife and the third consort of Chen Yi were considered symbolic of the 'bourgeoisfication' of the Party. (Zhou Enlai's wife, on her occasional appearances since the 'Long March', looked rough-hewn due to the hardship she had suffered during the March and the cave life, and she evoked unquestioned admiration.) The lifestyle of other Party leaders did not fit in with the spirit of Yennan.

We were proved wrong about the succession as Liu was dethroned when the Cultural Revolution was unleashed. The injunction to 'bombard the headquarters' came from Mao himself. The fact is that we did not know that the political centre of gravity in China was itself in turmoil. The Cultural Revolution was artificially seeded from above by Mao and, in subsequent years, it gained an unbridled momentum. When I left on transfer in May 1966, the process of party purification had not started, but in June 1966 all schools were closed, teenagers and pre-teens were told 'to make revolution' and imitate the 'Long March'. Mao's wife Jiang Ching and the Gang of Four assumed the right of direction over the established functioning institutions.

The problem ultimately is a philosophical one. Can those who gain authority in a revolution with violence and a militant universalist ideology resist the perks of office and not yield to corruption when an opportunity opens up?

Sino-Soviet debate on interpreting shared ideology

Stalin passed away in 1953; Khrushchev, in 1956, denounced the personality cult, but China continued to worship Mao for its unsupported triumph. In the post-Stalin period, they could not show off their independence. The US and imperialism threatened both, and the PRC was dependent on the Soviet military umbrella. Mao went to Moscow for the fortieth anniversary of the October Revolution in 1957. He was impressed by the launch of the Sputnik and declared that the 'East wind prevailed over the West.' However, he had to wait for months to get an agreement for the supply of a nuclear research reactor. The Peking reactor was eventually released but in 1958 China was distressed when the Soviets would not let China use Soviet nuclear capability in pursuit of China's national goals, specifically to force KMT forces to vacate the offshore islands of Quemoy and Matsu. In effect, Khrushchev would not permit a Chinese finger on the Soviet nuclear trigger. It became clear that, ideological unity or not, the USSR understood better the danger of instant retaliation by the imperialists.

There were other indications that the PRC had begun to feel that the Soviet Union was degenerating into 'soft' ideology described as 'Modern Revisionism', and that the revolutionary mantle of Marx and Lenin now rested on Mao's shoulders. Anyway, it was evident that communist solidarity was in a crisis, and the rift between the two giant apostles of the ideology was serious, if not unbridgeable!

One heard rumours of differences which had surfaced at the Bucharest Conference of Communist Parties in 1960, but secrecy was almost an article of faith in the practice of Marxism. While we were in Peking for the official talks in 1960, we heard rumours of trainloads of Soviet experts returning to Moscow, taking with them the blueprints of 250 projects, which they were building in China. Soviet interests as an industrialized nuclear power were different from those of China with its distinctive civilizational heritage and its unaided success in defeating both the Japanese invasion and the Kuomintang forces, and also its unfulfilled aspirations to climb to superpower status. The pamphlet 'Long Live Leninism' issued by the Communist Party of China (CPC) had come out in Peking in the spring of 1963. This was answered by the Communist Party of Soviet Union (CPSU). Thereafter regularly, new pamphlets with scholarly analyses would be issued by the CPC as open replies to the CPSU. While theoretically China drew inspiration from the 'First International' (1864) and the 'Third International' (1919), the CPSU was alleged to be banking on the pre-World War I 'Second International' (1889–1916), where Kautsky and Bernstein had urged moderation and maintained that the triumph of the revolution was possible without risking war. The CPC declared that 'Khrushchev was the greatest fraud', and praised Mao's analysis implying that pure communism was functioning only in China. It declared that the Cuban missile crisis illustrated the Soviet Union's 'nuclear fetishism' and 'nuclear capitulationism'. Studying the quotes from Marx, Lenin, Stalin, etc., and grasping the differences between the two communist giants was my daily preoccupation in Peking. Nuclear weapons in many ways were to my mind the crux of the Soviet–China rift.

Mao's biography, as written by his own doctor, said the Chairman had a lascivious sex life but we did not know it.* His corrective for the new generation born in a more stable country after 1949 was to replicate the old inoculation with the experience of blisters. His militant collaborators in the Cultural Revolution perpetrated excesses, dislocated the economy and even the educational system of the country. China claimed it alone was truly faithful to Marxism-Leninism while the USSR had degenerated into Modern Revisionism. For me, the differences were in the changing perception of national interest at different stages of great power, and this was illustrated by the approach to nuclear weapons and the Vietnam conflict. In one Chinese pamphlet titled 'Two different lines on the question of War and Peace', the gist of the argument was that true Marxist-Leninists must wage unrelenting war, but 'Modern Revisionists' were prettifying imperialism, 'getting fearful of war', 'trumpeting Peace on Earth and Disarmament'. The tenth and last of the series which came out after Khrushchev was ousted in October 1964 had the title 'Khrushchevism without Khrushchev'.

Western Foreign Offices, notably the US administration, were slow to understand the Sino-Soviet rift. The differences, in fact, proved the abiding resilience of nationalism, and the effects thereof were incomprehensible to those imprisoned by ideology. The gallop of technology had led paradoxically to the atrophy of absolute state power, and accentuated as well as moderated national separateness.

One stray example of China's militant mood in 1964 was when Sir Paul Gore-Booth who had been UK High Commissioner in India came on his way to take over as Permanent Under Secretary in London. It happened to coincide with a special cultural function for the Diplomatic Corps where each invitee was provided with earphones and translations. The play was about Lumumba and it

*Li Zhisui, *The Private Life of Chairman Mao*, (Random House: 1994)

was a 'hymn of hate' with words such as, 'The river Congo is red with the blood of the Blacks shed by the Whites', etc. Sir Paul, who was a devout Christian Scientist, was shocked. Even at the height of the Indo-Pak War, he said he had never experienced such vicious hostility. I told myself that we had gained one more friend for India.

It was during this period that, for the first time, the CPC organized an open street demonstration of one communist government (China) against the Embassy of another communist state (USSR), showing that the erstwhile senior members of the communist fraternity were now publicly at loggerheads. In the Embassy we heard about the protest rally by a telephone call from a junior Soviet official. I quickly got into my car and, without the Chinese driver knowing it, took photographs of the surging crowd as it approached the Soviet Embassy, with my pocket Minolta.

The Vietnam conflict and Sino–Soviet differences

Vietnam illustrated the problem of differing goals under the façade of a proclaimed united purpose. When Vietnam, like China and France, refused to sign the Partial Test Ban Treaty (PTBT) in July 1963—sponsored jointly by the US, the USSR and the UK—it provoked Khrushchev into cutting off all aid even to a communist country currently under attack by the 'arch-imperialist'. The rationale must have been that the US possessed nuclear weapons, and as in Cuba, retreat by the USSR was preferable to a nuclear conflagration, worldwide destruction and rampant radioactivity. The paradoxical result of the stoppage of aid to Vietnam was that some non-official parties, notably the Communist Party of Japan, switched allegiance from Moscow to Peking. It was in this context, after the dethroning of Khrushchev that his successors, Brezhnev and Kosygin, realized that the CPSU must not be seen as being unconcerned about the struggle of the Vietnamese people. In February 1965, Kosygin stopped off in Peking and called on Mao but the latter, I believe, said that Soviet support in Vietnam was not required. Kosygin, nevertheless, went on to Hanoi and pledged to resume supply of military hardware to the country. The hidden purpose was that Soviet arms supply would dilute dependence on neighbouring China; indeed, arms supply was a method of arms control. For example, no fighter planes were supplied because that would increase the chances of aerial dogfights and so, of escalation of conflict with the USA. The military hardware was initially sent by the safe overland route through China but the Chinese, it was alleged, retained some of the sophisticated equipment. Thereafter, Soviet military hardware was sent by sea to the port of Haiphong even at the risk of observation and interruption by American agencies. Incidentally, Kosygin's visit coincided with the 'Tonkin Gulf' incident which was used by President Lyndon Johnson to obtain Congressional support for increased US commitment to the war in Vietnam.

The Soviet Ambassador was quite friendly with me and told me of Kosygin's visit. I was one of the few diplomats at the airport when he passed through Peking. I have never seen a colder reception for a head of government. To me it was abundant proof of the ineptitude of the CIA not to have seen its significance.

Political belligerence and military prudence

It was, however, obvious to me that although China was helping Vietnam, it did not want to provoke the US. I had long concluded that unless China's own integrity was perceived to be threatened—as when US forces approached Yalu in 1950—or there was certainty of military victory, as against India in 1962, China's political belligerence was combined with military prudence. While food rations, non-military essentials and logistic help were being sent from China, Chinese 'volunteers' were withheld. I got proof of China's non-provocative intentions when Ahmed Al-Shukairy, then Palestine Liberation Army (PLA) leader, was visiting Peking. He felicitated the PRC for its help for the Democratic Republic of Vietnam and added that he had heard that thousands of Chinese volunteers wanted to fight shoulder-to-shoulder with their

Vietnamese comrades. I was there and could perceive that Zhou Enlai felt embarrassed by this statement; the next day this was confirmed when the New China News Agency (NCNA) printed a report about the Palestinian representative endorsing China's solidarity as a 'lip-and-teeth' friendship with Vietnam, but there was no mention of Chinese volunteers fighting in Vietnam! The PRC did not want to shed Chinese blood for Vietnam nor provoke the US into a direct attack on the mainland. China and the Soviet Union were tailoring their attitude towards the struggle of Vietnamese nationalism to their own selfish national goals: for China it was to cause the maximum embarrassment to both the US and the USSR without risk to its own security, and for the USSR it was to minimize the risk of escalation.

The USSR was the only secret well-wisher of the USA in Vietnam

Surprisingly, despite the thousands of books on Vietnam very little has been written on the divergence in the attitudes of the communists. To me it was abundantly clear, as was confirmed by my reports to the Ministry, but was not obvious to Washington, that the best ally the US had in Vietnam was the USSR! There was an unspoken interest on the part of the Soviet Union in the early negotiations to defuse the ongoing conflict. If, in desperation, at the prospect of a shameful American defeat, Washington had used nuclear weapons, it would have posed a serious dilemma for Russia who claimed to be guardian of the communist bloc. The Russians supported, at least tacitly, every initiative for peaceful resolution of the problem. There were several. The British Prime Minister, Harold Wilson, and the Polish Foreign Minister made separate but plausible recommendations to avoid the risk of a humiliating defeat for the US. On the other hand, the Chinese purpose was best served by fuelling the conflict and proving that these nuclear superpowers were simply 'paper tigers'. Amongst the many proposals for solving the Vietnam problem was one from de

Gaulle, suggesting that the five permanent members of the Security Council, the P5, mediate in Vietnam. This would have ensured that the French were included. The Chinese, however, did not encourage de Gaulle. Mao wanted to expose the secret 'love feast' between the two superpowers.

The Vietnamese were, of course, only interested in expelling the foreigners with whatever support came from the Soviet Union or China and through international official or non-official opinion, and in reuniting with South Vietnam. It was when Soviet military support overtrumped China's help that the Democratic Republic of Vietnam (DRVN) agreed to start talks in Paris.

Soviet–China relations were, of course, of interest to India, but our Ministry and even our experts did not grasp its full significance. I went to Ulan Bator (Mongolia) to meet with Ambassador T.N. Kaul from Moscow, when he came for the Mongolian National Day celebrations in July 1964. We discussed at great length what was happening within the communist world. According to him, all these were superficial ideological differences behind the unity of the communist movement. I argued that the two giants were deadly set against each other. In one of my last reports from Peking, I suggested by the same logic that the USSR might give arms to Pakistan's military regime in order to out-trump Chinese influence as in Vietnam, but Ambassador Kaul, back from Moscow, thought I did not understand the strength of proletarian internationalism.

The ultimatum to India for collateral support to Pakistan

What was of primary interest to me was the Chinese attitude that would have a bearing on India's security. China had exploded its first nuclear device on 16 October 1964. Its significance had been extensively analysed in strategic literature but although China's political hostility to India had become obvious, and the corrective defence measures had long been debated, I was not alarmed by a likely repetition of 1962.

I shall not repeat what has been described at length in my book on negotiations.*

In March 1965, Ayub and Bhutto came to China to solicit collateral support for the planned 'Operation Gibraltar' to seize Kashmir. Since the India–China War (1962), Bhutto seemed convinced that China would give unconditional help and felt reassured by the Chinese statement. 'We will not stand by idly.'

Contrary to Bhutto's reading of Mao, 'One spark did not light the prairie fire.' In the disappointment over non-support by the 'locals', Pakistan's army attacked the Chhamb sector of Jammu. Pakistan had not reckoned with the sagacity of the little man, Lal Bahadur Shastri, who was PM of India at that time. We did not confine our operations to J&K only, as we had done in 1948–49, which meant a long detour through Pathankot. On the advice of military commanders, India attacked across the international line towards Sialkot and Lahore.

As it happened, on 3 September, two days after the Pakistan army had launched its direct offensive in Chhamb, by a long-scheduled commitment, Rama and I were due to have dinner and play bridge with Ambassador and Mrs Raza. While dealing hands till the small hours in the morning, the four of us talked about everything except what was topmost in our respective minds—our war. But this 'diplomatic socialization' did mean that there was no propaganda between our two embassies. I had asked Col Khera, the Military Attaché, to invite all the other service attachés to his house on September 4. I had authorized him to display the confidential maps of the western sector to explain India's military problems. In accordance with a pre-arranged understanding, I dropped in later and asked the military attachés for their operational advice 'if you were India's generals'. They all said there was no alternative but to go for Sialkot and Lahore. On 6 September when the Indian army attacked on the western front, the rumour

---

*Jagat S. Mehta, *Negotiating for India* (Manohar: 2006).

circulating in the Diplomatic Corps in Peking was that Mr Mehta was the only one briefed on the operational strategy of the Indian army which, of course, was far from the truth!

China, 'We will not stand idly by': our professionalism demanded risk-taking

China advertised to the world and especially to the people of Pakistan that the government of China was being a good and faithful friend. Following Stalin's practice, on 16 September, in the middle of the night I was called by the Foreign Office. I said I would reach in ten minutes, but then I was asked to wait until the translation was ready! I imagine the decision must have been taken at the highest level but Yang Kung-su, a mere deputy director and hardly my opposite number, was told to summon me for a meeting. I asked Damodaran, the First Secretary and my deputy, to come with me. I was given an ultimatum that within three days the bunkers built across the Sikkim frontier should be demolished and the 'stolen' sheep and yaks returned. After reading the ultimatum, I reacted by saying that the accusations were absurd and I wanted clarifications. He was visibly flabbergasted at my request and wanted all the questions put together. I said my subsequent questions would depend on his answers and would have to be seriatim. He had, of course, no answers to my questions. He had expected me to rush to the Embassy and transmit the text. The PM's reaction to the first ultimatum was to offer inspection by impartial international observers who would prove that the alleged provocation was false. On 19 September, a second ultimatum was served. One of my questions on 16 September had been, 'At what precise time did the three days begin?' The second ultimatum specified that it would end at midnight of 22 September. My final question on 19 September was that, if we could not satisfy the totally unjustified demands, whether the PRC would go to war with India. Yang Kung-su was flustered and at about 2.30 a.m.

said that he had another appointment and put his hand out to say goodbye. I refused to shake his outstretched hand and I put mine dramatically behind my back. Not since 1 September 1939, when Neville Chamberlain, the British PM at the time, had any ultimatum been given as a possible prelude to military operations. We were naturally anxious and perplexed and I took some precautions such as ordering the burning or shredding of our secret reports, and keeping just one cypher in the Embassy. I also announced that anyone wanting to send away his family was free to do so and they could proceed at government expense. I am proud to recall that not a single one of the India-based staff availed of the offer.

On 21 September, there was a buffet reception in the Ghanaian Embassy. Rama was making small talk with Ambassador Raza when, suddenly Raza said he had to leave and without even saying goodbye to the host or waiting for the dessert, he rushed off.

I never could understand how the Chinese would have wanted to give collateral military support to Pakistan—as expected by Bhutto—in order to let Pakistan seize Kashmir. Both India and Pakistan have wishfully misunderstood the great powers. The Chinese only wanted popularity with the Pakistani people. When Rama told me that Raza had left without waiting for dessert, this confirmed my speculative analysis. The Ministry had not asked for the Embassy's assessment of the developing situation. Before the ultimatum was due to expire and after consulting the officers of the Embassy (who discouraged me from volunteering my own analysis), I sent a telegram to the PM and the Foreign Minister which would reach well before midnight. After giving my reasons fairly exhaustively, I vouchsafed that the Chinese would *not* violate Indian-held territory or the Sikkim frontier. My guess was that since we knew that the decision to accept the ceasefire had the backing of both the US and the USSR, any unilateral action by China would create complications for Pakistan. We now know that Ayub and Bhutto paid a secret visit during the week but I did not know it at that time. My guess was that Raza had probably rushed off to meet Zhou Enlai to inform him of Pakistan's decision to accept the ceasefire and prevent China playing the devil's hand against the superpowers.

As it happened, my surmise proved correct. As a cover-up, next morning, the *People's Daily* asserted that India had complied with the Chinese demand for demolishing the bunkers. The delivery of the *People's Daily* (where this item was the lead story) was unusually delayed suggesting a last-minute change of the headlines.

Apparently I was the only one to anticipate that the Chinese would not make good on their threat. Needless to say, we had given no provocation, nor stolen any sheep or yaks, nor constructed bunkers across the international boundary. But I was conscious that Nehru's and Krishna Menon's prediction on 7–8 September 1962 had proved fatally erroneous and I was needlessly running a risk. However, I felt I must live by my own civil service ethics that we had a duty to *volunteer* honest and timely advice in national interest.

After the ceasefire, I was asked to come back to Delhi for consultations. I stayed on in Peking until 1 October, which was China's National Day. After 16 September and for the next fortnight, every night there would first be a call to the Chancery and when there was no answer, I would be woken up in the middle of the night. I got used to waiting for the call and finally, on one occasion before the voice could tell me it was the Foreign Office, I spontaneously cursed the caller for disturbing me in the middle of the night! There is nothing like playing games with the Foreign Office at a time of acute stress!

Diplomacy of walking out of banquets

During this period, I had also innovated (or was it merely revitalized) the 'diplomacy of walking out' as a public protest over false accusations of aggression hurled at India. At the banquet on 30 September on the eve of the Chinese National Day, the speech was only in Chinese. Mao himself was present. English, French and Russian translations were provided to senior diplomats who had, of course, been invited to the banquet in the National People's Hall but no English text was distributed to my table, perhaps deliberately, so I got the French version from the Swiss Ambassador at the adjoining table. After reading the paragraph which unmistakably accused India of aggression, Rama and I walked out, which, according to the Chinese, was an unpardonable insult to their revered Chairman. The Chinese had anticipated my possible reactions and planned the maximum harassment to the Indian Chargé. Our car had been hedged in, so Rama and I shivered for a good half-hour at the top of the grand steps before the car could be extricated! After my innovation, subsequently, even the Soviets mustered the courage to practise the 'diplomacy of walking out' in Peking.

I received the text of a note dated 24 September 1965—the day after my telegram—obviously dictated by the PM personally, conveying his felicitations to the Embassy on our risky but correct anticipation. On arrival in Delhi, I was promptly received by Prime Minister Shastri, who gave me a hug and asked me in Hindi how I dared make such a prediction—no one in the Foreign or Defence Ministry, or any newspaper in India had expected the Chinese to back out of their repeated ultimata. I was naturally gratified by his appreciation. Apparently the PM had spoken very warmly about 'whoever was in charge in Peking' to L.P. Singh, then Home Secretary, saying, 'This young man had the courage.'

After talking to various officials at headquarters, I was told to accompany Mrs Vijaya Lakshmi Pandit to some West European capitals to explain the Indian stand on the recent conflict with Pakistan and our relations with China.

We still speculate over the extent to which China encouraged Pakistan in its attempt to seize Kashmir, and whether there was deliberate ambivalence in the statement 'not standing idly by', which Bhutto interpreted as a definite promise to rescue Pakistan if defeat or a stalemate faced them. The operations obviously did not go as planned; the expected quick victory was belied at every stage, and the battles between modern American tanks on the one hand and World War II antiquated ones in our armoured division on the other, led to a stalemate. Pakistan did not anticipate the predicament of alienating both the US and the USSR. My guess is that had the Chinese pledged a full-scale attack in Sikkim and NEFA (Arunachal), and not just tried to prevent India from overrunning East Pakistan, it might have changed the end result. However, I felt that China did not really go back on its promise as the pledge was deliberately ambivalent. Anyway, I knew I was putting my own career on line by predicting that the ultimata was deliberately vague or amounted to mere psychological pressure. China would remain militarily prudent but still demonstrate to Pakistan that it was not reneging on the promise to Ayub and Bhutto, and making known that the PRC was a reliable friend!

I returned to Peking only in December. India had broken off diplomatic relations with Pakistan after the attack in Kashmir. My colleagues were in the throes of Christmas celebrations but of course, confined to the incestuous Diplomatic Corps. General Raza was once again talking paternally to Rama and suddenly asked her in Urdu, 'Bibi, will you dance with me?' She replied, 'Certainly.' I saw this and promptly rushed across to Begum Raza and took her to the floor. I recall two ambassadors leaving the party for their chanceries, presumably to send telegrams to their headquarters signifying that rapprochement between India and Pakistan had been made. No such thing had happened and Tashkent was still weeks away; it was only local, unauthorized socializing. As it happened, the Soviet Ambassador was in our Embassy on 11 January 1966 to celebrate the Tashkent talks but we did not know our PM had passed away at midnight.

The death of Lal Bahadur Shastri was the second prime ministerial death during my tenure in Peking. Zhou Enlai came on both occasions to sign in our condolence book. Subsequently, it has been asserted in a recent book by a Pakistani author, Fakir A. Khan, that both Mao and Zhou Enlai had spoken disparagingly about Nehru to Nixon and Henry Kissinger, but in 1964, as Zhou Enlai was getting into his car, he said to me, 'Nehru was a great man and my good friend.' Zhou Enlai was being hypocritical either in 1964 or in 1972! Another fact I recall is that I had asked my colleagues to be formally attired and not to carry any cameras. Several Foreign Office photographers clicked away during Zhou Enlai's visit. Even though we requested several times, a copy was never sent to us. The Chinese obviously did not want publicity, even for a formal courtesy call, at that time in India–China relations.

Surreptitious import of technology

The twice-yearly Canton fair was the entry point for China's trade with the world. Extensive import and export deals were concluded with initial hard bargaining but once a deal was signed, the implementation was businesslike and faultless. Special trade delegations from some select countries were also welcomed. One such delegation came from Tanzania, an approved 'radical' country. All incoming and outgoing visitors had to stay in a hotel in Canton. Much of the Tanzanian commerce was handled by Asians, including persons of Indian origin. Bhupat Oza happened to be doing the courier bag duty run that week. He ran into the Tanzanian delegation in the dining room and found two of its members not eating anything, talking to each other in Gujarati, and with fellow members in Kiswahili. Gujarati is Bhupat's mother tongue. Bhupat became friendly with them and discovered that the 'Tanzanian Indians' were so conservative that, for the entire ten-day trip, they were living on pre-cooked chiwda (a fried savoury snack), as they did not want to eat anything cooked by the Chinese. (By definition, the Chinese used what, for strict vegetarians, were polluted ingredients and cooking fats). Bhupat invited them home in Peking and the delegates welcomed their first opportunity to have an Indian meal at the house of a Brahmin! In the process, he got to know a great deal of China's trade and semi-secret sales of hardware to Africa.

The basic problem in the pre-Deng Xiaoping's ascendancy was that, while China was anxious to acquire modern technology, it did not want its skilled and unskilled persons to study abroad and risk being subverted. China, therefore, encouraged Japan and the Western Europeans to hold exhibitions in Peking. The invariable pre-condition for the exhibitions was that the exhibitors had to bring their latest technology products and the Chinese would have the option of purchasing the equipment brought in. The appropriate experts from approved public sector enterprises, all wearing identical blue Mao suits, would visit the exhibitions in hordes and get to know a part of the process. Somebody else would come the next day and ask about some other circuit and, by the end of the week, the entire know-how would have been surreptitiously acquired. The strategy was that, without patented rights, China could replicate foreign innovations. Policy changes occurred in the eighties when 50,000-odd Chinese were financed and sent to the West every year but, in the sixties they found these devious methods to breach the patent laws.

There was a sudden regime change when Sukarno was ousted in October 1965. The Indonesian Ambassador was a crypto-communist and took refuge overnight. The poor Counsellor did not have any directions and came to our Embassy to obtain guidance from his Foreign Ministry.

President Nkrumah in Peking when neither he nor the Chinese knew that he had been overthrown in Accra

Ghana was the first country in Africa to be decolonized in 1957, and Nkrumah had been President ever since. During his years in power, Nkrumah had become an arrogant dictator and broken relations with the Commonwealth. With his special equation with the PRC, he thought he could act as an international mediator and solve the Vietnam problem. China was reluctant but could not refuse his intervention. The airport had the usual VIP paraphernalia of gaily attired children waving Chinese and Ghanaian flags to receive a VIP. He landed at four in the afternoon. As I calculated, the time differential between Peking and Accra was ten hours. In other words, when we of the Diplomatic Corps set forth from our respective embassies to receive the Ghanaian President, we did not know Nkrumah had been effectively dethroned. President Liu Shao-ch'i, Premier Zhou Enlai, Foreign Minister Chen Yi and others too, did not know that, while they were driving to the airport, their guest had been ousted. By the time we got back to our respective residences at about 5.30 p.m., I received a telephone call from Donald Hobson, the British Chargé d'Affaires, who sarcastically asked me where had I been. I told him he knew perfectly well where I had been. And that, even if the UK had broken relations with Ghana, there were other countries who wanted to continue with Commonwealth solidarity. He laughed and said, 'Nkrumah ain't President any more.' The Chinese must have been equally taken aback when they found that they had a pretender on their hands.

All heads were invited to the welcoming banquet scheduled as usual to begin at 7 p.m. It seems the Chinese debated whether or not to still treat Nkrumah as the President of Ghana and risk alienating his successors. After all, what mattered to China were the people of Africa. But it would have been insulting if the banquet were summarily cancelled. 'Our Excellencies' had assembled in an anteroom of the National People's Hall. Finally, the dinner was held as if for a visiting President and the speeches delivered were unchanged. The streets of Peking kept the oversized portraits of Nkrumah, but the banquet was the first and last public event held in Nkrumah's honour.

The problem was how to get rid of Nkrumah in order not to forfeit the friendship of the people of Ghana. Despite his attempt to assure the Ghana Embassy that he would be back in the saddle soon, the Mission had immediately switched its loyalties. The Chinese were getting anxious about their guest's security while he was in China. A Ghanaian diplomat's son, aged no more than twelve, who innocently bought a penknife for school was arrested within an hour because he was considered likely to attack Nkrumah while he was in Peking! Nkrumah finally left via

Moscow on being promised that he would be made the joint Head of State of Guinea, another radical country.

This incident, however, gave me the only entry into the vast complex of guesthouses in Western Peking for visiting VIPs. Nkrumah sent for the Indian Chargé d'Affaires, and the Chinese could not very well refuse his request. Nkrumah asked me to send an immediate message to 'his sister Indira' to stop the special Viscount in which he and his entourage had flown to Rangoon, from where he had switched to a Chinese aircraft. The Viscount had, indeed, landed in Bombay, re-fuelled and fortunately already taken off when I telephoned Delhi. This gave me a second opportunity to visit the guesthouse complex and convey our regret. Being at the tail end of the Diplomatic Corps, I must have been the last person to shake Nkrumah's hand when both he and I thought he was still the President of Ghana!

Transfer orders

Even though in the doghouse, I was enjoying the posting in Peking. I had asked the Ministry to let me stay for another term, which was only two years. However, soon after Mrs Indira Gandhi became PM, the Foreign Secretary wrote to me that the PM had approved the opening of a Policy Planning Division and had chosen me to launch it. So at the end of April, I packed my bags and came back to the Ministry. It was my third stint in the Ministry. I had been away for less than five years. I had grasped that ideology in international affairs was merely a convenient cover for national interest; professionally, one must learn to see through the written word to unearth the reality. Being asked to start a Policy Planning Division and chosen for the job by the Prime Minister left no scope for hesitation.

11

Policy Planning and its Subjective Benefits; Interlude at Harvard (1966–70)

On arriving in Delhi, when I called on the Foreign Secretary, C.S. Jha, I asked what the directives were for the new Policy Planning Division (PPD) for which I had been recalled from Peking. His words were to the effect that the PM had announced the constitution of the division in the MEA and had specially chosen me for the task. I had to work out its structure and also, how the proposal could be implemented. I was a little taken aback by the lack of even broad outlines of my responsibilities. Something occurred to me spontaneously. If Policy Planning (PP) were to be useful, we had to have the right to suggest policy modifications, no doubt confidentially, but we should not be penalized for identifying avoidable failures. I said frivolously, 'You, Sir, must write the ACRs (Annual Confidential Reports) of the Policy Planners, not every year, but say, after three years, and judge if, in our crystal balls, we had seen the changing realities, at least for the medium term. We should not be expected to find new reasons for old mindsets and provide justification for unwarranted national self-righteousness. Successful foreign policy in diplomacy hinges on grasping the misperceptions of other sovereignties, as this alone would enable courageous innovations and peaceful solutions.'

Planning the structure for policy planning

I worked out what I thought should be the organization and procedure for the division. Of course, even foreign policy planning has to respect the constraints inherent in a democracy, which can be unforgiving about mistakes like China. The division should not be operationally involved in current decision-making, but all telegrams and reports on important political and economical questions, should be marked to the head of the division to glean out what is significant. The PPD should not duplicate the existing divisions. My suggestion was that under the Joint Secretary, there should be, at least in the beginning, two deputies who, in foreign postings, had shown analytical independence. They must be able to pose searching questions, listen to and not dispute with their interlocutors. The three—the head and the two deputies—should evaluate how world developments might affect India in the future. Besides coordinating the work of the division, the Joint Secretary himself should concentrate on some problems. For me, India's relations with her immediate neighbours was of critical importance for its security and economics; one of the deputy secretaries should dwell on the developed world—communist and non-communist (Europe and North America)—and the other, with the developing countries, which are unified by problems of delayed development as a legacy of colonialism.

Policy planners should invariably start by consulting with functional officers. Policy planning may be expanded but always kept small. They will be expected to keep abreast of published material in journals and books, at home and abroad and, within affordable means, allowed to attend think tank meetings and to consult freely with scholars and known experts. Planners should enjoy some prestige for having been entrusted with the delicate assignment of getting out of rigid ruts, but in pursuit of the PM's decision, other divisions and ministries must not consider them to be intruders.

There have been a few examples of policy evolution which emanated from considered policy planning. George Marshall, who had proved himself with his masterful leadership of the Allied victory in World War II, was already assured of a place in history when he was appointed Secretary of State. He willingly entrusted policy planning to George Kennan. After Kennan's 'Long Telegram' from Moscow in 1946, which eventually fructified into his 'Mr X's Article' in *Foreign Affairs*, he evolved the policy of 'containment' of communist USSR. Though his original recommendations were interpreted as having laid too much emphasis on the military element, on closer reading and subsequent clarifications, it was perceived that his analysis detected the inner weakness of the Soviet Union under Stalin. While many, even in India, thought Soviet communism was the inevitable wave of the future, Kennan proved prophetically farsighted. The disintegration of the communist bloc was caused by inner distortions rather than its military weakness. The Marshall Plan emerged from Kennan's policy planning which declared that twentieth century 'decolonization' required domestic development as collateral.

The marginalization of policy planning

I was nominated the MEA representative on the Joint Intelligence Committee (JIC), which met weekly. It was upgraded with a full-time Chairman at the Additional Secretary level after the 1962 conflict, but we were only fed tactical intelligence, mostly on Pakistan, and never given details of our own deployment. The result was that assessment of the JIC was never really credible, at least not as a useful input for long-term policy planning.

In the original structure I had recommended that the Foreign Secretary, as head of office, should automatically preside over the policy committee. This, in my view, was so that independent policy planners with their recommendations could interact with the secretaries who had current operational responsibilities. After I left, policy planning was virtually ignored or relegated to minor tasks such as rationalizing current policies. Few papers were written, and those which were, had been done without extensive consultations; there was little emphasis on independent thinking and policy modifications, practically surrendering the right of forward-looking innovations.

During my limited experience, I felt that major policy was not debated. When the Chairman of the Policy Planning Committee became a pseudonym for a non-official, non-foreign service advisor, it became a transparent mockery of the envisaged role. This designation was conferred on D.P. Dhar—an experienced and shrewd politician but not inclined to reflect on the years ahead; later, also on G. Parthasarthy—a non-official with experience of ambassadorial appointments, but one who had never written any papers, and who probably scoffed at long-term perspectives. The challenge of policy had died even though it was not ceremonially buried. And yet, policy-making in the twentieth century is an abiding challenge to understand the consequences of empowered poverty and the new informed defiance of the people. This requires a new definition of security where nations must weigh opportunity costs for the rich and the poor. In the last hundred years, policy projections in Foreign Offices have generally failed, and this underlines the need for modernized anticipation and thinking ahead. The world would be very different if we could start again but it requires not only not rejecting policy planning but also not paying only lip service to it. It critically depends on decision-makers having the self-confidence to seek advice, and that is rare.

Ad hoc utilization of the Policy Planning Division

Policy planning, let me confess, has made little contribution to timely major policy adjustments. The initial prestige has gone and the post of head of PP has become a sinecure. When it first opened, it was not entirely without clout. At least on issues which straddled several divisions, I was asked to make a quick analysis; at times it was a short background note, a banquet speech or a general brief for a VIP visitor. PP was treated as a kind of semi-high-powered fifth wheel to the coach which, at the discretion of the Foreign

Secretary, served either as a replacement or as a supplementary, but it was not considered quite the same as an in-house think tank.

Assigned an operational role: the Raghunath–Vijay episode

One specific problem which the Foreign Secretary, C.S. Jha, asked me to handle operationally was the Raghunath–Vijay incident. I have described the incident in some detail elsewhere but it bears summary repetition, as it was a major episode which illustrated my rationale in diplomacy—of innovation, improvisation, initiative and discretion in the national interest.

In a short overlap during which Raghu was showing his successor Vijay around Peking in the western hills they were seen taking a photograph of a demolished pillar typifying the destructive licence during the Cultural Revolution. Some Red Guards who happened to be around while this shot was being taken had reported it to the police station as an 'insult' by two foreigners. Once it was discovered they were Indians, vindictive official action got underway. Raghu was declared a spy and Vijay was to be banished as persona non grata even before he could start work. Ram Sathe, my successor as Chargé d'Affaires, refused to accede to the demand that Raghu should present himself at the Red Guard kangaroo court. He wisely assembled the Indian families in his residence. Raghu was bloodied on the tarmac on his way to the plane and throughout the outward flight he was bombarded with Maoist propaganda over blaring microphones.

All this was reported not just to the Ministry but also by Reuters and in the international press. It enraged Parliament and roused public opinion in India. On arrival at Palam, Raghu and Vijay were given a massive welcome organized by the Jan Sangh. The Red Guards, in retaliation, surrounded our Embassy in Peking, stopped all our Chinese servants from carrying out their normal duties and held up supply of essentials like milk sent to the inmates herded in the Mission.

I called the Chinese Chargé and warned him that if the Chinese government did not lift the boycott within twenty-four hours, our authorities might do the same to the Chinese Embassy in Delhi. I held a daily press conference and told the correspondents that the provocations violated international conventions on diplomatic immunity. I also hinted that I had been reading about measured retaliation during the Cuban missile crisis for defusing a possible provocation. The Chinese did not expect India to pay them back in their own coin. The next day, all Indian employees of the Embassy were stopped from entering the Chinese Mission in the Diplomatic Enclave. After one more day, the government authorities in Peking allowed the Chinese servants to re-enter the Indian Mission in Peking with essential supplies and, correspondingly, we did the same in Delhi.

Coping with public and Parliamentary anger

In Parliament there were vociferous demands for the severance of diplomatic relations with China. Breaking relations is easy but I knew re-establishing them would be more difficult. The problem was to uphold national dignity in the face of unprovoked insults and injuries to our diplomats. The Jan Sangh decided to demonstrate in front of the Chinese Embassy. The Chinese diplomats, showing off their militant loyalty (hoping that it would reach the Red Guards headquarters), were fearless: they came out to 'fight' the surrounding crowd, which had broken through the police cordon. As it happened, while the Embassy was being besieged, the Chinese Chargé was sitting in my room. We had already declared one member of the Chinese Embassy as a 'spy' and another as a 'persona non grata'; one of these two had come as interpreter with the Chargé but I told him to go back as he no longer had diplomatic status.

Anyway, I was the one to inform the Chargé that his Embassy was surrounded. He flushed and was visibly anxious not only about his Mission but also about his personal safety. I told him to wait for a while and that I would make sure of his returning safely to his Embassy. From the next-door office of my PA, I requested the police authorities to arrange an escort. This took time and it became dark. Finally I got one of my PAs to accompany me and the Chargé in one of our vehicles. We leaned forward so that if there were any brickbats, they would hit us and not the Chinese diplomat. When we approached the Chinese compound, the largest in Chanakyapuri, there was still altercation and fighting around the front gates of the Embassy and so I asked the driver to go around. The gate of the house roughly opposite Mansarovar, Karan Singhji's house, was of course locked. I told the Chinese Chargé to get down and jump over the four-foot wall. (There were no barbed wires and spikes as there are now). Once back in his Mission, he regained his colour and confidence. He then asked me to come across and see what damage had been done by the 'hooligans'. I told him that my promise had been only to return him to his immunity. I used my discretion, because I was not prepared to see any damage which may have been caused by demonstrating Indians. I did not want to be a witness against my own countrymen. Meanwhile, the PM had been kept informed; the Cabinet had been called and they were all awaiting my arrival for almost an hour. After restoring the Chinese Envoy to his immunity, I went straight to Parliament House and described what had happened. I arranged for any injured Chinese to be taken to the Willingdon Hospital (now re-named Ram Manohar Lohia) and I visited them the next day. The Chinese expressed full satisfaction with the treatment accorded to them.

However, the crisis was not over, certainly not in Parliament. Immediately afterwards, the Chinese proposed sending an aircraft to take back their officials who had been injured. I consented to this suggestion but only on condition that an Indian aircraft, which would be stationed in Hong Kong, could fly simultaneously to Peking and evacuate Indian families. Obviously the Chinese did not want our plane in their airspace and so they did not accept the idea of reciprocity. A few days later, at about 4.30 p.m. the Chinese

Embassy delivered a note that the following morning one of their aircraft, with a specified call sign, would approach India from East Pakistan to take away their injured personnel; in other words, they were proposing unilateral action. It was late afternoon and I had to tell all concerned, but specially the Chinese Foreign Ministry that no such aircraft would be allowed into Indian airspace without our consent. I informed the Chinese Embassy in Delhi but I was at a loss as to how to make sure that this had reached Chinese officialdom in Peking. I sent an un-coded telegram direct to the Chinese Foreign Office, and also conveyed its substance on the telephone to Sathe that since they had not agreed to simultaneous flights, we could not allow their plane. 'We have as much sovereignty over our airspace as they have over theirs.' To make doubly sure, I called Ashok Bhadkamkar, a colleague and friend who had a room two doors away, and told him to convey our firm negative reply in Marathi. As soon as Ashok started speaking in Marathi, the telephone went dead. After I came back on line speaking English, the telephone was live again and I knew immediately that my message had been monitored by the Chinese authorities!

Meanwhile, I alerted Air headquarters that some fighters should be prepared to take off in case the Chinese aircraft invaded our airspace from the East; it should be ordered to land at the nearest airport, but in any case not allowed to reach Palam. (I suggested Allahabad which had an air base.) After taking all these immediate actions I tried to inform the Foreign Secretary but had difficulty in reaching him. Late that night, Defence Minister Sardar Swaran Singh, called me in my flat on Wellesley Road. He spoke in Hindustani, but instead of being his normal suave self, his manner expressed anger. He told me that I had no authorization to take such a decision as it could lead to the outbreak of hostilities between China and India; it should have been reported for a Cabinet decision. I assured him that there was no reason to apprehend a conflict; I did not believe that the Chinese would order a military or a civil plane to intrude into our airspace but, anyway, I had had to take immediate action. Our air force would only be discharging its normal duty safeguarding our skies. In the end, as I had expected, no Chinese aircraft came.

However, we were still left worried about the reaction in our Parliament to the uncalled-for humiliation suffered by our young diplomats. We expected that the Chinese Embassy would plan to send its officers back to China by some other means. After a couple of days, we gathered that the following morning, the Chinese officials were booked to fly to Kathmandu by a scheduled flight of Air Nepal. I put on my thinking cap and requested the police to prepare for the exercise of some muscle power. We had guessed correctly that the 'spy' and the other officer would come with the Chinese Chargé in his car. I was discreetly present at Palam airport. In accordance with International Law, the person declared 'persona non grata' was allowed to leave as a diplomat but, as planned, the one dubbed a 'spy' was sharply segregated and taken into a 'secret' part of the airport. When all the other passengers had boarded, the 'spy' was marched across the tarmac with two tall uniformed policemen on either side. By previous arrangement, the 'spy' was photographed 'in custody'. (No harm had been done to him in detention.) The Chinese Embassy personnel in Nepal, to show off their own militancy, had already demonstrated and so provoking insults to the portrait of King Mahendra of Nepal. The Chinese Embassy staff vociferously welcomed their colleagues from Delhi. Anyway, when the photograph of the 'spy' with uniformed policemen appeared in the Indian newspapers the next morning, members of the Parliament including those of the CPI, felt that India's honour had been redeemed, and the crisis was summarily defused! The demand for the break of diplomatic relations was never raised again.

The Hazards of Impetuosity and Constriction

The Red Guards had acted equally impetuously when they attacked the British Mission. Donald Hopson, the British Chargé, and his colleagues 'fought' them. (Donald had been highly decorated in WW II for his bravery.) For having defied the Red Guards and tried to save the Embassy residence, Hopson was incarcerated in the counsellor's flat for a whole year. Denise, his wife, also a heroine of the 'Resistance' had left prior to their ordered transfer. During his confinement Donald fell in love with Anne-Marie, a Third Secretary in the Danish Embassy. He was knighted on returning to London and appointed Ambassador to Venezuela. There was a sense of terrible disappointment when he announced his divorce from Denise and marriage to Anne-Marie. She was 'Lady Hopson' after Donald passed away while Denise was left running a small shop in Paris. This is an example of the hazards of constricted diplomacy in a place like Peking in the sixties.

The lesson: the imperative of professional sagacity

I have dwelt in some detail on the Raghunath–Vijay incident. It was a proof of good professionalism that we had guessed correctly that the Chinese Foreign Office and the security agencies themselves were on the defensive against the Gang of Four and the rampaging Red Guards. India had handled the crisis with firmness, avoiding national humiliation but, at the same time, without any setback to long-term relations. As a diplomatic episode it had some amusing or at least unusual aspects. It is not often that an envoy's protection from brickbats is entrusted to host officials, and that he is then made to jump over a wall to get back to his diplomatic immunity! More seriously, though without seeking formal permission, I had done no more than exercise my best and prompt judgement in the pursuit of perceived duty, including asking fighter planes to be ready to take off against a foreign aircraft which was likely to violate our airspace despite our prior refusal. Even in the twentieth–twenty-first century, diplomacy permits sophisticated initiative for demonstrating domestic national sovereignty after all precautions against escalation have been taken. Lack of prompt action, in my view, carries far worse consequences. At one stage, not just the Jan Sangh opposition but many parties in Parliament, including the Dange-led CPI (Left), were clamouring for breaking off diplomatic relations with China. No minister, or even senior bureaucrats, could have countermanded my initiative but some might have hesitated or delayed it. It may also be worth recalling that even in 1967 we were still facing China's anti-Indian and pro-Pakistan tilt. Vajpayee, as Foreign Minister, might not have gone to China in 1979 if we had no diplomatic relations during the previous decade. Shrewd diplomacy has to find ways of not succumbing to public anger or Parliamentary opinion in order to safeguard long-term national interests. Academics can indulge in armchair reflections but diplomacy must weigh the future with sagacity.

Accompanying the PM to Eastern Europe (1967) and Latin America (1968)

Apart from these two incidents related to my posting in China, although my responsibility was policy planning, I was occasionally roped in for other 'jobs' and tours abroad with no particular logic behind my inclusion. I was told to accompany the PM, the Foreign Secretary and others on a visit to Eastern Europe in 1967. It was a sort of goodwill visit after Mrs Gandhi had assumed responsibility as head of the government in Delhi. We went to Moscow, Warsaw, East Berlin, Bucharest, Belgrade and finally, Cairo. These were all well trodden grounds and everywhere there was goodwill for India and unqualified admiration for Mrs Gandhi.

More interesting was the tour in 1968. It was my first-ever trip to seven countries in South America and two in the Caribbean, in all, nine countries in not more than three weeks. Next to the PM and the Foreign Secretary, I was the most senior and the only one with a major load of responsibility in a fifteen-member delegation. There were S.K. Bannerji, Sharada Prasad, Natwar Singh of the PM's Office, Usha Bhagat, (a lady-in-waiting), S.K. Singh on behalf of the Commerce Ministry, various security personnel and some representatives from the press. Instead of the territorial division head I was supposed to brief and record the political talks. Not that there were any big problems in Brazil, Uruguay, Argentina, Chile, Peru, Colombia, Venezuela, Guyana and

Trinidad, but it meant mastering a fat briefing book which no one except me had read from cover to cover. In Brazil and Argentina, the halts were for three days each but in other places, for not more than one or two days. Everywhere we went through virtually the same formal rituals—arrival ceremony, speech at the airport, laying of a wreath at the statue of the national hero (generally Simón de Bolívar), meeting the Indian community, a welcome banquet and perhaps, an hour or two of conversation thrown in which included the time taken for translation.

The hypocrisy of joint communiqués

I was supposed to 'negotiate' the joint communiqués, which had to be 'pithy' as an Asian VIP was visiting the continent for the first time. Many in Latin America had heard of Mahatma Gandhi, some of Tagore, a few of Nehru, and all were thrilled that Nehru's daughter was coming. After seeing a draft of the scheduled programmes, I wondered when there would be time to make 'profound declarations' and hammer out joint communiqués appropriate to such a visit, which had aroused great public expectations! Moreover, one had to be careful that each successive declaration did not echo the previous one. In Buenos Aires, it had to be different from the one in Brasilia. After studying the nature of regimes—democracy, military rule or dictatorship—and after taking care that each had appropriate individuality, I drafted nine joint communiqués and left them on the file in Delhi. Just before landing I would whisper to the PM, the name of the President of the country, the nature of the regime, perhaps the name of the Foreign Minister. On arrival I would quickly give my draft of the communiqué, for subsequent finalization, possibly after dinner. (The secret in all multiple declarations is to draw 'first blood' so that it becomes the working draft.) Of the nine communiqués—except for one small paragraph in Brazil, which incidentally pertained to nuclear weapons as the country was then contemplating making the bomb—all finalized communiqués were exactly as I had left them on our file before we started! The ultimate exercise of imagination was that I had even improvised conversations between the heads of government!

The PM, with her elegance, her saris, shawls, coats, hairstyle and indeed, her youth made such a great impact on the Latinos that she really overtrumped the political profundity of President de Gaulle who had trod the same trail a year earlier. The visit was an undoubted success.

A sudden coup in Peru

There was, however, one unforeseen crisis. On the eve of our scheduled departure from Santiago (Chile), we heard that there had been a coup in Lima, which was to be our next halt. Such sudden changes of government were not unusual in non-democratic South America. Our man in Santiago, who was concurrently accredited, had no idea what to make of it. It was left to me to ascertain if it was a benign coup or if it would create embarrassment for India. We knew Mrs Gandhi was particularly anxious to visit Machu Picchu, the remnants of the old Inca civilization in Peru. I had to telephone various sources and piece together instant advice. I finally recommended that it was too risky to plan a two-day stay in Peru. We were eventually flown to Valparaiso and so we had two leisurely days, observing the South Pacific Ocean! In Bogotá (Colombia), we visited the jewellery museum, and Mrs Gandhi was presented with a huge uncut emerald.

Amusing incidents: an impostor as Indian Ambassador and a 'husband–wife controller'

Two incidents regarding Colombia are worth recalling. An impostor who arrived in Medellín, dressed as a maharaja and claiming to be the Ambassador of India was fêted lavishly. A boy from his home town recognized him; it became a national joke and was recorded on a long-playing record. I traced the Spanish record and bought it.

The other was a small purchase in Guyana made of straw, called a 'husband- or wife-controller'. When fixed on a finger, it could not be removed except by the partner! Mrs Gandhi was amused and she wished Usha Bhagat had bought one for use by the recently married Rajiv and Sonia!

At the end of an enjoyable but fairly active three weeks, we landed in New York in early October. At the reception in the Indian Consulate, I managed to stop the long queue of invitees to enable Prof. John Kenneth Galbraith to present a copy of his book on Indian Miniature Painting—jointly edited with M.S. Randhawa—to the Indian PM. As a reward for my shamelessly holding back the long queue of American dignitaries, Ken took me along to an election meeting in Sergeant Shriver's apartment where Ken was addressing a meeting in support of the Democratic candidate for the White House.

While in New York, I took Rajeshwar Dayal, the Foreign Secretary, to call on Henry Kissinger whom I had met a few months earlier at Harvard at the Pugwash Conference led by Vikram Sarabhai. Kissinger had been working for the nomination of Nelson Rockefeller but by October, Nixon was chosen as the Republican candidate. As we were leaving, I said to Henry that if Nixon won the election, he would probably be in McGeorge Bundy's job as the National Security Advisor. He lectured me that I did not understand the American system, and that he was irrevocably identified with Rockefeller. The basis of my prediction was simply that Kissinger was the only Republican I knew who had written on nuclear weapons and foreign policy. In January 1969, he wrote to me acknowledging that I was the only person who, in October, had predicted that he would be given the position of National Security Advisor in the Nixon White House!

Secret visit to Bhutan

Another 'odd' job which I was asked to undertake was a secret visit to Bhutan. I lied even to my family about my destination.

The Cabinet had commissioned me to persuade the King to make a public statement that he had asked India to take up the question of China precipitating a territorial claim against Bhutan. This remains the last occasion when, according to our interpretation of article II of the Treaty, Bhutan had not only to seek India's guidance but also follow it. (Thereafter, with India's sponsorship, Bhutan became a member of the UN and has held direct bilateral talks with China.) My visit remained secret even from colleagues in the division, but some weeks later, Hitchcock, the American Consul General in Calcutta, asked me about my visit to Thimpu. I was naturally surprised, but obviously the CIA had informers even in Bhutan!

Socialism and non-alignment versus the logic of economic development

During those PP years, Kosygin paid a visit, and urged greater economic dynamism in India. I was sitting at the back with the other Joint Secretaries, but I was taken aback when he said India must not allow the Trade Union who were pro-Soviet communists to impede production. One could have sensed the difference between ideology and economic development.

Tripartite cooperation with Yugoslavia and Egypt

In the claimed high noon of non-alignment, there were attempts to work out a triangular economic partnership with Tito and Nasser. The Commerce Ministry was dutifully promoting the idea of a joint component-manufacturing arrangement. I thought even then that the political-cum-economic logic of partnership between three countries in different continents was dubious. Despite a shared faith in non-alignment, the economic cooperation never took off. Policy planning however, was not consulted on these but at least I was invited to sit in.

Gesture of response to Singapore

There were occasional flashes of policy opportunities. The visit I especially recall was one where we succeeded, without having uttered a word. In 1968, I had urged the Foreign Secretary to respond positively to an invitation from Singapore to send an observer to the 1968 meeting of the 'Ministerial Conference' on South-East Asia. Recalling the ugly memories of World War II, PM Lee Kuan Yu, who had succeeded David Marshall, believed that India could politically balance the economic surplus of fast-developing Japan. Manu Shroff, an economist and director in the Finance Ministry, and I were named observers. What was in the offing was a variant of Japan's old Co-prosperity sphere, which came up to and included Burma, but excluded non-aligned India. Our visible presence as 'observers' from India put an end to the Japanese grand design. Later, as leader of the Indian team, I had a long one-to-one interview with the Singapore PM. We did not follow up with South-East Asia until thirty years later but by then these non-communist countries had progessed economically and made a success of ASEAN. We had stood aloof on the grounds that most of South-East Asia was America-dominated. We are now at last 'looking East'.

Nuclear Non-Proliferation, 1967–68

The implications of nuclear weapons demanded deeper examination. It illustrated the conflict between historic notions of military power and peace as the twin child of non-utility of nuclear weapons in the twentieth century.

The Chinese nuclear explosion in 1964 naturally aroused anxiety about India's security, and we debated the seeking of a nuclear umbrella consistent with our non-alignment policy. An idea was put forth for a nuclear declaration jointly with a superpower, but with no strings attached. In 1967, a treaty supported by both the USA and the USSR was in the air. We were taken aback when Kosygin told a delegation led by C.S. Jha and L.K. Jha, Principal Secretary to the PM, that 'there was no such thing as automatic security but India should sign the treaty.' We still stuck our faith in the 'time-tested' friendship with the USSR, little realizing that the Soviet Union was working out a balance between anti-USA military preparations and advocaing non-proliferation in the rest of the world. The USSR did not want the International Atomic Energy Agency (IAEA) safeguards to be bypassed even by India.

The treaty gave a special, privileged position for the five who had already 'tested', and they happened to be the permanent members of the Security Council who had the right to retain and develop Weapons of Mass Destruction (WMD). My personal recommendation, on which I elaborated in a policy paper, was that India should not stand aloof on a question of nuclear disarmament even if it were flawed. I felt WMDs were not usable, and we should not abandon our Nehruvian approach to nuclear disarmament. Prestige, which the WMDs were alleged to give, was dubious. Our interest, I argued, was in collective security and in pressuring the Nuclear Five towards disarmament as we had been doing. In 1968 (by which time C.S. Jha had gone on to Paris), I thought his successor, Foreign Secretary Rajeshwar Dayal, saw the logic of my viewpoint but he did not assert it strongly enough to the PM or in the cabinet meeting. He simply suggested further examination of the implications of the problem. Mrs Gandhi was strongly in favour of not signing the treaty. I gave my advice but the Cabinet decided not to sign the treaty.

Policy planning really contributed to my own education. It gave me a broad canvas but, to tell the truth, we made no visible impact on policy. However, it is with immense satisfaction that I still re-read the twenty major policy papers, which I wrote in 1966–69, even if the members of the Policy Committee had no time to discuss them or pay any attention to their recommendations.

The emancipation of an only son: Jagat Mehta in 1928 in his first pair of shorts. This was a dramatic change from the feudal dress of a 'Bhanwerji' (grandson)

Portrait of Mehta Jeewan Singh, the author's grandfather, in ceremonial court dress on the Maharana's birthday in 1936

Panditji during a visit to Paro, Bhutan, 1958

The feudal household inside the haveli: family servants and children, 1961. Jagat Mehta (second row, first left), Bhabi (second row, second from left) and Rama Mehta (second row, third from left) in everyday Mewari dress. Vijay is seated at her feet

Pandit Nehru and Indira Gandhi at breakfast in front of one of the huts, on the way to Paro, 1958

Jagat S. Mehta with Indira Gandhi just before crossing the Nathu La pass, 1958

Panditji trying on a Bhutanese hat, 1958

Jagat S. Mehta in the Foreign Secretary's room

Jagat S. Mehta with External Affairs Minister Atal Bihari Vajpayee in Damascus, 1978

Midnight of 1 October 1977. The signing of the Agreement on Farakka with M.A. Abbas of Bangladesh

The author with Jaiprakash Narain in Patna, 1977

During the Non-Aligned Movement Summit of 1971. (From left) Prime Minister Indira Gandhi, External Affairs Minister Y.B. Chavan, Principal Secretary P.N. Dhar and Jagat S. Mehta

In Moscow, 1977: (from left) I.K. Gujral, Leonid Brezhnev, Morarji Desai and Alexei Kosygin. A.B Vajpayee is on the far right and the author is second from left, second row

The author with Manmohan Singh at Jeewan Niwas, in Udaipur, 2003

Jagat S. Mehta with Henry Kissinger at Jeewan Niwas, Udaipur

The author with the Dalai Lama at Dharamshala, 2005

Jagat S. Mehta at John Kenneth Galbraith's home, 2004

Interlude at Harvard

I was about to complete my term of three years, and there was talk of my being assigned an ambassadorship somewhere. Yugoslavia was mentioned. But I had made it clear in advance to the Foreign Secretary and to Foreign Minister Dinesh Singh that I would like to have a sabbatical year. In the fifties, Robert R. Bowie, a professor of law at Harvard who had served as head of Policy Planning, had broached the idea of an International Fellowship programme consisting of a one-year sabbatical for senior diplomats. Nehru, had approved India's participation in the programme. But it was appropriated by the Cabinet Secretariat. L.P. Singh was the first to avail of this Fellowship and then successively, A.D. Pandit, Mangat Rai, A.N. Ray, and all senior ICS officers. Our Ministry thought that IFS officers should not join as they might get 'contaminated' by American influence. The Fellows from the rest of the world were notable diplomats who had availed of this opportunity for high-level interaction with internationally respected faculty members. I voluntarily surrendered my diplomatic passport in exchange for an ordinary one and The Fellows representation grant. We 'Fellows' had faculty status and could attend any lectures that we wanted. The only obligation was to write a paper on the subject of one's choice. Nobody from MEA had been on the programme before me. I was unanimously elected spokesman for the Fellows group. In 1969–70 we had some Americans but the programme was largely dominated by distinguished diplomats from other countries.

Apart from Prof. Bowie, I met and befriended many distinguished professors like Samuel Huntington, Reischauer, Ray Vernon, Stanley Hoffman, Joseph Nye, John Fairbanks, Ben Robert Schwartz and Adam Ulam among others. Far from influencing us, they were anxious to learn from our experience. We visited the White House and met Henry Kissinger and Patrick Moynihan. There was a memorable visit to Archibald Cox of Harvard Law School, who, later, took leave of absence to accept appointment as the first Watergate special prosecutor.

I was invited to lecture at many universities and even visited think tanks like the Hudson Institute under Herman Kahn soon after he had written *On Thermonuclear War*. I wrote a monograph on China's foreign policy and then extended it. Altogether, I advanced the theory that an unarticulated, unforeseen, overriding community of interests was emerging between nuclear adversaries, and that arms supplies to Vietnam by the USSR was, paradoxically, a method of arms control and of promoting negotiations. All the five chapters are almost of book length. The thesis was heresy as most faculty members were refined Cold Warriors. The thesis should have been published but I was still in the service and this unorthodox definition of non-alignment may not have been approved.

1969–70 was a year of turmoil on the campuses of American universities with protects against the war in Vietnam and the invasion of Kampuchea. Our centre was stormed by radical students; the person in charge of the Fellows Programme, Ben Brown, was injured. While the other Fellows evacuated their rooms, I refused to leave. When the attacking militant students barged in, I told them to take a second look and then they would see that I could not possibly be an agent of the CIA. The acronym for the Center for International Affairs (CIA) was changed to CFIA. I never regretted having chosen academia rather than fly the flag for a year in one of our missions. I have long been convinced that enlightened patriotism does not get contaminated by travel, postings or sabbatical exposures. But I did not realize that I had incurred the suspicion of my new Foreign Secretary.

12

Exhilarating in the Banishment to Tanzania (1970-74)

As High Commissioner to Tanzania, I succeeded somebody who was twenty-three places below me and was followed by another sixty-two places and ten years junior to me in the seniority list. I knew it was intended as a penalty for being too independent-minded and not 'committed' to the then intellectually fashionable approaches. My experience in China was cited as justification, but the hidden sting was patent. I did not even murmur a complaint. In fact, the posting turned out to be the most satisfying of my career.

The fact was, that after Apa Pant's tenure in Nairobi, postings to Africa were either an unwelcome stint in a 'hard station' on the rotational principle, or were given to an officer who was considered unsuitable to hold a heavy charge in the Ministry, or had been rejected as number two in an important country and so was banished to Africa where he could rejoice at being an 'Excellency'.

Though other posts were vacant and my availability had been known for months in advance, I had to mark time for four months until my predecessor attained superannuation. Later, as Additional Secretary when I was put in charge of administration, or as Foreign Secretary, I made a point of elevating the level of most African and immediate neighbourhood postings, sending abler and more promising, direct IFS recruits. Not all of them measured up but I made it a regular condition that, unless an officer had served in a developing country or on the economic side, he should not be brought in as Secretary at headquarters.

At a chance meeting with Mohan Lal Sukhadia, then Chief Minister of Rajasthan, I had suggested that India should have a Peace Corps of its own to help in the progress of other developing countries. The palace in Sajjangarh, the Monsoon Palace, located on the highest hill near Udaipur, was ideally suited to be the National Environment Development Centre.

Soon after I got to Dar es Salaam and presented my credentials, I started preparing for the visit of President Nyerere who was to be the Chief Guest for our Republic Day parade in 1971, then only a few weeks away. Nyerere came after attending the meeting of the Commonwealth Prime Ministers which was held in Singapore. As was customary, I went back to Delhi to be present for the Presidential visit.

Amin takes over, and Obote takes refuge in Tanzania

While the Prime Ministers' Meeting was on, Idi Amin, the Commander of the Ugandan Armed Forces, displaced Milton Obote as Head of the State; Obote and Nyerere had both been freedom fighters in their respective homelands. Obote's initial reaction was that the military takeover would collapse, and his own popularity would ensure that he would soon be able to return to Kampala. This, of course, did not happen and Obote was obliged to stay on in Tanzania. Harbouring Obote enhanced the suspicions against Tanzania. On encouragement Obote's, Tanzania even embarked on a military intervention against Amin's illegal takeover, but it failed, and Obote remained an honoured but helpless guest of Nyerere all through my tenure.

Bangladesh in Dar es Salaam

The other event which, through 1971, got international headlines was, of course, the developments in Pakistan leading to the breakaway of Bangladesh. Sheikh Mujibur Rahman had gained overall support of the Pakistan electorate in the elections of December 1970, and should have been made the PM of the country. West Pakistan had treated its eastern half as a kind of colony, exploiting its resources, appropriating its exports, giving it a stepmotherly treatment in development, and a disproportionately small representation in the Pakistan army and senior establishment. Following the brutalities of the West Pakistan armed forces, there was widespread sympathy in Tanzania for India who had to cope with millions of refugees. The High Commissioner for Pakistan, Dr Ghani, was a distinguished Bengali academic who had been given the assignment to show adequate representation to the constituent parts of Pakistan, but his First Secretary, a career officer from the Punjab, one assumed, had been told to keep a vigilant eye on his 'boss'. Dr Ghani's sons were teaching in Dhaka University, which was the hotbed of Bangladesh's aspirations for independence. While he was officially obliged to represent Pakistan, Dr Ghani's sympathy was with the freedom movement led by Sheikh Mujibur Rahman. Rama and I inwardly sympathized with the problem of Dr and Begum Ghani. They both came to visit us in our residence in the middle of the night, driving their own car when the African servants had gone to their homes or quarters. We came to an understanding that Dr Ghani would denounce India and me personally for subverting Pakistan's sovereignty by interference in its internal affairs and, in turn, I would publicly give as good as I got, pointing to the nemesis of the two-nation theory, the ruthless killings by the Pakistan army, and pleading that the world must recognize the inevitability of Bangladesh as a separate nation for its distinct culture, geographical separation and electorally proven, alienated majority population in the province. It was a clear case of sub-decolonization. This artificial hostility amused the diplomats but seemed to have carried credibility among the local Tanzanians, sufficient to prove that Dr Ghani faithfully represented Pakistan. This belief saved Dr Ghani's sons from being targeted by the West Punjab military forces trapped in Dhaka. Finally in

December 1971 when hostility broke out between the Indian army and the West Pakistan forces, through our discreet intervention, Dr Ghani managed to escape to London and from there was able to fly back to Dhaka. I understand Dr Ghani was made Chief Scientific Advisor in Bangladesh. Years later, I visited one of his sons outside Washington DC. He expressed gratitude to us for having helped his parents when they themselves were in near-fatal danger, and when so many academic colleagues had paid the ultimate price.

Catherine Galbraith has her luggage stolen

Catherine Galbraith came to visit us and we took her to the game parks in northern Tanzania. To visit the Ngorongoro crater, personal vehicles had to be left behind and a four-wheel wagon hired. One could see all the local fauna—lions, zebra, elephants and even flamingoes—in a small area on a lake. When we got back, we found that, while the driver had wandered away, Kitty's elegant bags had been stolen. Not only her clothes but also her passport and travellers' cheques were gone. All the other things were replaced, but Kitty was sorry that her five-year diary of travels with her famous husband was not returned despite my promise of a lucrative reward. We felt really guilty.

Tanzania under Nyerere's leadership

Tanzania, thanks largely to the enlightened leadership of Julius Nyerere, had established a respected position in Africa. From his student days in Edinburgh University, Nyerere had shown a vision and an unambiguous commitment to the liberation of Africa.

The Tanganyika African National Union (TANU) was founded in 1954. Even in its original idealism, it had underlined secularism, racial equality and non-violent struggle for the liberation of the whole continent. Unusually, it was committed to non-tribalism and socialism. Not unlike Nehru, Nyerere was an intellectual and his three books* remain an abiding compilation of his ideas and idealism.

Although Mwalimu (teacher)—the title given to him—Nyerere remained the unchallenged President for nearly twenty-four years, until he voluntarily stood down, he never got intoxicated with power. Till the end, he was respected for his integrity and faith in the dignity of peasants and farmers. He wanted development through village consolidation (Ujaama), broad-based social services and, above all, rapid progress in education. The Arabs had been the old slave-drivers; the 'Whites' had ruled; the 'Browns' had been the instruments of colonialism and had often shown contempt for the 'Blacks'. Nyerere, however, argued that all domiciled residents, whether they were white or brown, were entitled to be considered citizens; he resisted the tendency of the Blacks to avenge centuries of humiliation and discouraged the notion of dual citizenship, but he expected loyalty to the country of residence. Nyerere was truly a statesman and in many ways in the mould of Nehru.

Tanzania, the spoilt child of diverse donors

Tanzania received development aid from all blocs and from diverse sources. Nyerere inspired confidence that the aid would be used purposefully and not for self-gratification. Until World War I, Tanganyika had been a German colony; between the two wars it was a League of Nations Trust territory to be administered by the British, and they created an Anglicized infrastructure, amalgamating it with Kenya and Uganda, and the three had formed the East African community with a common currency and linked services. The Scandinavian countries were particularly impressed by Nyerere's goal of democratic socialism, and the UN had a programme of

---

*Julius Nyerere, *Freedom and Unity/ Uhuru Na Umoja* (Oxford University Press)

Julius Nyerere, *Freedom and Socialism/ Uhuru Na Ujama* (Oxford University Press)

Julius Nyerere, *Freedom and Development/ Uhuru Na Maendeleo* (Oxford University Press)

technical help for Tanzania. In the background was the East–West competition with projects being financed by both sides.

The People's Republic of China sought to make Tanzania a showcase of its own interest in Africa. It made pledges in Zanzibar, but the biggest commitment since 1964, when Zhou Enlai had toured Africa and declared that it was ripe for revolution, was to build the Tanzam railway to enable the export of Zambian copper through Dar es Salaam, avoiding Mozambique on the East and Angola on the West, both of which were still under Portuguese colonial rule. Estimated to cost half a billion dollars, the Tanzam railway project was next in size only to the Soviet commitment to the Aswan Dam on the Nile in Egypt. This was all to demonstrate the Maoist strategy that Asia, Africa and Latin America were the 'villages of the world' which, like the PLA in China, would surround and smother the 'cities' of North America and Europe, including the USSR and Eastern Europe.

Dar es Salaam also became the headquarters of various African Liberation movements to complete the unfulfilled agenda of the continent. The different movements were committed to end apartheid in South Africa, liberate Southern Rhodesia (Zimbabwe), support Samora Machel and FRELIMO against the Portuguese occupation in Mozambique, and help Sam Nujoma to get freedom for South-West Africa, which was under the trusteeship of South Africa. It gave me an opportunity to meet many future presidents and dignitaries of their respective countries who looked to India for inspiration and support.

There were frequent visitors from liberated Africa: Kenneth Kaunda of Zambia, officials from the OAU (Organization of African Unity), from Addis Ababa, including HM Haile Selassie of Ethiopia. Dar es Salaam was never like a backwater of Africa.

India and Tanzania

Diplomacy for India was particularly difficult. We had no comparable aid-giving potential but at one time, 1,10,000 persons of Indian origin were domiciled in the country and under British direction, they had provided the infrastructure for the country—both on the mainland and the island of Zanzibar. Indians had brought monetary economy to the country outside the capital and the port cities. Most Asians had worked hard and saved, and apart from some regular remittance for the families in India (in accordance with middle-class priorities), invested in houses, plantations and real estate. Many had taken local nationality but 'Indians' had already been asked to move into towns. When I arrived, Indians still had some coffee and sisal plantations which were the country's principal export earners. In general, in 1971–74, the non-official economy had remained in the hands of the local Asians but there were apprehensions that the Indians had a limited future in socialist Tanzania. However, this had been their home, in some cases for several generations. They knew Kishwahili but decolonization had left them at the mercy of the Blacks whom they had habitually looked on only as 'hewers of wood and drawers of water'. It posed something of a dilemma for me as I could not but sympathize with my ethnic kinsmen but at the same time, not question directly the right of an independent country to pursue socialism and a policy to rectify historical inequities. Every real estate property more than ten years old was to be nationalized; national service was compulsory and every girl or boy, after leaving school, had to go to a work camp. The socially conservative Asians often decided to leave the country rather than have their girls mix with the local boys in such close proximity.

China's interest made the task for the Indian Envoy even more difficult. The fact that I had been posted in China and had negotiated with them, gave me some special respect. China did not have the legacy of a resident population brought to Africa, often as indentured labour, as the British Empire did. I had the feeling that I was being specially watched.

While there was recognition that India had started the process of decolonization and deserved deference as a consistent crusader for African liberation in the UN and the Trusteeship Council, one could not help feeling that the relationship was one-sided. Africa appreciated India as the defiant leader against colonialism and racial discrimination, but when it came to India's own national interests such as conflict with Pakistan or China, then Africa including Tanzania, was inclined to be hesitant and neutral.

I did not, however, want our relations with Tanzania to be vitiated by the ups and downs of subcontinental problems. Recalling the betrayal of non-alignment and the principles of coexistence by mentioning India's disappointment with China, would not improve our relations locally. My thrust was that India, for all its problems, was transparently an open, multiparty democracy and a sort of development laboratory, which could provide guidance to other developing countries! This was my polite method of underlining that Tanzanians visiting China were showpieces of achievement.

I wanted Tanzania to become an example of India's different pattern of cooperation with Africa. The Economic Division under Sanyal, the Additional Secretary in Delhi, proved a consistent supporter. He managed to pilot through a proposal for a ten-crore loan for Tanzania, the first to Black Africa. We innovated on the technical assistance to the country. Sanyal suggested that the government of India could help by subsidizing select technical personnel who would be deputed to assist in the development of Tanzania. I argued that, paradoxically, Tanzania would respect us more if we did not give any subvention except for incidentals like travel and housing. I suggested that the Tanzanians should first give us a detailed description of their needs, and be ready to depute someone to help the selection committee choose from a shortlist prepared by us, but the final choice should be a shared responsibility. This made it unique in technical cooperation.

The Tanzanian salaries were generally much higher than those in India. The stipulation we made was that the Tanzanian government must allow tax-free repatriation of one-third of the basic salary as savings or for the maintenance of families in India. Compared to the salaries of those, including Indians, recruited by the UN, Canada and other western countries, the net emoluments in our programme were small, so there was some resentment that similarly qualified Indians, possibly from the same professional college, were being paid at least four times more in comparison with those who came on the Indian government procedures. I sought to explain that India was not in favour of demanding extravagant salaries when working in fellow-developing countries. Most were content to be able to remit the equivalent of their basic salaries, and our personnel had to be serious about transfering technology to the local people. Thus, if an automobile engineer was provided for a district, he would be obliged to train his understudies, and this would command greater and more lasting respect in Tanzania. We thus demonstrated realistically South—South cooperation.

My predecessor had preferred to be legally correct, and seldom socialized with Tanzanians of Asian origin. I changed the approach and mixed freely with the Indian community. I contacted residents in upland districts without excluding Muslims or Christians (mostly of Goan origin). In fact, I constituted a Committee of Asians in the district headquarters and met all Asians on my visits. To allay any suspicions, I even took Tanzanian district officials with me. After all, the problems in Tanzania of Hindus, Muslims, Bohras and Ismailis were similar and, except when there were conflicts, Hindus and Muslims (the latter, largely Gujarati-speaking) had good social relations with each other. The message went out that the Indian High Commissioner was interested in the problems of Asians as a whole and did not want to probe into whether, after Partition, any had switched allegiance to Pakistan. The socialization between communities was welcomed by Jamal, an Ismaili, and an old socialist-minded colleague of Nyerere. He was the Finance Minister in my time. In fact, the Tanzanian Minister designated to the East African communities was also of Ismaili origin.

My predecessor, at the annual functions celebrating India's Independence on 15 August and Republic Day on 26 January, only used to notify that Indian nationals were welcome. Apart from the inmates of the High Commission and a few protocol officers, very few of the local Asians came for our National Days. The Asians living in the country were reluctant to be seen as 'Indian nationals'. I changed the wording of the notification to 'Indian nationals and friends of India are welcome.' The result was that there was a congregation of thousands who came because they were prepared to be seen as 'friends of India'.

President Giri's visit

The high point of my time in Tanzania and of the growing cooperation with India was the visit of President and Mrs V.V. Giri in 1972. However, this posed problems which I had never before encountered. They had very orthodox requirements; they wanted new cooking utensils and a kitchen in which meat had never been cooked. We bought new utensils and I managed to find Andhra-origin volunteers among our technical personnel—or rather, their wives—who were thrilled with the idea of cooking for the President!

Nyerere had his office in the State House but he himself lived in a small cottage on the beach. As a rule, no one visited him in his private home, but President Giri insisted that he wanted to call on him in his house as he had heard of his modest style of living. The visit was duly arranged and, to President Giri's surprise, and frankly to my embarrassment, in Nyerere's small study, lying prominently on his table, were two books written by Rama. Earlier, President Nyerere had asked Rama to come and do a sociological study of the women of Tanzania. Rama had promised to come after her husband retired but that was not to be as she passed away in 1978.

Another incident during President Giri's visit worth mentioning was that the Ugandan papers had carried a report of large wooden boxes being unloaded from the special Indian aircraft which the party had brought from Addis Ababa. Idi Amin said that these boxes contained Indian arms which would be supplied to the Tanzanian forces which aimed to dislodge him. In fact these boxes, unloaded openly, only contained presents which had been brought for President Nyerere and other Tanzanian dignitaries. This report only reflected the Tanzania–Uganda relationship, and the deep suspicions of India being sympathetic to anti-Amin forces, particularly after he had decided to expel persons of Indian origin. I was embarrassed when Nyerere was paying a formal return call on our President and Mrs Giri barged in saying, 'I made him. Here is my record of Karnataka music!' Mrs Giri also told Rama, 'I like you as you are, "naat madern", who cut their hair.' (Rama had always kept her hair in a ponytail).

Visit to Nyerere's tribal village

There were some exceptional events which stand out in my memory. I was the only head of mission at that time, who was invited to visit Julius Nyerere in his country home in Butiama. Although his father had been chief of the small Zauaki tribe, his house was comparatively small with a thatched roof, and seemed to be without any ostensible security protection. It was on this confidential visit that I made bold to offer some unorthodox suggestions. While Tanzania was the spoilt child of international donors, in the whirligig of history, the only foreigners who had remained entrenched on the east coast of Africa were Indians. Most of the British had left, but our people faced a problem with the imposition of socialism. I had advised the local Asians to remain domiciled citizens, but in new Tanzania, their economic interests could be adversely affected, specially when China's presence was on the increase. India's strength after decolonization lay in democracy and was an open experiment in development. I repeated to President Nyerere the suggestion made earlier, that they could send a secretly planned delegation, which would be free to visit anywhere it chose, but in particular our military establishments which, I believe, were as good as any in the developed world. While we could not compete with the Chinese in the supply of military hardware such as the supply of a squadron of fighters or motor torpedo boats, in our training centres, the Tanzanians could learn how to repair equipment, take guns apart and reassemble them and become competent to handle it by themselves, rather than wait for experts from the manufacturing country. The select military-cum-civil delegation could travel in civil clothes, stay in military messes, not in hotels, and freely question our officers. They could also see some industrial projects but the emphasis would be on our training establishments and also on learning from the experience of our failed programmes!

This resulted in a military delegation going to India in civil clothes and coming back greatly impressed by the openness and thoroughness of the training programmes of the army, navy and air force. So the officers, after training in China, were sent to India for a more elaborate grounding.

The National Development Corporation of Tanzania asks India to take over a running cement factory

With the growing confidence in India's technological capability and friendship, the National Development Corporation (NDC) wanted to entrust India with a difficult task. The cement factory in Dar es Salaam had been set up by Cementia Trading AG of Switzerland, but the salaries and perks for the twenty-one expatriates resulted in practically no profits. I wrote to the Associated Cement Company. They sent Mr Hathangadi for an initial survey. There was resistance to his being allowed even to see the factory but finally nine Indians took over from the Swiss nationals at approximately one-twentieth of the previous expenditure. It was a rare case of our replacing expatriates and improving efficiency without an interregnum in production, and this further enhanced India's growing reputation.

Visit of the Indian naval squadron: Beating the Retreat in Zanzibar

Being a former navy person, I persuaded the Chief of the Naval Staff to send the Training Squadron consisting of the cruiser *INS*

Delhi and two sloops, *Krishna* and *Cauveri*, and the supply ship *Sita*, to Zanzibar and Dar es Salaam. Such a squadron of warships had never before been seen in these harbours. Without a rehearsal the ship's crew performed Beating the Retreat with buglers sounding the last post from the top of the Chinese-built stadium! This is the only time that a 'Retreat' was staged abroad. There were also friendly matches of football, hockey and volleyball with the local teams. I sailed in the *Delhi* from Zanzibar to Dar es Salaam and, in accordance with naval custom, and as a representative of the President, the national flag fluttered from the top masthead! After giving written authorization, I 'jackstayed', inspecting all the ships while they were underway, even though the sea was choppy—a difficult manoeuve.

The Tanzanian public was greatly impressed seeing the Indian naval ships entering the narrow harbour of Dar es Salaam. All ships were open for visits by the public. The culmination was that the German Ambassador Freiherr Muelleium-Rechberg—one of the survivors of the battleship *Bismarck* who knew that as the *Exeter*, it had chased the German battleship, the *Admiral Graf Spee*, leading to its scuttling in 1939—was so impressed to see that the fifty-year-old built for World War I could still get twenty knots that he sent a political dispatch about this to all German missions.

Chief Guest at the Caledonian Society Dinner

Another unusual event of my stay in Dar es Salaam was to be invited as chief guest by the local Caledonian Society. This must have been at the suggestion of Arthur Kellas, the British High Commissioner. All present had to drink only Scotch whisky with the meal, with Haggis (flown out from Scotland and ushered in with bagpipes and swinging kilts) and also with soup and dessert! In my groggy state, I had to make an after-dinner speech! I was the only head of mission to have been to the tsetse-infested Lake Tanganyika in Ujiji. In my speech I said that after carrying out local research could I confirm that when Stanley finally met Dr

Livingstone, he actually said, 'A Scotsman, I presume'. There was spontaneous applause and I was made an honorary Scot!

It was not all serious study and diplomacy. Rama and I used to visit the Makonde tribals who, sitting under shady trees, used to carve imaginatively on ebony wood without prepared drawings. The carved pieces would correspond to the shape of the branch, and often they would also carve out the 'Tree of Life'. Some were more modern and would carve shapely women with children. At one time, we had the largest collection of Makonde carvings in India, but some of the statues cracked because we did not oil them regularly and they could not survive Rajasthan's dry heat.

Downs and ups in relations with Zanzibar

Up to the mid-twentieth century, Zanzibar was ruled by Arab sheikhs from Muscat. In 1963, the British tried to 'decolonize' it by going through the standardized method of a constitutional conference, but the local Afro-Shirazi Party (ASP) led by Abeid Karume rebelled against this idea of transfer of power, which meant preserving the position of the Sheikh. 12 January 1964 was the 'Night of Long Knives', an uprising led by Karume. The Sheikh and his family had to flee, and many hundreds of foreigners including Indians were killed. Abeid Karume 'declared' himself the President of Zanzibar. After only a few months, the Union of Tanzania was formed with Nyerere as President, and Karume as the first Vice-President of the united country. Karume was uncouth, with little education and no refinement. He was assassinated in 1972, but before that, he had invited African heads of mission for the tenth year of his revolution, and wanted a five-star hotel for their stay. Being dictatorial, he had drawn up his own architectural plans and asked the British and the Dutch to complete the hotel in time. They refused and finally he turned to India. I personally wrote letters to Indian hoteliers including Oberoi, who responded positively and deputed Dilip Mathai. In a remarkable achievement, the hotel was completed, including construction of the dining and drawing rooms. Expense was no consideration, and India's stock shot up with a first-class hotel in place.

China and Tanzania

The Chinese commitment to build the Tanzam railway had ulterior motives. It made Tanzania a non-official trade promotion agency for China. All local costs had to be defrayed against the aid in Chinese imports. Tanzam was built in record time, importing 1,00,000 or more Chinese soldiers in civil clothes, but unlike in the cooperation with India there was no transfer of technology. The gauge corresponded not to the existing East African railway but to that of China. Each Chinese worker was allowed to take back a camera or a watch which Tanzania had to import with its own scarce, convertible foreign exchange.

The Chinese project was announced as helping Africa's liberation struggle but it was a comment on the presumed failure of decolonization. In fact, the Portuguese empire collapsed in 1974, and the exports of Zambian copper are again going through Mozambique in the East and Angola in the West. I suppose the Chinese-built railway is helping in the opening up of the southern hinterland but in the meanwhile China has 'liberalized' its own economy, and Africa is no longer considered 'ripe' for a communist revolution.

Incidentally from Dar es Salaam, I sent the longest-ever dispatch (thirty-six pages in single space) on China and Africa with an executive summary. Though I received felicitations from some missions, I have received no acknowledgement or comments on the dispatch to this day.

It was, of course, a method only of educating myself.

Supersession and the notice of transfer

While Tanzania was being held up as an example of diplomatic success, I had received notice in 1972 that I was to be superseded by somebody nine places junior to me in the seniority list. None of the other eight affected—there were several capable ones—protested against this arbitrary decision. I decided to make a representation to the Minister, S. Swaran Singh. I had been given exceptional responsibilities throughout my career (perhaps only because I was the nearest idiot reachable), but at various stages commended by the PM, and so this deliberate slap did not exactly please me. I got hints that I had earned the displeasure of the head of the service for non-sycophancy! The person who was responsible for this malevolent decision had himself retired in 1972. The new Foreign Secretary, Kewal Singh, wrote to me soon after he took over that, though I had done only one posting after my last stint in Delhi, he personally wanted me to come back as Additional Secretary. Since I had not received a reply to my representation, I made it clear that I would not accept coming back with this stigma of humiliation, but he assured me that it was a mistake which would soon be put right.

As I had already done three and a half years in Dar es Salaam, in April 1974, I had to move anyway. We packed our bags and went back to the Ministry, taking with us a used British Ford station wagon, and not the usual Mercedes without payment of customs duty, which was then allowed at least once in the career of returning heads of mission. Despite their partial scholarships, our children's education was costing us a pretty penny.

I was gratified that, a year after I had left, President Nyerere, in a speech which he delivered in Georgetown (Guyana), mentioned that I was the best envoy he had ever come across. This was morale-boosting from someone whom I had greatly respected. Nyerere, like Nehru, was a glorious economic failure but his integrity made him an icon for me. With this commendation, I should have retired, but I did not. Ups and final downs still lay ahead.

13

Back to Delhi under Subterfuge: Additional Secretary Administration (1974–76)

When I arrived at the Ministry, I was greeted by Ishi Rahman, the other Additional Secretary. He spontaneously said, 'I hope you are prepared to stay six years.' I was baffled by the statement, but he explained that I was destined for the post of Foreign Secretary and so was unlikely to get another foreign assignment!

Ishi's remarks were, of course, welcome as they implied that my colleagues, without envy, considered me suitable for the last step of the professional ladder. I used to remark frivolously that having only five foreign postings meant I was regularly rejected under 'export quality control'. In truth, I am the only one in the Foreign Service to have served in every rank at headquarters from Attaché upwards, but the benefit bonus was being entrusted more often with the negotiating of burdens and overcoming of stalemates. However, I myself was not so certain about my future. My representation was two years old, but it had not elicited even an acknowledgement and, with such obvious prejudice, there could be many stumbling blocks in the climb up the ladder!

I took over responsibility as Additional Secretary (Administration) from Avtar Singh, a senior colleague from my batch who (like Field Marshal Sam Manekshaw) had won an MC in Burma and that too, in an artillery unit. Like me, he had taken the risk of not accepting a permanent commission in the hope of getting into one of the civilian services. There was, however, a curious bracketing in my assignment. In addition to supervising the administration divisions, I was to direct the Policy Planning Division.

Pokhran

On 18 May 1974, just two weeks after I took over, we heard that India had made a Peaceful Nuclear Explosion (PNE) in the Pokhran desert. The Foreign Secretary and other secretaries, in separate relays, were meeting with accredited ambassadors, providing clarification that India had in no way violated its own commitment on nuclear disarmament. Later, Prof. P.N. Dhar, the Principal Secretary, walked into my office and informally inquired how we should defuse the inevitable critical world opinion. I suggested that if, in fact, there was no leakage of radioactivity, we should straightaway invite the members of the United Nations Disarmament Commission to visit the site and see for themselves that India was scrupulously adhering to the letter and spirit of the Nuclear Non-Proliferation Treaty (NPT). From what I had read, there was no real difference between a peaceful nuclear explosion and a bomb. Mr Dhar listened quietly to me; anyway, my suggestion of inviting the committee on disarmament from Geneva was not followed up.

Frankly, I held on to my minority view to ensure that the Nuclear Five took steps in good faith towards disarmament as pledged in article VI. But Additional Secretaries were out of the loop when it came to diplomatic firefighting or higher policy making.

Annexation of Sikkim

One morning, I innocently asked why it was necessary for us to mount a campaign against Sikkim and its Chogyal. The Chogyal had married Hope Cooke who came from an American East Coast patrician family, but even if she actually had the backing of the CIA, it was hard to believe that the Sikkim royal family could really undermine the integrity and viability of India. The lineal frontier was actually defined in the India–China treaty of 1890, even before the McMahon tripartite negotiations in Simla (1914). The Teesta starts by flowing southwards; in other words, it provides the watershed which has broad validity everywhere.

The Chogyal had been trying to establish Sikkim's pseudo-international personality but the dependence on India even for internal security had continued. We had started stoking the demands of an increasing number of Nepalese-origin persons who had changed the demography of the principality and who were in favour of amalgamation with India.

There is a long chapter titled 'The Merger in Sikkim' on the events of 1973–75 in P.N. Dhar's book.* The PMO, RAW, the FS and the Political Officer based in Gangtok succumbed to the idea of integration of Sikkim, with no regard to its wider implications. In 1975, Sikkim became a state of the Indian Union. For me, it vastly resembled Hitler's policy of first using the Sudeten Germans by stimulating their demand, and then annexing the whole of Czechoslovakia in 1938.

Administrative responsibilities

My main effort was to bring greater transparency in the day-to-day functioning of the Ministry's administration. The higher appointments of heads of mission were handled by the Foreign Secretary, sometimes in consultation with the Foreign Minister and, in politically sensitive postings, with the PM. At my level, one wanted to be scrupulous about observing the rotational system in appointments and transfers. In the case of postings for the selection grades, I consulted the Foreign Secretary. One had to

*P.N. Dhar, *Indira Gandhi, the Emergency and the Indian Democracy* (Oxford: 2000).

resist pre-conceived favouritism, but I did not invariably have success. I could boast that I had no relations in the service. I became known as being administratively fair-minded. I recently came across a book by someone from the information side who got a permanent mission appointment in New York. Apparently, I had insisted that he should leave for Tehran immediately, considering his earlier postings had been in Tokyo and Ottawa. He got out of it and arranged an assignment with the UNESCO. I have no regrets that my firmness had failed.

The Finance Ministry had a fixed notion that we in the diplomatic network had easy access to foreign education for our children at the expense of the taxpayers, enjoyed luxuries and immunities and so, our requests for greater allowances on the basis of comparison were to be taken with a pinch of salt. My own dealings with finances were relatively smooth as I seemed to have got a reputation for not being needlessly extravagant. I remember the Financial Advisor asking for my comments on a request sent at a lower level by my successor in Dar es Salaam who wanted more air conditioners so that the living room and the other rooms could also be artificially cooled. He said that the present Additional Secretary, just back from Dar es Salaam, had managed with just one AC in his bedroom for nearly four years. I was somewhat embarrassed and made an excuse that, being from Rajasthan, I was perhaps a little more accustomed to heat and could make do with less air conditioning, but considering the normal practice in other missions and the place being situated near the equator, the new head deserved better! The proposal eventually went through.

Visits to the LBS Academy in Mussourie

Unlike some senior colleagues, I always made it a point to respond to requests from the head of the Lal Bahadur Shastri Academy in Mussourie to address the foundation course. After speaking to the new probationers of all services about foreign policy, its difficulties and opportunities, I spent one long evening talking individually to those who had been selected for the Foreign Service. It was in such individual conversations that one could develop tentative ideas on language allocations and first postings.

A great deal more could be done to boost the morale of those in the Foreign Service and make them realize that there is scope for more recognition and achievement in the service than is commonly supposed. It is unpardonable that IAS officers, however able, should be sent as ambassadors to important posts by classifying them as political. (No Foreign Service officer has been made Chief Secretary of a state.) Diplomacy demands professionalism and there should be stricter uniformity in age limits for superannuation. This practice was less frequent in Panditji's time, but it has gravely damaged the morale and work ethics of 600 officers in the service; indeed it promotes cynicism and sycophancy. Except General Raina—a very special post-Emergency case—I do not recall recommending an officer from another service for a diplomatic appointment. They can be made governors or members of the Rajya Sabha if they have shown exceptional merit but not rewarded at the expense of Foreign Service career officers.

For example, whoever topped the Foreign Service selection list, could be attached to the office as an assistant for a few months. But Kewal Singh did not particularly relish the idea of a cadet prowling around top-secret telegrams. Ramu Damodaran topped the list in 1974, and Amitabh Banerjee, the son of a distinguished Defence Secretary, in 1975. Since the Foreign Secretary was reluctant, I took them into my own office. Both these young men subsequently had exceptional careers, including in the private offices of different foreign ministers. I suppose the disproportionate difference in salaries makes it difficult to resist the opportunities offered elsewhere, but I did tell them both that bilateral diplomacy could give much greater satisfaction. They certainly would have served the country with distinction.

AS (Administration) was supervisory head of the Foreign Service Inspectorate. We had a problem with the galloping inflation in South America. By an old tradition, our emoluments were paid in local currency at the prevailing rate of exchange for the rupee. We normally revised our foreign and representational allowances if there were a proven increase of ten per cent of the price index. In those wild inflationary economies, there would sometimes be a ten per cent increase almost between the dispatch of a letter through the post (with all the elaborate accompanying statistics) and its arrival a few days later in Delhi. Our small missions were justified in complaining that months lapsed before final orders were posted and when they came they were always out of date. I persuaded Vaidyanathan, the Additional Secretary in the Finance Ministry, to join an inspection tour and come to Santiago (Chile), Lima (Peru), Jamaica and Trinidad, which had so far not been 'inspected' but were apparently suffering great hardships. Kiran Doshi, a Deputy Secretary, and A.N. Rao, our financial wizard, also a Deputy Secretary, came with us to scrutinize the accounts. We reached an on-the spot commonsense decision, which ended this long harassment. We decided that the emoluments to be disbursed should be in dollars and not in the local currency so that the benefit would automatically absorb the inflation.

On our way back from South America and the Caribbean, we stopped for brief discussions on urgent administrative problems in Washington and New York. (These establishments were huge and we had a resident audit staff.) I cannot, however, forget the remark of the Deputy Chief of the Mission in Washington that 'These Americans are so obsessed by the fear of communism that, at any time, when we want aid, all we have to do is to make noises that we are about to turn to the Soviet Union again.' This was in 1974 and one more example of how our missions took the Cold War at its face value.

Some months later, we did another inspection lasting two weeks and visited Prague, Copenhagen and Oslo, which too, had not been inspected earlier. Ajit Majumdar represented the Finance Ministry. These were all beautiful cities. We sorted out some of their financial anomalies, raised some allowances, etc. I might add that I was not wholly impressed by the performance of the heads of some of these out-of-the-way missions.

Along with the Financial Advisor and a team of supporting officers from the Establishment Division, I also made a visit to settle one of the hardest problems that MEA had faced in decades—reducing the size of the High Commission in London and severing the automatic linkage with the Whitehall Establishment Code. By a mix of offering voluntary retirement and increasing the number of India-based personnel, I finally severed the linkage with Whitehall and in the process, halved the then strength of our High Commission.

On the sidelines of the Emergency

In June 1975, in Teen Murti Lane, we heard a crowd demonstrating in support of Mrs Gandhi. This was the first indication to us of the suspension of the Constitution and the proclamation of the Emergency. It did not affect my official duties, but by hearsay we came to learn of the arrest of Jaiprakash Narain and the other Opposition leaders, the brutalities, and the forcible of vasectomies.

Mrs Gandhi had seen me since my Allahabad University days. I knew Nanna Madan, a relation of Mrs Gandhi, and had even been invited to her wedding reception in 1942. She had seen Rama and me before she had become PM, and I had been asked to join the PM's party on various trips abroad, but I was never a close confidant.

Yunus Khan had also long been a family friend who dropped in from time to time. One day during the Emergency, he came and said that Mrs Gandhi had been given a longish list of possible authors of her biography and she had approved Rama's name. Yunus asked her if she would be willing to undertake such a biography. While Rama did not say 'no' she said she would like to have the opportunity of some exclusive interviews but, in any case, she must not be restricted in what she wrote. She heard nothing more after that.

My own conscience told me that we could not jettison old friendships even during the Emergency. I knew Kuldip Nayar and since I was aware that he had been taken into custody, we visited Bharati to share her anxiety and to inquire, even with our obvious limitations, whether there was anything we could do for her. We also knew Shri Mulgaonkar from our overlap in London. After his return, he had become editor of the *Hindustan Times* and later, of the *Indian Express*.

A more interesting problem arose when, one day, Mrs Subramanian Swamy telephoned Rama expressing distress at the way she was being harassed with inquiries about her husband's whereabouts. Subramanian Swamy was a member of the Rajya Sabha who had made a dramatic escape and was supposed to be in the US. Rama barely knew Mrs Swamy, said she was sorry but unable to help, but Mrs Swamy was welcome to our house. Knowing that Rama was married to a serving officer, she was surprised at this spontaneous gesture of friendliness. She came and at least unburdened herself of her woes.

While the Emergency was still on, and indeed, was leading to coercion, tensions and callousness in bulldozing and displacing people settled in the inner city of Delhi, I was continuing with my heavy but pedestrian non-political administrative responsibilities.

Portuguese-speaking professionals for decolonized Mozambique

When the Portuguese colonial empire collapsed, in 1974–75 it occurred to me that, apart from Macao and Brazil, only Goa and Mumbai had Portuguese speakers familiar with the laws, and the professional and administrative patterns of their metropolitan country. They could act as replacements for the departing Portuguese experts. I drew a classified list of such experts—doctors, engineers etc.—took it to Maputo (Mozambique), and suggested cooperation along the lines we had successfully had in Tanzania. At the time the independent government was enamoured of the Soviet model, and East Germany was prepared to underwrite help with aid. Even though I met Samora Machel, the President, and Joaquim Chissano, the Foreign Minister, our offer was turned down.

Told to go to Amin's parlour: Negotiating compensation for Indians

In 1975, Mrs Gandhi received a letter from President Idi Amin that he wanted a delegation led by the Foreign or the Finance Minister to come to negotiate cash compensation for the Indians who had left in 1972. The delegation, Amin mentioned, should be accompanied by journalists and a TV crew and that they would all be his guests.

Both the Cabinet Ministers declined and so did their deputies. The Foreign Secretary and the Economic Secretary did not want to go so I was ordered to proceed and fulfil the assignment. I pointed out that having been High Commissioner in Tanzania, I should be the last person to be sent for such negotiations as it was bound to aggravate Amin. But these reasons fell on deaf ears as no one else could be persuaded to go. I had to innovate furiously—described in *Negotiating for India*—including flattering the President and finally, 1.6 million dollars, about fifty times the Ugandan estimates was agreed upon, and individually allocated.

No instructions were given before I left and no guidance offered during the mission. The worst moment was when I reported that Idi Amin was going to give me this dollar cheque the next afternoon, and, on the Foreign Minister's instructions, and the Foreign Secretary rang back and told me that since we did not have individual powers of attorney, I should desist from accepting the cheque. This horrified me. It was a touch-and-go situation, involving refusing the President in front of TV cameras; I feared I might be the supper for the huge Nile crocodiles. I came back and talked to the various groups; they were gratified and indeed, surprised by the negotiated amount. I succeeded in persuading the Minister of State, Mr Kundu, to go and receive the cheque in Kampala.

De facto Assistant Foreign Secretary

The Foreign Secretary obviously had some special trust in me. Any difficult or heavy chore, he would assign to me. During the Parliamentary sessions, for example, it became a frequent practice that around 6 p.m., Kewal Singh would ring me up and say he had other heavy work or special engagements in the evening and would I handle the Parliamentary questions, which had come to his table. It was not easy to scrutinize replies, which had already been endorsed by the concerned senior officers, some by other Secretaries. Many were starred questions, and therefore I had to go through the notes for supplementaries. I would be stuck in the office till nine or even ten scrutinizing the proposed drafts.

Being treated as Assistant Foreign Secretary was no doubt flattering. There was however, ground for suspicion that he was delaying action on my representation which had been pending for three years. The restoration of my place in the seniority list had been a pre-condition to my coming to Delhi. Whether there was some hidden prejudice or partiality behind this sustained subterfuge I did not know.

Secret resistance to my promotion

I had come to suspect that I was being deliberately kept in the dark. I had a vague guess that Kewal Singh, after prior consultation or perhaps with deliberate purpose, wanted Ram Sathe to succeed him. He and Foreign Minister Y.B. Chavan had agreed that I should go as High Commissioner to Ottawa, but he wanted me to be around while he was in office. Ram Sathe had been a friend of mine and, although in the War Service selection he had not come through and was chosen in the overage selection, he was undoubtedly an able officer. His wife Shaila came to see Rama in our house and told her what a nice place Ottawa was, which confirmed my apprehension. Apparently, the secret intention was told to Ram, who had shared it with his wife. The recommendation that Sathe should be the next Foreign Secretary had already been endorsed by Y.B. Chavan, the Foreign Minister, but I was kept in the dark.

One Sunday afternoon, P.N. Dhar informally said to me that he wanted to discuss general foreign policy problems. We spent two hours walking up and down on the lawn of his house, ruminating on international affairs. I did not know that he was probing my attitude following the instructions of the Prime Minister. Subsequent to this talk, unknown to me at the time, he took the file back to Chavan and indicated that Mrs Gandhi was inclined to approve my appointment, and it would not look good on paper if she were to overrule his recommendation. The earlier recommendation was passed over.

In early February 1976, it was announced that Jagat S. Mehta would be the next Foreign Secretary. Kewal Singh's extension expired on 1 April. I was promoted from grade two to one and became Secretary for less than two months. Bimal Sanyal was senior to me, but was due to retire in a few months and raised no objection to my jumping over him. As it happened, my appointment was widely welcomed. Khushwant Singh, in his 'Malice Towards One and All' column headlined 'The right man in the right job', even published a photograph of the family. I took over as Foreign Secretary on the prescribed date—April Fools' Day 1976!

14

Catapulted to Foreign
Secretary; the Emergency;
Unprecedented Fruitful
Negotiations
(1976–77)

Walking into the big room

When Lutyens made the overall plan for New Delhi, he concentrated on the Viceregal Lodge. It was Baker who designed the South and the North Blocks of the Secretariat. I suspect there was some perverse logic in keeping the External and the Political Departments closest to the Viceroy's house, discreetly hidden until one approached the iron gates facing the Jaipur Pillar and Star. On the other hand, the office of the Commander-in-Chief of the Indian Army, just beyond the crest of the hill, was visible from far. Next to the Viceroy, the C-in-C was the symbol of imperial authority. His office had a slanting staff with a red flag with a crossed sword and baton, often with a wreath around it to signify the rank of a Field Marshal. Since 1970, this room has been the office of the Foreign Secretary. When the PMO expanded in the eighties, MEA was squeezed eastwards and the Foreign Secretary got the spacious room earlier occupied by the army chief. T.N. Kaul must have been the first occupant of the present room.

I was never one to demand refurbishing of an office which I

inherited. The elegance of an office makes only a marginal difference to actual diplomatic achievement. A board on the wall of the anteroom listed the holders of the post of Secretary General and scores of previous post-Independence Foreign Secretaries. (The Great Game in Central Asia had, of course, been directed by British Foreign Secretaries from Calcutta, but the field officers had not only bravery to recommend them but also latitude for improvisations).

In 1976, the Foreign Secretary was the only secretary who had a staff officer to assist him. Kewal Singh's alter ego, the DS/FSO, was K.V. Rajan, an extremely able officer, but he was soon to leave for Washington. For a while, he was succeeded by Shyam Saran, a young officer, who had impressed me by his analysis on China but alas! He was due for a posting. My own choice was G. Parthasarthy, who had worked with me in Dar es Salaam. We had great affection for him and his wife Shanti, but after his posting to Pakistan, he seemed to have abandoned faith in diplomacy as an instrument for long perspectives and problem-solving. The Foreign Secretary and the staff around him were handpicked and knowing that their long hours and exertions were likely to earn them a coveted post abroad, almost the first thing I did was to tell my PS to get people into the office who came from hard (category 'C') postings so that when, eventually, they got the posting which they wanted, no one would complain that this was an out-of-turn reward for working with the Foreign Secretary!

I had no illusions about the Foreign Secretary's lot being a happy one. However, my colleagues formed an able team; apart from Bimal Sanyal and Vishnu Ahuja as Secretaries, there were K.L. Dalal, K.R. Narayanan and Jagdish Ajmani as Additional Secretaries. Two months later, Narayanan was assigned to upgrade our mission in Peking to the ambassadorial level.

My guide, of course, had to be Kewal Singh, who belonged to the ICS cadre of undivided Punjab and was eight years my senior. Apart from small administrative matters, the only advice he gave me was not to dispute suggestions given by the Defence Ministry and RAW when it came to security matters. I did not dare disagree with him but this really went against the grain when I was on the threshold of a new appointment. As it happened, my first assignment as Foreign Secretary vindicated that national interest can be truly advanced by forward-looking diplomacy.

Beginning normalization and catalyzing an improved climate of relations with Pakistan

On 27 March 1976, four days before I was to take over, Z.A. Bhutto, the Prime Minister of Pakistan, wrote a letter to our PM that he proposed to withdraw the complaint filed in 1971 with the International Civil Aviation Organization. (An IAC Fokker on a scheduled fight from Delhi to Jaipur was hijacked by pro-Kashmiris and, though the passengers were released, the plane was destroyed on the Lahore tarmac. Bhutto himself had led a triumphant procession through the city.) We had suspended the over flights between East and West Pakistan. This delayed the flow of reinforcements during the Bangladesh struggle which followed a few months later. During the Bangladesh crisis, diplomatic relations too, were severed and so they remained for five years and were not restored even under the Simla Agreement (1972). Bhutto's letter was thus a unilateral acceptance that Pakistan no longer wanted to continue to bear the heavy cost of the diversion of PIA flights either via Sri Lanka or over Tibet to reach China, Japan etc.

Armed with cabinet authorization and accompanied by a large delegation with representatives of civil aviation, transport, home, railways, customs, commerce, etc., in the middle of May, we set forth in a special air force plane for Islamabad. These negotiations had attracted wide international attention and quite a few journalists and correspondents—foreign, Indian and, of course, Pakistani—had congregated for our arrival. We were met by Pakistan's Foreign Secretary Agha Shahi and other Pakistani officials but the press were impatient to sense our intentions. The bland statement of 'hoping to resolve existing problems' did not satisfy them so I added that I also looked forward to saluting my old Commanding Officer of Navy days, Hamidullah Burki. Burki was a first class navigator; with him commanding and me assisting, we had been entrusted to take the LCAs and the LCMs, assembled for the invasion of Malaya, and to scuttle them in the Bay of Bengal as transporting them elsewhere would have been too expensive. My statement distracted the assembled journalists from their serious questions and I had lent a human touch to their reporting.

Some journalists must have telephoned Burki and he rang me up in the hotel. After using the familiar obscene naval language, he seemed touched at my remembering him from 1945. It provided me with an opportunity to convey that I was utterly sincere in making the negotiations optimally successful. He was known to be close to Bhutto and must have conveyed this to the Pakistan PM, a far less formal interlocutor than Agha Shahi.

My anticipation of the Pakistan position turned out to be more accurate than that of the Pakistanis. Bhutto, even in his climbing down, wanted to have something to show for five years of needless confrontation. I wanted a new beginning with no reference to the past, not even complaints and counter-complaints. The Pakistan PM tried to get me to persuade the Indian PM by telephone to incorporate a clause that the compensation question would be discussed when diplomatic relations were restored but, I myself was opposed to his suggestion. However, I could not very well refuse the Pakistani PM's request to try. I got through to P.N. Dhar, the Principal Secretary, and managed to be even less coherent than usual! I elicited a reply that I had better return to Delhi and explain the matter. I interpreted it as non-approval—exactly what I had wanted. I was also right in guessing that Agha Shahi and others would listen in to my conversation. Since Pakistan was more or less desperate to resume direct overflights, they dropped their insistence on the subject of compensation. We had delayed the departure of the Indian air force plane by seven hours, but we concluded signing the MOU and held a joint press conference for the weary journalists, announcing a comprehensive agreement.

Two important points in the negotiations deserve a mention. I knew that though they did not want a long discussion on the future of Kashmir, Agha Shahi could not face the Pakistan press with no mention of it. It was raised by him at the last minute and was promptly dismissed by me as outside our agenda. The mention of Kashmir barely lasted half a minute. Agha Shahi could claim that the Kashmir question had been raised and I could affirm that it had not been discussed!

What totally surprised Agha Shahi and also most of our own delegation, was when I suggested that the proposed comprehensive normalization of diplomatic relations, civil aviation, road and rail communication, and state trading in specified items—some requiring detailed technical preparations and agreements—should all be completed within two months and, in a synchronized manner the two High Commissioners would present credentials precisely at the same moment to the respective Presidents. The members of our delegation were visibly taken aback at this peremptory time limit. None of them had orders regarding a time limit. As we had no mission in Islamabad, the Pakistanis could either refuse or accept my deadline; my proposed innovation put them in a spot. While one must not try to score points against a foreign adversary, there is virtue in being forward-looking although it might involve taking risks.

Accused of exceeding the brief

Before I left New Delhi, the Chairman of the Policy Planning Committee, G. Parthasarthy, and Prof. P.N. Dhar had told me that I should negotiate constructively, and then get Bhutto to sign the MOU with Mrs Gandhi in India. On reflection, I had become convinced that this would be unwise and only likely to create delay and friction, and reinforce suspicions. On my return, I was told politely but unmistakably, that in signing the MOU in Islamabad, I had 'exceeded' my brief. It was not part of the cabinet decision but would have made it look like an Indian triumph, and implied a riposte to Bhutto for reneging on his Simla promise. It reflected the old attitude of scoring points rather than creating a constructive climate for the future. These complaints were completely dissipated when congratulatory messages from all over the world started pouring in. It was led by TASS, the official news agency, on behalf of the Soviet leadership. Once again I felt I understood the USSR better than some of our dedicated ideological votaries. At crucial moments, the Soviet Union had been helpful to India by exercising its veto but basically, the USSR's preference was for India–Pakistan normalization. Many officers in the Ministry and in our Embassy in Moscow understandably wanted to believe that the USSR must be hostile to our neighbour because the latter was allied with Washington, but it was not so. I was not surprised at the outcome of Tashkent.

Mrs Gandhi herself never raised the question which my critics had; in fact, she thanked and praised me, and I felt this reinforced her confidence in me for the rest of my overlapping tenure. She never discouraged me from giving honest advice in the period 1976–77.

Implementing the normalization agreement

The unexpected success of the normalization proceedings with Pakistan led to a transformation of the atmosphere between our countries. While in defence we remained vigilant, India's real opportunity and challenge lay in constructive diplomacy. Assembling personnel and equipment for a major mission with diverse representatives required immense effort. I selected Kiran Doshi, a Deputy Secretary/Director at headquarters as Deputy High Commissioner-designate, assured him full support in finding personnel including people from other ministries, assembling the equipment and manuals, etc. It all had to be done with a sense of urgency. Meanwhile, technical details had to be worked out on civil aviation, rebuilding or strength the enough of road bridges, relaying of rail tracks and rail schedules, all within the time limit. The major hurdle for me was to find a suitable High Commissioner in order not to default on the deadline suggested by me.

Immediately after the Pakistan visit, I had to go to London for official level consultations. I asked K. Shankar Bajpai, who was our Ambassador in The Hague, but nowhere near the end of his tenure, to meet me at Frankfurt airport where I persuaded him to seize this chance to reopen the mission in Pakistan. The official talks in London with Sir Michael Palliser, the Permanent Under Secretary (PUS) in the Foreign Office, were friendly but not worth recalling. On the last day, the PUS, following a brief by the Board of Trade or the Defence Ministry, I suppose, made a pitch for the sale of squadrons of Jaguar aircraft to India. The aircraft industry of the UK was tottering and this contract could have helped rescue it. I had no instructions on the subject. In any case, it went against my own grain to divert resources to military hardware, thereby providing Pakistan with an excuse to look for matching capability. I remember leaning back and saying to Sir Michael (who subsequently became a good friend) that I was glad that the British government thought that India should be better armed against Pakistan. He got the hint and the conversation ended.

Let me mention some developments, which followed my return from Islamabad. Afghanistan, under Daud Khan, was showing greater non-aligned flexibility. Daud was the brother-in-law of King Zahir Shah, who had been obliged to abdicate in 1973, but the tribal feudalism had continued. Internally, Afghanistan was by no means stable, but there were signs of improvement of relations with the Shah of Iran and Bhutto's Pakistan. I accompanied Mrs Gandhi when she visited Kabul in July with a large delegation, including Mir Qasim from Kashmir. Incidentally, when she went to Ajmer (by plane to Jaipur and from there by helicopter) for the centenary celebrations of Mayo College (where my sons had studied) at my request, she took me along. I also accompanied her when she went on a short trip to Mauritius and Zambia. I remember she asked me to sit next to Bansi Lal, the Defence Minister, as this was his first visit abroad and to tell him a 'little' about foreign policy!

There were other instances where reasoned analysis was considered objectively, and Mrs Gandhi showed constructive statesmanship and gave latitude to me as her Foreign Secretary.

The dividends of comprehensive normalization—successful handling of another hijacking in August '76

The hijacking incident which took place in August 1976 was in sharp contrast to both the destruction of the *Ganga* aircraft in January 1971 and the Kandahar incident in 2000, in which Foreign Minister Jaswant Singh himself handed over proven terrorists in exchange for the release of our passengers. Mrs Gandhi personally telephoned me within fifteen minutes of the hijack. The Cabinet Secretary and the crisis control group assembled at Safdarjang airport in half an hour, from where we could keep in touch with the pilot. Handling hijacking requires instant decisions and not a lackadaisical attitude as was displayed in the 2000 incident during the two-hour flight from Kathmandu to Amritsar, when the aircraft had been allowed to take off after refuelling in Amritsar, and then to fly to Lahore and Dubai before the final, shameful deal in Kandahar. On my advice the aircraft was told to land in Lahore and stay there rather than go to the Gulf or Libya.

It was quick action on the part of the Pakistan Additional Foreign Secretary Shah Nawaz who drove down from Islamabad following my urgent telephone call to Agha Shahi and who promptly established liaison with the Lahore authorities—which helped rescue the passengers unharmed, and the aircraft to be returned undamaged.

The critical situation for us in Delhi was to understand the dilemma in Pakistan of not wanting to betray its sympathizers and at the same time, not cause a major incident with India. Shah Nawaz understood the implication when I told him on telephone that the hijackers should be 'seen' to be taken into custody when they left the aircraft. I was certain that asking for the repatriation of Pakistani hijackers for trial in India would only invite a rebuff.

But seeing them arrested was likely to satisfy Indian public opinion. When the hijackers were released a few months later, it really caused me no surprise or offence.

Successful diplomacy was a by-product of the normalization of relations with Pakistan and the Indian PM's trust in her officials. We were right in judging that the Pakistan government was not behind the pro-Pakistan hijackers. It was proof that professionalism, which commands the confidence of decision-makers, served our interests better than succumbing to the old knee-jerk hostility—as we again did in December 2000 following the terrorist attack on Parliament. Retaliation must be calibrated and flow from good contemporaneous judgement.

Salal

Even after eight years, with almost a score of discussions between the Indus Commissioners and two meetings between the Foreign Secretaries, we had not been able to overcome the stalemate on Salal, a hydel project with a potential of 700MV of power on the Chenab which, under the Indus Treaty, was assigned to Pakistan. Exacerbated that the recommendations of the Central Water and Power Commission (CWPC) had not been followed, the Prime Minister had approved the utilization of the procedure envisaged in the treaty for arbitration. The entire process could take years.

I was taken aback that despite our bitter experience over Kashmir, we had again consigned a bilateral problem to internationalization. I expressed my honest concern to the PM. I suggested, 'Let me try further bilateral talks.' I was aware that I was running a risk in recommending a reversal. The PM, who had approved going for arbitration, straightaway agreed to my recommendation. It is another illustration of how we civil servants, sometimes on the basis of 'technical advice', surrender the constructive role of diplomacy.

I wrote to Agha Shahi for a further round of talks. I got no reply from Pakistan for several weeks but I kept telling him that this hesitation could have a setback effect. We saw no harm to Pakistan, but, in keeping with the treaty, it could provide substantial economic benefits to India. Finally, Pakistan could no longer refuse to talk. We had two sessions in October 1976, first in New Delhi and then in Islamabad. (After I retired, I learnt from Mubashar Hassan, who was Finance Minister in Bhutto's cabinet, that the majority in the cabinet were opposed to a resolution on Salal.)

The fact was our previous negotiated stance had been badly conceived; we actually needed power for our Green Revolution. My colleagues made fresh calculations along guidelines given by me to prove that Pakistan's reservations on the grounds that the Indian plan was for a military contingency and that the economic purpose was only a cover-up, were simply not tenable. However, the entire Pakistani press was convinced that our purpose was to prepare for possible operations. When I called Mr Bhutto, I told him not only that we had no malevolent intentions but also that our data showed that it would be suicidal for India to do what was feared. Bhutto told me to postpone my return.

The Pakistani chief engineers (civil and military) were all called by Bhutto to scrutinize our calculations and they found them credible. What prevailed was the indisputable fact that if we were to empty the Chenab and use it for an attack on Sialkot (or to drown the onrushing Pak tanks in the Kashmir Valley) rather than as a run-of-the river project, with no storage beyond three days, we would be doing disproportionate harm to ourselves as the turbines would stop. There would be greater damage to power availability in India than any we could inflict on Pakistan. Salal is a case of how nations get gridlocked in hostility by perverse fears.

Our own technical experts despite many meetings had failed to assuage Pakistan's unjustified fears. It was a miserable failure of diplomacy. It was not difficult to guess that Bhutto did not want to go into the proposed domestic elections risking a charge of having made a concession to India. He could not articulate this, so privately I volunteered the assurance that I would use the prevailing Emergency not to publicize the climb down. It was thus that the agreement was initialled in October 1976 instead of being deferred further or consigned to arbitration.

Farakka

In July 1976 I accompanied G. Parthasarthy (senior) in the ongoing negotiations on Farakka, but we were talking at cross purposes. The dam begun in 1960 had been completed in 1975, by which time Bangladesh had come into existence and Mujib was still in power (he was assassinated in August). After Mujib was killed, disregarding even his reservations and the damage being done downstream in the Padma (as the Ganges is called in Bangladesh), we persisted with our right to flush the Hooghly by diverting 40,000 cusecs from the river. Mrs Gandhi, of course, was pondering over the assassination of Mujibur Rahman. The Bangladesh delegation was deeply worried by the decrease of the flow and had widespread international sympathy. They were inclined to place the matter in the UN General Assembly beginning in September 1976. Parthasarthy who had been Ambassador to the UN should have led the Indian delegation at least for this particular case, but knowing the general hostility towards India, he backed out. I was charged to deal with the matter. I tried to flatter Admiral Khan and Abbas and pledged that we could negotiate a compromise but not under the shadow of internationalization of the question. It was the first time in the history of the UN that an item on its agenda, which would certainly have gone against India, was withdrawn before the voting. The item then would have become a running sore between Bangladesh and India in the following years. While G. Parthasarthy had refused to handle Farakka in the General Assembly, Mrs Gandhi upheld my recommendation that bilateral negotiations should follow immediately.

Jagjivan Ram, the Minister of Food and Agriculture, was deputed to lead the delegation to Dhaka when, as I had pledged, we wanted to explore a realistic compromise. The atmosphere had improved because of my friendlier attitude and a second round followed in Delhi in January 1977. Before a compromise could be reached, the Emergency was lifted; the Opposition leaders were released and Farakka had to be postponed till after the elections. River projects are doomed anyway, and we simply had a myopic view of our stakes in the stability of Bangladesh.

What was not widely known at the time, and certainly not publicized in either country, was that the Pakistan Ambassador to the UN had discreetly advised Bangladesh not to persist with an internationalist stance. This, to my mind, was the direct result of the improved confidence built by the bilateral negotiations in May.

Diplomatic rigidity and overreaction

There were, of course, some instances where I was disappointed with Mrs Gandhi's rigid attitudes. She was needlessly cool to Admiral Khan, the Deputy Chief Martial Law Administrator of Bangladesh when he, along with Abbas called on her prior to the reference of placing the Farakka question in the Assembly. This meeting between equivalent heads of government barely lasted a few minutes because she observed a stony silence.

Mrs Gandhi also did not quite encourage my suggestion of trying to improve relations with Nepal by separating the question of Trade and Transit.

Let me recall another incident not involving the PM, but where our diplomacy failed to advise the Foreign Ministry correctly. Since I was to handle the Farakka item, I had postponed my visit and did not go with Foreign Minister Y.B. Chavan to New York. It was an easy anticipation—an annual ritual—that Pakistan would again refer to Kashmir in its address and trot out the familiar arguments against India. Since the FM was in town, he asked Rikhi Jaipal, the Permanent Representative, and Al-Hashmi, his deputy, to exercise 'the right of reply' in order to show the Indian public that we had not taken the reference to Kashmir lying down. I would have advised against it myself and Pakistan's speech would have gone unnoticed and unpublicized. Our 'reply' invited Pakistan to rebuff, and so the ding-dong of arguments followed. This amused the international audience and got local headlines that the South Asian twins could be relied upon never to exercise restraint.

The Emergency period in our own diplomacy

I took over as Foreign Secretary in the middle of the Emergency. Though it did not fall in the orbit of my responsibilities, I was aware that the suspension of the Constitution had not carried much conviction in democracies abroad. The USSR, the communist countries and the assortment of authoritarian governments did not offer trenchant criticism, but they had not prompted its adoption and did not see validity in its defence. However, the Emergency was a fact and, in accordance with civil service ethics, I accepted it; the normalization with Pakistan had augured well for Mrs Gandhi as it proved to be more comprehensive than any other agreement in her own or her father's time.

When asked, I did my best to give the most plausible defence of the Emergency—that its main purpose was the twenty-point programme, emphasis on controlling population, on ecology, encouraging reforestation, etc., but it carried little conviction. Mrs Gandhi did not personally overemphasize the subversion of constitutional rights. She did not lose her temper when I submitted to her that foreign journalists who had been expelled or withdrawn, including Mark Tully of the BBC, were much more critical of India than those who still remained in the country. Some of our diplomats abroad, in misguided zeal, notably in Washington, the Consulate General in New York and the High Commission in London, went well beyond the instructions sent from Delhi. Known friends of India like Prof. Robert Hardgrave were denied a visa by Washington. I did not understand how Mrs Thatcher and Michael Foot were hypnotized into applauding the Emergency.

Even after the Emergency was over, the 'official' engagements fixed earlier continued. In fact, foreign policy did not figure in the campaign either in India or in the parallel elections in Pakistan. It was during this period that I told the Pakistanis not to vitiate the atmosphere by issuing pamphlets on Kashmir or wherever the thrust was anti-Indian.

In February, we went to have official talks in Moscow. Nikolai Firyubin, the Vice-Minister for our part of the world, was my opposite number. (While we were in the Soviet capital, one heard of the change of party allegiance by Jagjivan Ram.) The Russians went to town urging caution that India should beware of friendliness with China. Across the table, I said that, while we wanted to normalize constructive relations wherever possible, it would not be by sacrificing a trusted friend like the Soviet Union. Firyubin was not quite satisfied. During the coffee break, I said to him that I was prepared to show my top secret analysis dated 1959 with theirs of the same period, then we could tell which country had been more naïve about China! Firyubin laughed and kissed as only Russian males do! It was during this visit and in front of Purushottam and Arvind Deo, both accompanying Joint Secretaries, that Ambassador Sudarikov said to me, 'Please come to Moscow as Ambassador; Gujral will soon be finishing his term.' After my experience in Peking, I had always had the feeling that I understood Russian diplomacy much better than some of our left-leaning intellectuals.

International conference on Water: Indian general elections

On March 14 or thereabouts, a long prepared UN conference on water was held in Mar del Plata (Uruguay). Abbas, who had an unmatched international standing among civil engineers, especially when it came to questions related to water and rivers, led the Bangladesh delegation. He told me that he had been to 150 conferences where Farakka figured prominently. Not surprisingly, Abbas was made Chairman of one of the main committees. Fortunately, I had established a fairly good rapport with Abbas in New York. We were still concerned that the subject of Farakka could be raised in the international forum. It was a sort of triumph for India that the Farakka question was not directly referred to and so we were saved from international embarrassment. I was leading the Indian delegation and felt immensely relieved.

Meanwhile, the results of the general elections were about to be announced. After delivering the main speech, halfway through the conference, I left. Eight hours to New York, then almost eight hours across the Atlantic, lunch with B.K. Nehru, the High Commissioner, and his Deputy Natwar Singh in London, where I learnt of the first results that the Congress was trailing. Natwar Singh was, of course, confident of Mrs Gandhi's victory. I remember his remark, 'I am Mrs Gandhi's chamcha (flunkey).' I said nothing, but felt he should have gone into politics much earlier.

We could not land in Cairo because a plane had crashed on the runway. We were diverted to Athens and as the crew had to have their prescribed eight hours' rest, I spent 21 March in Athens, marking time. I went to the Acropolis and paid homage to democracy while the Indian electorate showed its unmistakable independence and the Congress suffered a humiliating defeat. For the first time since Independence the people voted to change their rulers at the centre. When I got back to Delhi, the final results were already public. I went to call on Mrs Gandhi and thanked her in the garden of 1, Akbar Road. She was sombre, but she congratulated me on the Mar del Plata success, and that was the last time I had a one-to-one conversation with her. Mrs Gandhi never forgave me for my efforts for the Janata government. But as Foreign Secretary, I had never had any hesitation in offering her honest advice and she in turn paid me attention and deference. My counsel to Mrs Gandhi coincided, so I believe even thirty years later, with the enlightened national destiny.

15

Straddling the Change in Government: Bipartisanship continues in Foreign Policy (1977–79)

The climate before the elections and the service reactions

Within External Affairs, we were not too affected, at least not in policy-making, by the Emergency, but we knew it had vitiated our image in many countries. We had got accustomed to western-oriented sophisticated personalities like Nehru and Mrs Gandhi as head of government, and we had banked on the continuation of a person in whom we could take pride abroad. The timing of normalization with Pakistan and the subsequent developments were independent of India's domestic politics. Some colleagues were natural sycophants and openly pro-Emergency, but most considered it safe only to go along with those who presumed that Mrs Gandhi would head the next government. We pretended to believe the assessment of RAW, IB, and diverse sympathizers that said the Congress would be re-elected. Anyway, as far as my own professional duties were concerned, they continued as before and one discouraged speculation about a possible change in the government.

The result of the elections was, however, openly welcomed by most as it lifted the constraint to maintain silence, and restored freedom of thought and expression. We also knew that the electoral defeat of the Emergency would fortify our international image as a truly functioning democracy.

Immediate reactions after the formation of the Janata government

The Janata coalition was a hotchpotch of opposition parties cobbled together in a hurry. Even though Morarji Desai knew me, I had not tried to reach the new PM, but I was present at the swearing-in ceremony in Ashoka Hall, which was to be followed immediately by a press conference. I managed to edge my way through as the PM was walking down the main staircase of Rashtrapati Bhavan on his way to Vigyan Bhavan. In the middle of the crowd milling around him offering felicitations, I managed to tell him he might like to make a positive mention that there would be a basic continuity of non-alignment in foreign policy. I hoped that this might be a peg for his answer rather than unthinkingly launching forth on a criticism of Mrs Gandhi and the Emergency. It stuck in his mind but he interjected the adjective 'genuine' before non-alignment. This provoked speculations whether this might mean a turning away from the Soviet Union and a tilt towards the West. In my view, these apprehensions reflected the common perception that non-alignment did not mean independence but the leveraging of blackmail. I myself felt that this kind of kite-flying could harm India but the media was now uncontrolled, and such opinions could be expressed.

Vajpayee appointed Foreign Minister

A few days later, the names of the cabinet ministers were announced and the new Foreign Minister would be Atal Bihari Vajpayee. All of us who had had occasion to hear him from the Officials Box in

Straddling the Change in Government

the Lok Sabha, had been greatly impressed by his oratory and intelligence; of course, his speeches were in Hindi. One recalled that Panditji had praised him but I had never met him personally. As soon as I heard the announcement, I drove to his house on Ferozeshah Road. I was ushered in straightaway. I announced my name and present appointment, and made some sort of a declaration that it was up to him to retain or to transfer me but, as a civil servant, I could assure him of faithfully implementing the new government's policies. I was somewhat nervous that he may have heard criticism of some officers for having projected the Emergency too earnestly. He was gratifyingly reassuring towards me personally and said I must continue in my job. In my best Hindi, I added that I had only one request. Even if my recommendations went against governmental thinking, I should be allowed to tender my recommendation before any important decisions were finalized. Though Vajpayee does not recall it now, I think I added that if I were stopped from rendering counsel, the implementation of policy may well be half-hearted or even sabotaged. He perked up his ears and he must have shown some non-verbal form of displeasure, but he did not say anything. Clearly he was not expecting any such reservations in a courtesy first call. Let me add, however, that in all my time of service with him, he never interrupted me when I sought to volunteer an opinion. He was akin to Shastri in allowing the liberty of dissent and this was part of his greatness as Foreign Minister.

He arrived punctually the next morning and I took him to his room and then invited him to address the senior officers in our committee room: it would be an opportunity to clarify the new government's policy approaches. He spoke in Hindi but I have never heard anyone, not even PM Nehru, give such a lucid statement of what the role of professionalism should be in foreign policy-making. Everyone, he said, could bank on his understanding and objectivity; there should be no hesitation or inhibition in expressing honest opinions. The elections had shown that ours was a functioning democracy, and civil servants were expected to serve the government of the day, always keeping long-term interests in mind. All the officers left, visibly relieved that we were not going to lurch to a 'Jan Sangh' foreign policy!

Subsequently, we explained the organizational structure of the Ministry, our respective duties and the ongoing problems. We were however a little taken aback when, instead of choosing at least one private secretary from the IFS, he brought two from the IAS. I accepted that it was his discretion to select his personal staff, but I felt that someone from the department would better field liaison.

There were some internal worries too, as we were all habituated to working and, even thinking in English. One of my recently appointed colleagues was M.A. Vellodi, who was from Kerala. He was frank enough to tell the Minister that he could not even speak coherently in Hindi. The Minister assured him that he should have no hesitation in writing and speaking in English.

Corrective prophylactic action: the USSR and Pakistan reassured

The immediate policy worry was that the Janata coalition would cause anxiety in the Soviet Union and in Islamabad. On my advice, an invitation (which, in fact, had been pending for a long time) was sent to Andrei Gromyko, the Soviet Foreign Minster, to visit Delhi as soon as convenient. Gromyko came posthaste and went away fully satisfied that the well established relations with the USSR would not be diluted.

The Pakistan government was satisfied with the normalization negotiated the previous year under Mrs Gandhi. Meanwhile, following parallel elections in Pakistan, internal developments had led to General Zia-ul-Haq re-establishing military rule and arresting Bhutto. Agha Shahi had been elevated to Foreign Minister by the General. Pakistan was worried about the possible deterioration in relations with a coalition which included the old Jan Sangh. Agha Shahi came to Delhi ostensibly to offer congratulations to the new government but really to get a feel whether it would repudiate the improving climate of relations between the two countries. Like Gromyko, the Pakistan Foreign Minister had suppressed his anxieties over the rejection of the Congress. Agha Shahi also went back satisfied that there would be a basic continuity in India's Foreign Policy, and that no deterioration in bilateral relations was envisaged. The calls on the PM and the Foreign Minister were transparent, successful and forthright. The government, within weeks of assuming office, had succeeded in establishing its credibility as regards the continuity of Foreign Policy.

Resuming Farakka negotiations

One unresolved issue to be tackled by Morarji Desai's government was to resume the negotiations on Farakka. There was deep anxiety that the massive transfer of waters in the Hooghly was creating damage downstream in Bangladesh. In the January negotiations, the proposed allocation for Bangladesh was greatly increased but the differences had not been bridged. Jagjivan Ram, who had led the delegation before the elections, was then Minister for Food and Agriculture, but he had changed his allegiance to Janata in February, and was now the Minister for Defence. It was decided that he should continue to head the delegation. With G. Parthasarthy as his deputy, I now became the deputy leader of the delegation from having been number three. We still had with us C.C. Patel, the Chairman of the Central Water and Power Commission (CWPC), and a string of officers from MEA and the Commission.

Before departure, I had occasion to mention to the PM confidentially that, if success of the negotiations was to have an even chance, we had to remove irritants likely to be taken as evidence of malevolence towards the post-Mujib government in Bangladesh. While we in MEA had no official information, we gathered that Tiger Siddiqui and the Mukti Bahini, earlier involved in supporting the liberation of Bangladesh, had been redeployed along the Garo hills in Meghalaya. From those heights, they made nightly raids into Bangladesh; they were sometimes caught and then shown on TV as proof of India's hostility towards the country. The PM straightaway called R.N. Kao, the head of RAW, and point-blank asked him whether the remnants of Mukti Bahini were, in fact, in the Garo hills and engaged in destabilizing operations. While External Affairs could be kept in the dark by RAW, it was not possible to deny information to the PM. When it was confirmed, the PM ordered that, within three days, the whole of Mukti Bahini should be removed from the neighbourhood of Bangladesh and transferred to the vicinity of Darjeeling. This decision could not be kept hidden from the Bangladeshis; it dramatically improved the climate for the resumption of talks on Farakka.

The mood was distinctly more propitious on both sides. In the leanest period, normally the first days of May, statistically the total flow in the Ganges was 55,000 cusecs upstream of Farakka; the last figure mentioned during the January talks in Delhi had been 33,000 cusecs for Bangladesh and 22,000 for the Hooghly. In the talks, India's share was reduced to 21,000 while Bangladesh would get 34,000 cusecs. At the restricted talks between General Zia-ul-Rahman, the Chief Martial Law Administrator, and Jagjivan Ram, Tabarak Hussain, the Bangladesh Foreign Secretary, and I were the only ones present; the residue difference was split. The general and Jagjivan Ram agreed that India would limit its share to 20,500, allowing Bangladesh a flow of 34,500 cusecs. It was less than what Bangladesh had expected and certainly less than what our engineers had considered the minimum required for the proposed flushing action. It reflected the spirit of accommodation and defused the brewing storm of anger amongst the Bangladeshis. Only a man of the stature and political courage of Babu Jagjivan Ram could have agreed to this reduction. He told the Chairman of the CWPC to accept it in the larger interest of good neighbourly relations.

There still remained a great deal more to be negotiated between our delegations including the commitment on long-term solutions. It hinged on whether the Brahmaputra and the Ganges basins were to be treated as one so that waters could be transferred from the surplus in the eastern river to replenish the flow in the Ganges above Farakka, as proposed by India, or a separate watershed (as wanted by Bangladesh) with storages being built in Nepal to increase the water availability during the lean months. There were also questions of guarantees in the event of exceptionally poor monsoons, the duration of the agreement and other semantic problems. Resolving these problems was left to me for India and Abbas for Bangladesh. We had several more meetings in the following weeks. The final meeting was fixed for September 1979. Muchkund Dubey, Joint Secretary, subsequently High Commissioner in Dhaka and eventually Foreign Secretary, had reservations over some aspects of my approach but he dutifully hammered out the compromises and eventually conceded I was right.

However, at the last minute there was an impediment from our own Finance Minister, Charan Singh. We had already conveyed our agreement to the basic wording of the MOU. Charan Singh now said that the period of the MOU should be changed. I was greatly embarrassed that our own draft was being repudiated. I was due to leave for New York to be with Foreign Minister Atal Bihari Vajpayee for his first speech in his new capacity. I somehow managed to persuade Abbas to incorporate the extended period as suggested by our Finance Minister, but he said it required the approval of his President, who was on tour and so, not easily accessible. We waited anxiously all day. At 8 p.m., Abbas got his President's approval by long distance. Then it had to be typed on parchment paper. I took the two delegations for dinner to Karim's in Jorbagh and we initialled the Farakka Agreement at forty minutes past midnight in our committee room with 'Satyamev Jayate' (Truth triumphs), and took off for New York at 2 a.m. The formal agreement was signed by the new Minister for Food and Agriculture Surjeet Singh Barnala, and Admiral Khan, Deputy Chief Martial Law Administrator in charge of Water and Rivers, in Dhaka in October 1977.

The Farakka episode was an experience of early friendship under Mujib turning into deep political hostility after his assassination, followed by diplomatic ups and downs. The final settlement was only possible because human equations enabled an acceptable last-minute compromise. The agreement assured Bangladesh that if, in some lean years, the flow was less than 55,000 cusecs, we guaranteed that their allocation would not be reduced. I felt satisfied that through this concession, diplomacy had reduced the ugly hostility between neighbours, but in 1982, when the period of this agreement ended, in the revised text this guarantee clause was omitted. This must have caused irritation to the people of Bangladesh.

The Commonwealth Prime Ministers' Conference, May 1977

The first major conference for the Janata Government was the Commonwealth Prime Ministers' Conference in May 1977 which coincided with the silver jubilee of the accession of Queen Elizabeth to the British throne. Morarji Desai commanded admiration as did India's democratic resilience. There were comments about Morarji's dietary habits and sniggering ones about his personal therapy but the proof lay in his remarkable health at eighty. Since he was born on 29 February 1896, he had had only twenty birthdays! It was widely recognized that India deserved credit for transforming the Commonwealth into a multi-racial and multi-continental body by enabling a Republic to stay in the old monarchical empire. I casually related to our PM what had transpired in the second Prime Ministers' Conference held in 1949 when the Indian republic was allowed to stay in the Commonwealth in the face of strong royalist sentiments. During the conference, Sir Girija Shankar Bajpai had suddenly quoted from the Statute of Westminster. When the British PM was somewhat incredulous, Sir Girija had said he alone had been there in 1931. As it happened, I was the only one who had attended the first two post-war conferences. Morarji said that the 'Commonwealth would have long perished or been confined to the White dominions if India had not "stayed" in it. We should now have an Indian to head it. You should take over as the Commonwealth Secretary General after Ramphal's term expires.' This was the beginning of my aspiring for the post but more of that later.

Preserving the morale of the service

The hardest problem for me as Foreign Secretary was to preserve the morale of the service after the cataclysmic change of government. As head of the Foreign Office, my primary concern was that it should not lead to witch-hunting and damage the confidence of the service. The FM was amused when 'Hindiwallas' showed off their loyalty, hoping to flatter him by reciting their own poetic compositions. Most officers had dutifully followed the official line justifying the Emergency but some had shown an uncalled-for zest in harassing the known sympathizers of the Opposition. After the election surprise, many non-official residents sent their complaints through their private or party connections. Some reached the Foreign Minister who mentioned names to me and thought they should be removed from key positions. I parried these accusations and prevented serious harm to the service. Not a single officer was transferred or downgraded.

But the problem was where duty went beyond direction. While I will not name individual cases, one particular episode does deserve mention. Even as a civil servant, K. Natwar Singh had openly identified himself with Mrs Gandhi. He had almost finished his term as Deputy High Commissioner in London; I remember asking Mrs Gandhi when she was still PM about his next posting. I recommended—and this can be corroborated by the minutes of the Foreign Service Board of January 1977—that he be sent to Mauritius, as High Commissioner. Mrs Gandhi had expressly approved the proposed posting. Natwar had absented himself during the Silver Jubilee Commonwealth Prime Ministers' Conference, but he expressed outrage that he was being sent to a small island totally below his experience and ability. He eventually got himself posted to Zambia which, at least to my mind, was politically and trade- and investment-wise, less important.

The Foreign Minister's impact

Foreign Minister Vajpayee, though it was his first time in government, made an early impact in various meetings in Delhi and abroad. He took my advice to heart about starting by strengthening relations with India's neighbours. Our relations with Nepal had gone through a patchy period. King Birendra was distancing himself from India and becoming friendlier with China. Vajpayee's visit to Kathmandu was ritualistic but his oratory made an unforgettable impact. Speaking in Hindi which was widely understood, he *inter alia* said, 'Where every stone is an image of Shankar, and the waters flow to enrich the holy Ganges, how could India not have friendship with Nepal?' The entire hall burst into applause.

The big challenge for Atal Bihari Vajpayee was his first speech in the UN General Assembly. Al Hashmi having been the first to use Hindi in a UN Committee, Vajpayee welcomed the opportunity to address the General Assembly in our national language. Having finalized the agreement on Farakka soon after midnight, I had joined the Foreign Minister in New York for talks with some other ministers. I must have prepared some sort of draft in English focusing on the return of democracy and constitutionalism in the country. I had given it to our official Hindi interpreter, who had been specially asked to be in New York, but I did not feel too happy with the translation. However, I had no alternative except to pass it on to Vajpayee for his scrutiny. He sat through the night, translated my draft into immaculate Hindi, incorporating all the nuances and delivered it in the Assembly. We had made special arrangements by which N.P. Jain, a colleague, read out the English text, which then was interpreted in the official UN languages. It was a notable event, both because democratic India had regained prestige and Vajpayee had for the first time delivered a major speech in the language of several hundred millions.

Prime Minister's visit to the USSR, October 1977

More important was the next visit when Vajpayee and I accompanied Prime Minister Morarji Desai to Moscow in October

1977. Gromyko, after his visit to Delhi, had gone back and reassured the Kremlin hierarchy about the continuity in our Foreign Policy, but even so it was natural for the Indian PM to make an early visit to the USSR. Recognizing the importance of the victory of the Janata coalition, not only Kosygin but also Brezhnev, the President, came to receive Morarji Desai at the airport. The PM and the Foreign Minister, V. Shankar (the PM's Principal Secretary) and I stayed in the Kremlin suites. The same suites had been used by Nixon and his entourage, and we were told of the landscaping improvements made to please the American President! The Russians noticed that as soon as the Indian PM had washed, he opened his charkha and started spinning! We had already told the Russians that he would carry no health certificates as he objected to injections. We had also notified his diet—nuts, fruits and juices, etc. At the banquet I was within earshot when Brezhnev and Morarji had an intellectual duel on healthy food: the former said that in their climate they needed meat protein but Morarji countered by mentioning that the biggest animal on earth was the elephant, which was a vegetarian!

The formal conversations were held in what had been Catherine the Great's drawing room, which reminded me of Versailles with its opulence. In the conversations, one could see that Brezhnev was bordering on senility and Gromyko had to prompt him in not so soft whispers!

There was an old-fashioned radiogram in the common dining room. I was curious to see which records were kept. I was astounded by the collection of long-playing records of American jazz and pop singers! The flight on Aeroflot was not comfortable; the heating was inadequate for the October night. Comments have been made about Vajpayee, sitting just behind Morarji imbibing some brandy and vodka and ignoring the Prime Minister's strict abstemiousness.

Carter visits India in January 1978

Throughout the winter of 1977–78, we had an unending stream of visitors from round the world coming to pay their respects to the revitalized democracy in India. We were informally cautioned that the PM should not plan an immediate visit to the United States. The reason soon became obvious. The US President himself undertook a many-nation tour. Apparently Zbigniew Brzezinski, the National Security Advisor, had identified Iran, India, Saudi Arabia, Egypt and Nigeria as 'hegemons' who could be entrusted to keep regional peace. After visiting the Shah of Iran, President and Mrs Carter and a large party were due in Delhi on New Year's Day 1978. Every year, on 31 December/1 January, a large group of the Delhi elite celebrated the twin birthdays—first at Charat Ram's and then at Romesh Thapar's in Kautilya Marg with glasses of punch and dancing. The walls were plastered with slogans of sarcasm against the government and the Opposition of the day. Romesh had voluntarily stopped the publication of *Seminar* and so this year was somewhat special. There was another reason why this day remains embedded in my memory. While we were whirling around in a waltz on a crowded floor, I dropped my buttonhole badge issued by the CIA to only the few who could have access to Palam airport for the arrival of the US President. Mala, Romesh's daughter, embellishes the story of how she cleared the crowded floor of all dancers to look for my CIA buttonhole!

The big item was a one-to-one conversation between President Carter and PM Morarji Desai with India being asked to accept the US Non-Proliferation Act or risk the denial of further supplies of enriched uranium fuel for the Tarapur reactor. Morarji Desai's reaction was apparently firm and uncompromising. He said that while he himself thought nuclear weapons were an abomination, as long as some countries including the US continued to work military reactors, India would refuse to accept US domestic legislation. The Indian PM's rigid stance, even at the end of an extended talk, exasperated the American President. The rest of us including many Indian ministers and senior secretaries, and from the American side, Cyrus Vance, the Secretary of State; Brzezinski and Harold Saunders, the Assistant Secretary for South Asia and the Middle East, etc., were waiting in the conference room on the ground floor of Rashtrapati Bhavan. Finally after we had taken our seats, there was a brief photo opportunity for chosen members of the press. The NBC correspondent, with a long vulgar looking microphone, was one of the correspondents. While he did not hear anything himself, the sensitive instrument picked up the whisper from Carter to Cyrus Vance, 'The old man will not accept; we must write a rude and blunt letter to him.' The formal conversation was friendly. The NBC correspondent filed his tape and went for sightseeing. As scheduled, a small group—including me—was invited to lunch at the residence of Robert Goheen, the US Ambassador. At the initial photo opportunity, one of the bearers was caught swatting a fly on the flower vase. One could almost guess—and we were proved right—that the next day the front page photograph would be of the fly and not the VIPs! What took us by surprise later when President Carter was describing his service with nuclear-powered submarines, Purushottam, the MEA spokesman, came to the Embassy and said that the microphone had picked up Carter's whisper to Vance about the 'rude and blunt letter' and this had automatically been distributed to hundreds of journalists. I was deputed to go to the Ashok Hotel, which was the Press centre, to field the angry questions over the remarks of the American President. Morarji had told me to play down and not to inflame the Indian protests.

Carter also visited a nearby village which was named Carterpuri. My wife Rama had been selected as a lady escort for Mrs Carter. The next morning, President Carter signed what we had hoped would be a ringing declaration of two large democracies, affirming principles with no mention of any current issues.

The idea of an unusual kind of joint declaration had occurred to me when I was flying from Chicago to Washington. I scribbled a draft, which was typed in Washington and given to the White House. It was refined by many hands, but principally by Tom Thornton, who was the South Asia expert in the White House. I had borrowed a phrase from the book jointly authored by Catherine Galbraith and Rama that this grand declaration would remain valid 'now and through time'. This had survived the editing process. In fact, I was glad to find that most of the original draft had been approved by the principals on both sides. Alas, the NBC leakage, the swatted fly incident and the eventual fall of the Janata coalition smothered the hoped-for longevity of the high-sounding principles of the 'Delhi Declaration 1977'.

Vajpayee's historic visit to Islamabad, February 1978

The high point in a year crowded with negotiations and events was the visit of Foreign Minister Vajpayee to Islamabad in February 1978. It has been compared to Anwar El Sadat's historic visit to Jerusalem (1977) and Nixon's to Peking (1972), leading to diplomatic reversals of settled hostilities. In 1972, as he had led a march against the Simla Agreement, there must have been opposition from hardliners in the Jan Sangh; some Pakistanis too, opposed Vajpayee's being invited, and many distrusted him personally. His visit transformed India's policy. We have had setbacks like Kargil but Vajpayee has never gone back on the rationalization that India's own future hinges on the stability and prosperity of Pakistan.

MEA told to separate Trade and Transit Treaties with Nepal

It was also in 1978 that I was able to persuade Morarji Desai that we had to make serious efforts to repair our relations with Nepal. (I had failed in this respect with Mrs Gandhi.) From British days, Nepal had been treated as an economic adjunct of India. Though nominally independent, Nepal had no international trade, its foreign economic needs and employment opportunities across the border were provided by India. The Gurkhas were considered the bravest soldiers of the Indian army. But after India built the Tribhuvan Rajpath (Highway) and the Gauchar airport, and Air Nepal started flying directly to Bangkok and Hong Kong and further afield, and it had become a full member of the UN, it was incongruous to deny it the right of independent transit. Initially, in response to Nepal's request, a separate warehouse at Calcutta port had been provided to facilitate bonded goods transiting India. But since the border was now virtually open, we had maintained that the residue of the old practice was necessary to control smuggling, which undermined our national policy of import substitution. The Nepalese felt that we were free to control smuggling but that Nepal must also have the same rights as other landlocked countries. There was quite a tussle in the Cabinet. Finance Minister H.M. Patel was opposed to the proposed separation. I was constrained to point out that the old imperialistic attitude, which previous Commerce Secretaries like K.B. Lall and P.C. Alexander had shown, was jeopardizing our strategic interdependence. Anyway, there was even more smuggling from Dubai despite the vigilance, regulations and customs posts.

Cabinet approval was finally given that trade, transit and illegal smuggling be covered in separate treaties and that the negotiations be handled by the Foreign Secretary. I obtained approval from George Fernandes who was the Minister of Industry to further liberalize the duty-free import of Nepalese-origin goods.

I was thanked by King Birendra and was also told informally that it was the first time that India was treating Nepal as a fully sovereign independent country (with rights like Austria and Switzerland, or even Afghanistan vis-à-vis Pakistan). Not that the separate treaties made any difference to the volume of smuggling, but it augured well for constructive negotiations on riparian cooperation and the sale of surplus power from Nepal for adjoining states in India, which alone made Nepalese hydroelectric power projects viable. I had privately hoped that in the wake of this breakthrough, negotiations could begin on the Karnali project which had been pending for a long time and promised immense economic benefit both for Nepal and India. Alas, my own tenure, as indeed that of the Janata government, was not long enough to move it forward. Meanwhile, widespread deforestation had continued; in fact, the Commerce Ministry listed timber as one of the items for export from Nepal, little realizing that billions of tons of Nepalese topsoil was adding to the clogging of our rivers, and that poverty would become more and more explosive.

Prime Minister's visit to Washington, June 1978

Another notable milestone in my term as Foreign Secretary with the Janata government was in June 1978. However, it happened to coincide with a sad event in my personal life. On 4 June 1978, Vijay, our daughter turned twenty-seven, and our youngest son Uday came of age and turned twenty-one. I came down from Simla that Sunday morning and the entire family was together, after many years. Vikram took a photograph of Rama in the evening when all of us and Vasundhara Raje—a close friend of Vijay and Vikram before she joined politics—were relaxing around Rama. Early morning, the next day, accompanying the PM and the Foreign Minister, I left for what was planned as a longish trip abroad. We stopped in Tehran, flew by helicopter to the Shah's palace (his last VIP call when the Indian PM confidentially advised the Shah to democratize) and resumed the flight for Brussels for talks at the headquarters of the European Union the same day. However, after the banquet—about 2.30 a.m. in Delhi—I got a call from Vikram that Bhabhi (as the children called their mother) had suffered a massive heart attack and had been taken to the Dr Ram Manohar Lohia hospital. Next morning, I turned around from London, arriving on the morning of 7 June and drove to the Pant Hospital where she had been moved to the ICU. She was still in a coma, though I believe she opened her eyes and saw me, but I never talked to her again.

I did not take part in the talks in London. The PM went first to the West Coast of the US. The Foreign Minister rang me up and delicately hinted that he knew that the customary twelve days were not yet over but he wondered if I could join them in Washington and then go back. Apparently the PM wanted me present. After the cremation in Delhi, we had motored to Udaipur. I decided to go, and reached Washington in time to join the PM at Blair House. I was touched by the condolences of the President and Mrs Carter.

Even though differences persisted, it was a highly successful visit. Carter and Morarji Desai were kindred spirits who prized morality and principles in politics and had a shared faith in national democracies. There was no progress on Tarapur fuel but that did not come in the way of their fundamental beliefs. Jimmy Carter took Morarji Desai to pay homage at the Jefferson and the Lincoln Memorials on the Potomac.

Reassurance to Muslim countries

The Janata government fundamentally continued the broad outline of foreign policy as pursued by Mrs Gandhi, but it did not seek to score points over its predecessor. Atal Bihari Vajpayee grew in stature when he made a point of making a special trip to some Muslim countries. I accompanied him on a tour to the Gulf and Syria. He carried conviction when he said that he believed India's future lay in broad friendship and cooperation disregarding national religious beliefs; in our domestic policies, all religions commanded equal respect. Janata's relations with Pakistan, and the free and fair elections in Kashmir (in 1977) reinforced the claim.

I gained individual recognition of my role, commencing in Mrs Gandhi's time and continuing with the Janata, by being invited by the Saudi Foreign Minister to Jeddah. I persuaded the Saudis to attend the Non-aligned Conference being held in Belgrade and I was astounded when the Saudi Ambassador from Geneva came to our delegation 'to be briefed by Mr Mehta'!

I had come to sense that I enjoyed Vajpayee's trust but, with his political and parliamentary preoccupations, it was truly difficult to find even fifteen minutes every day to discuss foreign policy problems. I always had my lists and piles of files ready whenever he called me so that I could report developments and sense his reactions on controversial issues. I found his perspectives were akin to my own of greater reliance on diplomacy. I did not have to be at a loss if he was not available, as for example, when he undertook internal tours.

Prophylactic diplomacy after the Saur Revolution in Afghanistan, 1978

One such case was the sudden developments in Afghanistan. In April 1978, as described in my book,* I acted spontaneously. President Daud and his cabinet were unexpectedly massacred in Kabul. Without specific authorization, I took prompt initiative to inform the Acting Pakistan High Commissioner not to imagine that India had a hand in it, or that we would exploit the uncertainty in Afghanistan by a pincer movement with the Soviet Union. I assured the Acting High Commissioner that while we would recognize the new government, there would not be the addition of a single battalion on our western front. The following morning, I called Ambassador Goheen and urged him not to repeat the mistake of 1953 by imagining that, because there was a semi-communist coup in Kabul, which had proclaimed itself as a 'Democratic Republic', there was a need to further militarize Pakistan. In fact, Agha Shahi did go to Washington the next month and advance the old anti-communist arguments but he was refused the sale or gift of military hardware by the Carter administration. The request for A7 aircraft was summarily turned down. This, I think, is the only time where prophylactic diplomacy prevented military hardware flowing into Pakistan.

Leasing Gan Island belonging to the Maldives

I suggested to the Secretaries Committee that Gan, which was separated by 400 miles from the cluster of the main Maldives islands and was beyond its administrative reach, might be leased by India and made into a non-aligned non-armed outpost. I chartered a special small aircraft from the Maldives and we landed on the long-abandoned landing strip. I brought back the Officers' mess book which had been left behind when the base

---

*Jagat S. Mehta, *The March of Folly in Afghanistan* (Manohar: 2002).

was wound up but alas! The Finance Ministry thought a million dollars a year was too expensive for a mere tourist centre; its strategic significance was overlooked. To combat air-based piracy it would have been a convenient place for a turnaround after re-fuelling.

Origin of the 'Festival of India'

In 1976, Charles Blitzer brought a letter from Senator Moynihan and I asked him if he could come to office on Sunday morning. During the conversation, I found he had not visited the 'Aditi' Exhibition on Rural Arts-Crafts and Tribal Customs. As it was the last day of the exhibition, I took him and introduced him to Rajiv Sethi. Charles, after going round, said he wanted the whole exhibition for Washington. My daughter Vijay had a German friend take photographs of the exhibits. The Smithsonian saw the photographs and sanctioned a million dollars for bringing the exhibition to the American capital, and this became the 'Festival of India'.

The British had the first exhibition at the Brabazon in 1985. Subsequently the exhibition toured Paris, Tokyo, etc. If I am to believe Rajiv, the visit of Charles Blitzer launched him on his own career. Under Pupal Jayakar's direction (the 'Cultural Czarina' in Mrs Gandhi's time), with Niranjan Desai as the administrative coordinator, this display projected, as never before, the heritage of Indian civilization to the world.

Beginning of bipartisanship on Israel

On Mrs Gandhi's instructions, R.N. Kao, the head of RAW, had asked me to informally contact the Israeli Consul General in Bombay. The Consul came to Delhi but I met him only in Hyderabad House. This contact, however, became public during the prime ministership of Morarji Desai when Moshe Dayan paid a confidential visit to the PM. (We officials were kept in the dark about Dayan's visit.) Later I was given a letter by the PM to be delivered to Moshe Dayan in Washington. I can never forget the anxiety which ensued after my arrival. I drove to Princeton to see my son Uday, but at about 1 a.m., I found the staff car was missing. I was truly frantic, because I knew, as nobody else did, that my briefcase contained the highly secret, signed letter from the PM. Uday knew the only Indian in the Princeton police force and managed to contact him. The constable was able to locate the car in an obscure parking lot at 2.30 a.m. (Incidentally, Uday became a great friend of the Princeton policeman and helped him to choose a bride out of the many who had replied with photographs to his advertisement in the Indian papers!) These informal contacts took place long before we established diplomatic relations. Now there is a thriving cooperation with the country, but the surreptitious beginnings were bipartisan.

Overtures to ASEAN countries

During the autumn of 1978, pegged around a conference in Kuala Lumpur, I visited Bangkok, Singapore and Jakarta. In Malaysia, I was invited to deliver a speech at the university. I put forward the thesis that non-alignment, which meant combining independently oriented foreign policies with functional cooperation across ideologies, was now on the way to becoming universalized. (Détente had not yet become popular.) Economics, not politics, would prevail. Decades of mutual hostility between adversarial military blocs still had momentum, but my speech seemed to evoke wide interest.

I had long felt that India had neglected South-east Asia because of a prejudice that those countries had become western allies. In my view both South-East Asia and the Gulf in the West, had natural geographical, historical and cultural links with India.

I canvassed so that India might be invited as an observer to the annual meetings of the ASEAN. In principle, the Foreign Offices thought that India would be welcome, but it required decision and approval, which would be possible only at the next Heads' Conference due in 1980. India, I was told, could send observers to the 1980 meeting. I was satisfied that I had prepared the ground for an overdue correction. By 1980, however, when the invitation did come, the Janata government had been displaced and the Congress was back in power. Meanwhile, in accordance with a needless election pledge, Heng Samrin's government under the control of Hanoi had been recognized in Kampuchea. Foreign Minister P.V. Narasimha Rao did not attend the meeting in June 1980, ostensibly because of his mother's illness. It took two more decades for India to look 'East'.

Vajpayee's visit to China

1978–79 was yet another active diplomatic winter. In February 1979, for the first time after twenty-two years—since the visit of Nehru to Peking in 1955 and that of President Dr Radhakrishnan in 1957—Atal Bihari Vajpayee went to China as Foreign Minister on a high-level visit. Meanwhile, Sino-American relations had been resumed, and the Americans and the Chinese were suspected of conspiring against the Soviet Union. Vorontsov, the Soviet Ambassador in Delhi, visited me several times, expressing near-alarm that we were being naïve again. The Soviet fear was that India might develop more active trust in China and 'abandon' the USSR. I assured him that, consistent with our policy, we were functionally improving relations with all countries, especially with our neighbours, but we were careful not to endanger established friendships, notably with the USSR. We had not done so in Washington and were not likely to fall for this temptation in Peking.

There was, of course, reason for their concern. Deng Xiaoping had gone round America in January 1979 and practically in every speech denounced the Soviet Union. On our arrival in Peking, accompanied by Eric Gonsalves, I asked for an immediate call on Han Nien-lung. This was even before the welcoming banquet. I warned the Vice-Minister that India would be most embarrassed if the speech that evening contained adverse reflections on the Soviet Union. I believe the speech was edited. It was the only occasion in those months, where there was no criticism of the USSR. On all live issues—except the border, which was expressly excluded—Kashmir, Sikkim, arms to the insurgents in North-East India, there was satisfactory progress.

The Foreign Minister was still in China when the Chinese attacked Vietnam on 17 February 1979. The official discussions in Peking were already over and we were only making a tourist halt in Hangchow. Deng, in an off-the-cuff remark said, 'The operations in Vietnam will be of short duration like those against India in 1962.' Atal Bihari Vajpayee had to react to this development and so he cut short his visit by a day by not stopping in Canton. The Communist Party of India (pro-Russian) criticized Vajpayee's visit and the needless insult to India. The CPI was quite erroneous in its analysis. The attack on Vietnam was really timed to prevent the USSR from signing a Non-aggression pact with Heng Samrin's government in Kampuchea on that day. Some of our own officials tried to make out that the visit to China was a mistake and that Deng Xiaoping's remark was a deliberate insult to India, but, in fact, Vajpayee had made a good new beginning in China.

The second visit to the USSR, June 1979

The relations with the Soviet Union had not been adversely affected by the China visit. The proof of it came when, within weeks of Atal Bihari Vajpayee's visit, Premier Kosygin came to Delhi as return courtesy to PM Desai. He tried to get our support for the new government headed by Hafizullah Amin in Afghanistan but this was pro forma. We suspected that the pseudo-communist government had precipitated the insurgency in the tribal-dominated Islamic country. Morarji Desai stood his ground and refused to express support for Amin. Anyway, it was evident that there was no damage to our relations with the Soviet Union. Corroboration for this came again when Brezhnev asked the PM to make a stop over and not just to transit through Moscow during his proposed tour of Eastern Europe. Once again, Brezhnev himself received Morarji Desai. I do not know if any Indian PM has paid two official visits within twenty months, at least when there has been no change of leadership in either government. Though there were extensive discussions on various topics including Afghanistan, our position of not openly endorsing the Democratic Republic in Kabul seems to have been well understood in the Kremlin.

While the Prime Minister and the Foreign Minister went on to Warsaw etc., I stayed back and spent the whole day discussing Afghanistan with Ambassador Sudarikov, in charge of relations with South Asia. Reading between the lines, I got the impression that the Soviets themselves were unhappy about the policies in Kabul, and our mental reservations were fully appreciated.

Post-Emergency problems in MEA

Shah Commission probe on an aircraft imported for the 'Brahmchari'

While the Emergency had not seriously impeded foreign policy-making, we had some indirect fallout from it. The Shah Commission was appointed to examine the 'inequities' perpetrated during the Emergency. One of the officers of the Commission came in connection with an aircraft imported for the 'Brahmchari' without payment of import duty. I remember that it was brought to me by Teja, then Joint Secretary (America) with a plea of urgency as it had already been cleared by the Home, Civil Aviation, Commerce and Finance Ministries. I was asked to 'sign' it immediately, signifying concurrence, as no. 1 Safdarjang Road (the PM's residence) had telephoned for urgent clearance. I asked the Joint Secretary to leave the file on my table. I studied it quickly and sent it to the Foreign Minister with my reservations as I did not think that an aircraft could be gifted without some recompense. Mr Chavan overruled me and gave clearance, and the aircraft was duly imported. The Shah Commission investigator found the file in our section and came back to me and said, 'Sir, you do not have to appear before the Commission. It is about the only case we have found where reservations had been recorded against the automatic favouring of the Brahmchari.'

The other incident I want to recall is when Subramanian Swamy—a member of the Rajya Sabha, who had gone under ground during the Emergency—headlined a story in the *Illustrated Weekly of India* post-Emergency, that even senior appointments like that of Manmohan Singh (now the PM, then the Economic Secretary), and J.S. Mehta (as Foreign Secretary), were confirmed only after they had been interviewed by Sanjay Gandhi. (He must not have been told or forgotten that, at the height of the Emergency, my wife, at great risk to us, had invited Mrs Swamy to our house.) I wrote to the editor of the *Illustrated Weekly* that this was entirely false and demanded either proof or a published apology. The *Weekly* dilly-dallied for months but after several reminders, finally, in a small out-of-the-way report, published an apology and regret. It was, no doubt, hard to keep one's integrity in the vicious atmosphere of the Emergency, but I am glad that I managed to emerge unblemished by personal slander.

Defence Plan proposals

This is unrelated to the Emergency but it happened during the Janata rule and could have occurred before. The Senior Secretaries Committee was charged to consider national threat perception and in that light, plan for future defence requirements with minimum damage to our social goals. It was presided over by the Cabinet Secretary, Nirmal Mukherjee. All senior secretaries—

Home, Finance, Defence Planning, Foreign, and for this purpose, the chiefs of staff—were members. Its recommendations went to the Political Affairs Committee of the Cabinet. The Additional Secretary, who was Chairman of the Joint Intelligence Committee, K. Subrahmanyan, serviced the Committee.

The immediate request, supported by the Defence Secretary, was for squadrons of Jaguars, a bomber-fighter combination. Air Chief Marshal Latif justified the demand as the Air Force had to be prepared for fifteen squadrons of F15 having been made available by Saudi Arabia and several of F14 by the Shah of Iran to Pakistan. The consensus favoured the acquisition of Jaguars to meet with this hypothetical threat. I felt that the demand was hugely extravagant considering the opportunity costs and international political realities.

My reservations somewhat irritated the Cabinet Secretary. He pointed out that it had been a tradition to send unanimous recommendations to the Cabinet Committee. I said, while it was up to him to decide the final shape of the Defence Plan, on behalf of External Affairs, I could not endorse the projection. I was tauntingly asked whether I would record dissent and, to his surprise, I said I would do so by the following week.

I wrote a paper that the explanatory grounds for the Jaguar purchase were not plausible. Apparently, this was the first time that there was dissent in the Senior Secretaries Committee.

The Shah of Iran abdicated in February 1979, a few months later. Pak–Iran relations were never as close as had been implied. There has been no massive attack from Pakistan (Kargil came twenty years later, and that was a tactical ground intrusion.) I have no regrets over my dissent. Only Vajpayee expressed reservations about the purchase of Jaguars. I have heard that when the purchase was finally approved in the Cabinet, Pakistan put forward a demand for F16! The present Prime Minister recalls the incident. Foreign policy is of course only half the story. Ultimately what matters is domestic dynamism.

A high point in foreign policy

When, in June 1979, the PM and the Foreign Minister returned from the tour of Eastern Europe, and I came back from Moscow, I really felt that it was the nearest we had ever got, through diplomacy, to Nehru's promised 'tryst with destiny'. Between the governments of Mrs Gandhi and Morarji Desai, we had developed understanding and relations with both superpowers, all great and medium powers, all our neighbours—Pakistan, Bangladesh, Nepal, Bhutan, Sri Lanka—and got the promise of improving the climate with South-East Asia, West Asia, etc. The world once again saw India exemplifying the principles of international law, supporting national independence and functional interdependence, approximating to the vision which Dean Acheson had articulated in December 1946, when our Constituent Assembly stated that peace in the world for generations to come would depend on India. I must have made this kind of a claim to ambassadors who called on me during the period. There were, of course, still existing problems, such as fuel for Tarapur and the unresolved boundary dispute with China, but diplomacy had created conditions so that, given sensitive management, India could concentrate on economic progress, social and distributional justice, and fuller employment for its millions. The earlier highpoint was in 1955 when Churchill had complimented Nehru as the 'Light of Asia' but that was after Pakistan had already joined the western alliance system and we still had naïve illusions about China. Recently, we disagreed with the Soviet Union on Afghanistan, and yet did not lose their respect, nor have we been estranged for refusing to accept the discipline of the US Non-Proliferation Act.

16

Removed without Reason by a Government without a Mandate

The high peak we had reached in our foreign policy collapsed like a house of cards the very next month when the Janata coalition under Morarji Desai disintegrated, and Charan Singh took over as Prime Minister. S.N. Misra was appointed Foreign Minister. Even though they represented India they had no international charisma; nor were they known for sacrifice during the freedom struggle as Morarji Desai had been prior to the elections of 1977.

Some critics felt that Jaiprakash Narain should have placed the mantle of constituting the Janata coalition on Jagjivan Ram's shoulders. He had been a minister in every central government since Independence, and was more tactful and politically more discerning than Morarji. As far as foreign policy was concerned, I felt that if either Morarji Desai or Jagjivan Ram had completed five years in office—or even if Mrs Gandhi had been re-elected in 1977—India's international standing would have continued to ascend, but a government reluctant to govern was bound to be a disaster.

Administration

Let me refer to some administrative problems which went beyond my responsibilities as Additional Secretary. I had reason to believe that in general the morale of the service had improved considerably during my tenure. The rationale for promotions and transfers was generally accepted as fair-minded and transparent. Except those who had ulterior personal ambitions, officials felt that there was objectivity in rotation. I tried to revise the format of the annual confidential reports so that there was actual scrutiny of the quality, and an analysis of the author's political grasp and thoughtful projections for the future. I had heard whispers that my predecessor had made one relation move between Bonn, Paris and Rome, which understandably made others reluctant to go to hard stations. This made one cautious. There was one complaint, which has dogged me even after retiring and which, therefore, requires some explanation.

Accusations of gender bias

I tried to set up a process whereby all officers in higher grades like Secretaries and even Additional Secretaries would have a longish tenure so that they could render informed and independent professional advice, and thereby make optimum contribution to policy-making. I wanted good officers to reach the Secretary level with twenty-eight years, and Additional Secretary with twenty-four years, of service. The relevant vacant posts in 1978 were for Secretary (East) and Secretary (Economic). Eric Gonsalves was already in Delhi as Additional Secretary but only for a year. He would complete twenty-eight years of service in 1978 and in view of his excellent record, deserved to be promoted rather than be transferred prematurely. He had previously served in Korea and Burma, and came to the Ministry after a full and successful tenure as Ambassador in Tokyo. Ms Muthamma had been in postings west of India. She had also got grade one, the equivalent of Secretary, but she was not, in my view, equally qualified to superintend policies about Asia. Romesh Bhandari was below Eric but also of 1950 seniority. He had a degree in economics from Cambridge, was Ambassador in Baghdad and, therefore, familiar with oil politics, and was clearly suited for the post of Secretary (Economics).

I was surprised and inwardly irritated when I heard after retiring that Ms Muthamma had made an appeal to the Supreme

Court at not being called to the Ministry. Justice V.R. Krishna Iyer, without giving me or the Ministry a hearing, concluded there was 'gender bias' and this got a play in the press. Ms Muthamma may have thought a posting as Secretary would place her in line for Foreign Secretary, but the post of head of the office could be filled either from the Ministry or from a foreign posting. (Kewal Singh had never served in Delhi before being appointed Foreign Secretary.) In 1982—two years after I retired—Mrs Indira Gandhi as Prime Minister, decided that even though Ms Muthamma was two places higher in seniority, M.K. Rasgotra should be Foreign Secretary. Mrs Gandhi could scarcely be accused of 'male' chauvinism! It was simply the PM's prerogative.

My circular that women officers should be prepared for separate postings has also been adduced as reflecting male insensitivity. Why was it not sent to men in the service? Perhaps it was a mistake, but consider the background. Male officers had not gone and appealed to women MPs that their family unity would be jeopardized by separate postings. It was well known that posts which enabled working in tandem were mostly in category 'A' capitals and sometimes, the result was that other officers' terms were shortened or more strictly enforced, and this led to resentment that women officers were being favoured.

Gender equality must obviously be pursued as a contemporary rationality. It presents practical problems in the military, the police, the civil services and the corporate sector, but in diplomacy it has a special dimension. This profession presumes on the plurality of sovereignties, and success depends on persuasion. There should be no suspicion of malice or prejudice when decision-makers have to optimize national gains to the best of their judgement.

I might add that in my experience women colleagues were often more diligent and competent. However, the problem remains. Comparatively speaking, India has been very enlightened in upholding women's service rights. Couples have been posted together, as heads to adjacent countries several times. But we still cannot send women officers to some countries as it is discouraged by their sovereign discretion. While there has been evolution and progressively, gender equality, some handicaps and constraints continue; indeed, in Iran, they have revived. In some countries, one of the couple is given long leave of absence and the other is designated 'consort' until he or she can resume diplomatic service. I know I failed in establishing that good officers should reach grade one after twenty-eight years and grade two after twenty-four years of service, but I am glad that I tried. During my term as Foreign Secretary, even when the number of women in senior grades was smaller, far from bias we had seven women ambassadors, which was more than in any country at that time.

There was not an iota of reason which could prove my having a prejudice against women colleagues. The proportion of women even now is low, but that falls within the discretion of the Union Public Service Commission (UPSC). However, since the mid-fifties, disregarding gender consideration, MEA has maintained steady objectivity in selection and postings but, of course, we cannot force any domestic practice upon a foreign country.

Death of Mountbatten

On the eve of our departure for Havana, we received news of the death of Lord Mountbatten by terrorist attack. Not many knew that there was a fat file of correspondence emanating from Lord Louis himself on Indian representation in the event of his death. He had told Mrs Gandhi and me that he hoped the serving PM would attend, supported by an admiral, a major general and select staff from Rashtrapati Bhavan, including the members of the President's bodyguard. As it happened, only S. Swaran Singh, an ex-minister, attended.

When President Clinton came to India, I had suggested to the Foreign Minister that we might name a road after Chester Bowles. Since Independence we have had no better friend of India. While we have named roads after many dictators, naming a roadway after Chet would have been a good gesture.

Non-aligned Summit, September 1979

The Havana conference of the non-aligned nations in September 1979, though numerically bigger than ever, was confronted with ideological fissures within the fraternity. Under Cuban initiative, there was a revival of the proposal to declare that 'Socialist countries were the natural allies of non-alignment'—a falsehood—but to oppose it would have caused embarrassment to the host country so it was not challenged. During Cuba's tenure, the claim got vitiated when the USSR invaded non-aligned Afghanistan. The invasion was strongly condemned in the UN General Assembly. The Cuban government made sure that the Kampuchea delegation, which held a seat in the UN, was not allowed to come to the conference. President Tito made a statesman-like speech—his last—to the non-aligned nations urging unity of the movement. The conference was also notable as the Burmese delegation walked out of the movement.

The fundamental contradiction in non-alignment was that it was becoming an imitation of military blocs. This came to a head in Havana where the inclination towards the Socialist bloc was finally affirmed.

As usual, there was a large Indian delegation demonstrating our experience in drafting skills and taking an active part in preparing the declaration, but we had lost the position which India had commanded in earlier years. However, the Foreign Minister and I, with N. Krishnan, our Permanent Representative (PR) in the UN, were given time to call on President Fidel Castro.

Commonwealth PM Conference—defeat in the election for the post of Secretary General

It will be recalled that on the encouragement of Morarji Desai as PM, I had put forward my candidature for the next Secretary General as Ramphal's term was due to expire in 1980. But, in the meanwhile, the vitality and cohesion of the Indian government had deteriorated. The new PM was absent from the Lusaka meeting. Ramphal had toured most capitals and canvassed for a second term. Though he was from Guyana, a small country, he was more eminently qualified than I was. My asset was that it was India which had given a new incarnation to the old British empire and, as it happened, I had the longest experience of the post-war Commonwealth; and, as Foreign Secretary, had led constructive negotiations on important questions within and outside the Commonwealth. I had, incidentally, received encouragement from Mrs Thatcher, who had recently taken over as PM of the UK, because she was impressed by my unexpected success in negotiating compensation for expelled Indians by that 'monster' Idi Amin. The UK had given asylum to 25,000 and spent twenty-five million pounds in the process, but could not even start negotiations with Idi Amin.

Canvassing for senior international appointments hinged on national government backing. Our new government was shirking even from seeking a Parliamentary vote of confidence. It was clearly no longer the Nehru's India or the resuscitated democracy of 1977. I knew that individual officials could not be stronger than the government they represented and I was inclined to withdraw my candidature. But Foreign Minister Misra more or less forbade me to withdraw as he felt it would be a slur on him personally and the government which he represented. Misra was a new face amongst many old leaders and carried little persuasion, even when he solicited support. There was reason to suspect that our own High Commissioner in Lusaka, Natwar Singh, was personally not very enthusiastic about my candidature. At the retreat where Ramphal's request for continuation was openly canvassed by President Kaunda of Zambia himself, he announced that in his judgement the consensus favoured Ramphal being given a second term.

Mrs Thatcher had suggested informally that the next term could be split between Ramphal and me. Anyway, it was a mistake on my part not to carry out my intention to withdraw my name before Ramphal's re-election was announced. Quite apart from personal embarrassment, I knew my defeat caused needless national humiliation for India.

Summarily removed as Foreign Secretary

Soon after our return from Lusaka, the Cabinet Secretary, Nirmal Mukherjee—I suppose on the instructions of PM Charan Singh and with the concurrence of Foreign Minister Misra—informed me to be ready to hand over charge and told me that I could indicate where I would like to go next.

It is widely believed that my defeat in the election to the post of Secretary General was the reason for my sacking. I have some suspicion that there was also a political rationale behind it. The idea may have emanated from H.N. Bahuguna, who was in Charan Singh's cabinet. He had chosen a career in politics. He had climbed the ladder of UP politics and eventually became the Chief Minister but he had been removed by Mrs Gandhi. He then turned anti-Indira Congress and joined the Janata. Like many, he was a pro-Soviet votary. Apparently he advised Charan Singh that to get elected at the end of 1979, he should dramatically adopt a pro-Soviet stance. It was widely believed that I was pro-America, and by removing me, a meaningful message would reach the Kremlin, and Soviet support and sympathy would follow. Little did our politicians understand that the Cold War fallacies were already under review. The Soviets had, I believe, a favourable attitude towards me. Anyway, my summary eviction could not help electioneering manoeuvres. This may well have been the rationale, but it made not one iota of difference to the final result.

Unlike the elections in 1977, in 1979, Foreign Policy was very much the focus of the campaign. Mrs Gandhi made an accusation that the Janata government had spoilt relations with the USSR, which she would reposition on a healthier basis. The Congress election manifesto included a commitment to recognize the Vietnamese-backed Heng Samrin government in Phnom Penh—something entirely at variance with the attitudes of the ASEAN nations.

I informed the Cabinet Secretary that I would like to go back to Germany. I believed there was much greater scope for bilateral diplomacy even if there was not as much publicity as came with the post of the Permanent Representative in New York. Ishi Rahman, who was then Ambassador in Bonn, had been there for nearly five years by March 1980. Ram Sathe, who was back in Peking, was nominated as my successor and told to rush back. I handed over charge to him on 19 November, approximately six weeks before the date of the general elections.

I have mentioned earlier that I had had a glorious career with a succession of unexpected and possibly undeserved opportunities but, alas! It ended with a whimper. I went on leave when my aunt, who was my foster-mother, passed away in Udaipur. I moved out of 11 Akbar Road, assigned to me in order to be near the Prime Minister's and the Foreign Minister's residences. Overlooking this injunction given by the Principal Secretary, I had had to pay commercial rent as I had a house in Shanti Niketan. It came to nearly a lakh of rupees a month, for which we had had to sell some valuables.

While I was waiting for Bonn to become vacant, in February 1980, Ram Sathe kindly gave me an assignment to travel all over West Africa and write a report on India's interests and policies towards the region. But on the prompting of Natwar Singh—so General Brar told my son-in-law—my proposed appointment to Germany was cancelled by Mrs Gandhi.

Farewell to the Foreign Service

Had my service as Foreign Secretary not been prematurely terminated, even without the extension given to many, I would have been in the post longer than any other officer except S. Dutt. But even in the thirty-eight months given to me, it was one of the longest periods.

I have been to the Ashoka drawing room only once in the last twenty-nine years and that was to receive the Padma Bhushan award in 1998, nominated by Prime Minister Vajpayee. Earlier, I had been a frequent participant in official dinners for visiting dignitaries, but I have not been to the Banqueting Hall of Rashtrapati Bhavan even once since I retired.

Though I forfeited rewards given to most other former Foreign Secretaries, I do not really feel deprived. I had the unique privilege of having had occasion to work with and offer advice to four PMs and their governments. What was perhaps intended as a disgrace, I consider as proof of defiant integrity and honest counsel. Anyway, I have never felt a sense of shame. I can relive my years in the Foreign Service with a sense of pride and loyalty, and of an honest commitment to India.

Having been summarily relieved as Foreign Secretary by Prime Minister Charan Singh, and then the further two-year extension promised by him withdrawn by his successor, Mrs Gandhi, I remained a sort of in-house persona non grata. I was taken aback when I found that the heavy bundle of telegrams which were delivered every morning stopped coming. I guessed that this must have been done under orders of some higher-ups. However, many of my colleagues and accredited diplomats did not seem to believe in the denigration of my worth, and for months I continued to be feted by heads of missions at farewell functions.

Sir John Thomson, the British High Commissioner, gave a large dinner in my honour. He compared my tenure with that of William Cecil, first Baron Burghley, advisor to Elizabeth I. He was known for his loyalty to the monarch and had negotiated many agreements. This, of course, was unmerited generosity, but Sir John was a seasoned diplomat, who could have easily made a more formal after-dinner speech. What also remains in my memory is the sumptuous dinner by the Libyan Ambassador, who said that I had demonstrated India's principle of secularism which would regain for India the leadership of the Third World. There was an elegant dinner by Hasan, the Ambassador of Qatar who, though young for the appointment, was particularly active. His Embassy on Tees January Marg was made to resemble an Arab camp in the desert. He was active in disseminating Arab and Indian music and culture at Cambridge, where he was considered a real scholar in Islamic studies. I was given a large lavish dinner by the Libyan Ambassador which I took as a tribute to my secularism.

Learning through Teaching: Academia (1980–96)

Even before relinquishing charge at the end of July, I received an invitation from Ben Brown, Director of the Fellows Programme at the Harvard Centre for International Affairs (CFIA). It was, of course, an honour to be invited without asking, to Harvard.

Harvard then had no centre for specialization on South Asia. We were still under Prof. Ingle's *obiter dicta*. I found many old friends and made some new ones. Amongst the new ones was Richard Neustadt who had been in Washinton during the Kennedy presidency. I still possess a book inscribed by him which says, 'If we had had the benefit of JSM counsel we would have recognized the futility of the Cold War long ago.'

One memorable part was when I joined a party from the Centre which went to attend the annual meeting of the Canadian Northern Territories at Yellow Knife. The temperature was minus forty degrees centigrade. What I remember particularly was that the only doctor in the winter months was a Sikh. The area of the Northern Territories is roughly equal to that of India but the population is only 44,000. The representatives from distant islands provided some contrast to our North East India.

The two names I must specially mention; Roger Revelle and Peter Rogers, who for years, had had the Ganges and the Brahmaputra flowing through their personal computers. They were distressed that South Asian Governments had not seen that they could get 500 million tons of food grains if only they would cooperate with no more investment than six billion dollars.

There were some extremely able persons who brought great diplomatic experience to the centre. For example, there was Robin Renwick, who later became Ambassador to US. He wrote an incisive paper on the marginal effect of sanctions of apartheid on South Africa and Southern Rhodesia.

A Fellow at the Castle

Before finishing my academic year at Harvard, I learnt that I had been selected by the Woodrow Wilson International Center for Scholars (WWC) in Washington DC as a Fellow for the next nine months. Until then, no Indian official had been approved, or perhaps had not applied, to be a Fellow at the Center. To be able to claim that one was a Fellow at the 'Castle' when it was located on the Mall was a sort of feather in one's cap! (It has now moved to more modern and spacious premises in the 'Woodrow Wilson Plaza' but has lost some of the old prestige.)

The WWC was established in the name of the most scholarly American President. Funded by the US Congress, the Castle also housed the headquarters of the famous Smithsonian Institute. The WWC provided facilities for scholars, and adequate substitute finance to enable them to spend a sabbatical period and complete whatever writing they had in mind or in hand. There was not one whit of justification for the suspicion that insidious influence about current US policies was sought to bear upon orient incumbents. In fact, there were more doves in our ranks than strategic hawks in tune with Reagan's notion of the Axis of Evil threatening the United States. However, being near the US administration, there were frequent visits by high administration dignitaries at the pre-lunch meetings. My papers written at the time had no curbs on my independent thinking. I discovered that Madeleine Albright, also a Fellow at the Centre, was the daughter of Ambassador Korbel, who had been the Czechoslovak representative in the UN Commission for India and Pakistan (1948). I told her that as Private Secretary to the Secretary General, I had had the privilege of meeting her father. The next day she brought a copy of his book, *Danger in Kashmir*, and inscribed it to me in a friendly manner. Ten years later, she became the US Representative to the UN and subsequently, Secretary of State for America.

I first concentrated on international riparian problems which, to my mind, were the best symbols of the problem of finding a balance between national sovereignty and growing international interdependence.* I also wrote a paper titled 'Solution in Afghanistan: From Swedenization to Finlandization'.** I summarized the thrust of my paper in a seminar and following that, Charles Maynes, the editor of *Foreign Policy,* asked me to shorten it for an article which was then published in the summer issue under the title 'Afghanistan: A Neutral Solution'.

Unofficially meeting my former Chinese adversary

In 1983, I was invited to Harvard for the twenty-fifth anniversary of CFIA and asked to make a presentation to the founder, Robert Bowie. This was during Commencement week and as usual, Ken Galbraith had a party in the afternoon. There I ran into Chieh, who had been the interpreter for Chang Wen-chin during the Sino-Indian discussions in 1960. He accosted me and said that he was sure Ambassador Chang would be happy to see me in Washington. Sure enough, I received an invitation for a one-to-one lunch with the Ambassador. Since I was retired while he was still serving, I was more frank in the friendly meeting. I told him that the Sino-Indian War was a tragedy born of mutual misjudgements. We probably did not know that the Chinese would consider our Forward Policy provocative, but the Chinese had made a big blunder by accusing Nehru by name as responsible for the revolt in Tibet. Surprisingly,

---

*Jagat S. Mehta, *Rescuing the Future* (Manohar: 2008).
**Jagat S. Mehta, *The March of Folly in Afghanistan* (Manohar: 2002).

he did not demur. The friendly atmosphere can be judged from the fact that when I asked him if he would consider visiting Austin, where I would be professor, if an invitation were sent to him, he readily agreed in principle. He duly came. At a largely attended meeting in Austin, the Ambassador spoke on Chinese Foreign Policy. While introducing him, I said the only reason I was on the podium was because I had sat opposite him for six months.

Professor of World Peace at Austin

While at the WW Centre, I had a visit from Prof. Jim Roach of the government department in the University of Texas in Austin. I had met Jim earlier as he had been the US Counsellor for Cultural Affairs in Delhi. He asked me whether I would be agreeable to accepting the Chair as the 'Distinguished Tom Slick Professor of World Peace' at the LBJ School of Public Affairs for the year 1983–84. Amongst the previous incumbents were well known academics including the only husband-and-wife team of Nobel Laureates—Gunnar and Alva Myrdal (Alva had been Swedish Ambassador in Delhi in the fifties). One condition which went with the appointment was that I would have to teach a postgraduate course for one term and, in spring, arrange for a conference on a subject pertaining to World Peace. While the offer itself was flattering, I was inwardly very nervous. I had no doctorate degree, and except for six months and that too, as a lecturer in English literature to undergraduates in Allahabad way back in 1944, I had never taught and certainly not International Politics to postgraduate students. I showed interest but the offer was confirmed 'conversation' in Harvard and the Travellers Club, London at which apart from the Dean, Elspeth and her husband Walt Rostow were present.

My course was 'Misperceptions in Post-War Diplomacy'. After some reading, I began to realize that it was going to be either superficial or over-ambitious, but it was too late to materially alter it. I was somewhat taken aback when I found the seminar class was full. I distributed the structure of the proposed course with an attached list of books for reading. One book which I specially recommended, was Barbara Tuchman's *The March of Folly: From Troy to Vietnam*. By documenting four cases, the author illustrates her thesis of how decision-makers, throughout history, merely because of dated mindsets, had acted contrary to their own national self-interest even when alternatives were available. The last of the four cases was 'America betrayed itself in Vietnam.' I had a separate list of memoirs by American and non-American statesmen or diplomats.

I asked the class to choose one of the subjects listed in the course and also select one memoir for summary analysis. For each seminar there were to be two presentations. I urged that, with the benefit of hindsight, the students should analyse, debate and advocate what could or should have been done to minimize the adverse consequences. The second half of the course was on aspects of world economy and international trade relations. The students were expected to read through the whole of their chosen biography, but concentrate on a particular episode.

On the last day of the course, the teacher was told to stay away, at least half the time. The Dean's office distributed elaborate printed forms and every student, without giving his or her name, evaluated the teacher and the course. I was agreeably surprised when the grade point average for my first course was 3.8 where the maximum was only 4; but anything above 3 was considered excellent. (Any course graded 1 or below reflected that the course should be wound up or the lecturer changed.) My grading was never below 3.8, but one year I had the university record of getting 4, which could not be bettered.

Third World militarization:
A challenge to Third World diplomacy

The next term was the second half of my assignment as Tom Slick Professor. The title which I chose for the conference was comprehensive, but I was already committed. To crystallize the scope of the conference, I had written a long analysis of the problems covering Asia, Africa and Latin America—the text is available in my book *Rescuing the Future*—and sent it well in advance to possible invitees. The funds available for holding the conference were meagre, only 15,000 dollars. This included travel costs and so I requested all the invitees to book in advance and at the cheapest possible rate. Accommodation was arranged in a modest motel within walking distance of the university. To my surprise, we had thirty-four participants, of whom only eight were from the local faculty. They came from different universities, including distant ones. Among the distinguished participants were Harold Saunders, who had been Assistant Secretary for the Middle East and South Asia in the State Department, and Tom Thornton, who was the South Asia point man in the Carter White House. There were seven former ambassadors, and one— Olaru Ottunu from Uganda—who was then serving as Permanent Representative in the UN. Other participants were Peter Galbraith from the Senate Staff, Andrew Pierre of the Council on Foreign Relations, and Rodney Jones, Head of Nuclear Studies at Columbia. Aside from my own circulated advance paper, an overview was given in the inaugural address by Victor Urquidi, Head of El Colegio de Mexico, a much respected Mexican intellectual centre. It was gratifying to receive papers covering the major regions with some general statements on the total problem.

There was an intellectually incisive panel discussion after each paper. My own theme, which was outlined in my keynote paper was that Third World militarization was glibly explained away either as an imposition of the Cold War, or of ulterior profit-making by armament manufacturers by providing sophisticated military hardware to both combatants in a region. In most cases, the social costs from redundant militarization had been under-focused while the elite had had their 'cuts' deposited in numbered Swiss accounts. The reversal of unaffordable militarization depended much more on Third World countries themselves and this hinged on defusing regional or sub-regional tensions. In the paper written for the conference, subsequently titled 'Intellectual Paralysis and Socio-Economic Drift or Forward-looking Diplomacy', I encapsulated the consensus and listed ten points.

There had been no similar conference on the subject of 'Third World Militarization', at least up to that time. The edited book was well reviewed in US journals, including *Foreign Affairs*. John Kenneth Galbraith summed up the thesis and it is worth quoting:

'One encounters it in the newspapers week by week, month by month: some country—in Asia, Africa, Latin American—has concluded a purchase order for airplanes, tanks, electronic gear and other weaponry running to tens, hundreds of millions of dollars, sometimes more. So customary is it that we do not pause to consider the absurdity. It is regularly a charge against the desperate poverty of the people of the country in question. It is meant for a military establishment with no plausible enemy except the people—and government—of the particular country.

It is not only absurd, it is a scandal. The advanced industrial countries are rightly blamed for the sales. But the poor lands of the Third World must, even more, be blamed for the purchase. Let us stress also the importance of a boycott. The governments of the Third World countries must come together and unite in ending this scandal. No issue, the ending of the arms race exempted, is more important.'

The book is a university publication and did not have commercial backing and so it had limited reach of publicity. I never saw a copy in Delhi. In any case, no one should nurture illusions of the impact of such academic conferences (or lectures) on policy-making, but it might have been marginally more useful if it had reached some decision-makers in the Third World and the arms-exporting nations. I relished my visits. I got to know

Raja Roy, a famous Indian philosopher. One year R.K. Narayan, the novelist, was in residence for a whole year and became a friend.

Academia or Voluntarism

At the end of the academic year, the Dean, Max Sherman, told me that, while they had not yet settled on a successor as Tom Slick Professor for 1984–85, Sir Brian Urquhart, who had retired from the UN, had agreed to accept a nomination to the Chair. But Sir Brian had stipulated that he could not be in continuous residence. The Dean then said that he would like to raise a million dollars and create a corpus for a position for me to remain on the faculty on the same terms as the Tom Slick Professorship. It was a flattering offer, but at about the same time, I had received a letter from one of the trustees of Seva Mandir inviting me to come back as Chief Executive. In the light of straddling interest in international politics and grassroots development, I urged a compromise. I could come back every year to teach in the autumn term and work with Seva Mandir for the rest of the year. The Dean agreed to this suggestion and this pattern continued from 1984 to 1996.

Life in Austin

It became known that I came to Austin annually for the autumn term. The Chinese think tank sent a specialist, Xuecheng Liu, to meet with me and reflect informally on the Sino-Indian boundary question. With the presumed licence of intellectual freewheeling, we spent several evenings discussing the strength and the weakness of the respective cases. I mentioned that most of China's evidence was from Tibetan sources, but we had difficulty in affirming it, as India had already recognized Tibet as a region of China in 1954. In the book* subsequently published by the University Press

---

*Xuecheng Liu, *The Sino-Indian Border Dispite and Sino-Indian Relations* (Department of Government, University of Texas at Austin, University Press of America: 1994).

of America, he acknowledges he had conversations with me, but even the summary of the arguments, which I had advanced (and which were not challenged in the conversations), finds no mention. The book is an elaboration of the familiar official position, which I had heard during the official level discussions in 1960. I could not help noticing the contrast between the self-confidence of Ambassador Chang Wen-chin and Xuecheng Liu—the latter was merely pretending to be a free-thinking intellectual.

The most prestigious centre of University of Texas was, of course, the British Studies group. I spoke at the British Studies seminar myself, and it attracted many distinguished speakers like the British Ambassador Sir Nicholas Henderson, Baroness Shirley Williams and a host of British academics and authors.

One of the friends I met every year was Prof. Philip Bobbit. He was a nephew of Lyndon Johnson. Philip was from the law faculty, but despite his democratic connections, was respected by all Washington administrations. A Cold War hawk with faith in nuclear weapons, Philip is Director of the Center for National Security at Colombia and wrote a book published in 2002 after 9/11, called, *A Shield of Achilles: War, Peace and the Course of History*. More recently another book has come out titled *Terror and Consent: the Wars for the 21st Century*. His argument is that, notwithstanding the UN Charter, terror supersedes the old international law, which was based on the right of non-interference in the internal affairs of nation states. It implies justification of Al-Ghraib torture and prisoner abuse and the Guantanamo Bay prison. We disagreed frequently but he provided a stimulating provocation for my non-Cold War approach.

During those years, I visited many American universities and attended several conferences. I recall a major one in Aspen on International Security. Stephen Cohen asked me to come to Urbana (Illinois) for a conference on South Asia Security, which was attended by many from South Asia including cognoscenti from the subcontinent. The drawback was that most such conferences expected a paper to be written in advance.

Diplomacy at its best requires understanding and adjustment to different cultures—British, European, African, American and Asian—but without losing one's own national identity. My experience in academia gave me a plethora of lasting friendships, many of which survive. Some friends have visited me in Udaipur, and to this day many stimulate me with occasional epistles.

I coined the phrase Fresh Water Diplomacy and I encouraged David Eaton to hold a conference of all East Asian countries on 'The opportunity cost of delay in the development of the Ganges–Brahmaputra basin in the Gold Coast city on the east coast of Australia'.

The most respected person in the entire university was Barbara Jordan, the black lady who, but for her physical limitations, might have been nominated as Democratic candidate for the post of Vice-President. She was responsible for the near-indictment of President Nixon after the Watergate scandal. I cherish her signed photograph given years before she passed away. Her course 'Morality in Politics' was in great demand.

The LBJ School of Public Affairs was next to the vast Presidential Library. Harry Middleton was the overall custodian of LBJ papers. I participated in the discussion on Paul Kennedy's best-selling book, *The Rise and Fall of the Great Powers*. Middleton managed to invite Senator Pat Moynihan for an evening discussion. He had created a furore south of the Mason–Dixon Line for his remark that Civil Rights could be left to 'benign neglect'. While I was at Austin, at last the prejudice against Pat was overcome.

Back to the Origins: Voluntarism in Development, Education and Grass-roots Democracy (1985 to date)

'Although the early voluntarists of Udaipur cannot be said to be radical in terms of striking violently and immediately at the roots of social oppression, their efforts to develop Indian unity, self-confidence and progress, reveal a revolutionary zeal. These were peaceful men, more at home at Vidya Bhawan's open-air session, enlightening their pupils, than as satyagrahi or potential prisoners. Yet, revolutions are fought in many guises, and the most enduring changes are often those wrought in less confrontational ways. In the history of Udaipur, perhaps the greatest tribute that can be paid to the founders of Seva Mandir and Vidya Bhawan is in the number of local people who remember and revere either the organization ideals or Dr Mehta himself.'

Gregory Jones

This extract is from a monograph titled 'Peaceful Revolutionaries', which was written by a British volunteer who came to Seva Mandir after getting an Oxford degree, and stayed on for a year. He interviewed the surviving teachers, rovers and colleagues, who had worked for a pittance with my father between the 1920s and 1940s, before Independence. I quote it, as something of this spirit must have moulded my values through my education and career which eventually brought me back home to Udaipur for the last part of my life.

While Vidya Bhawan must have made me sensitive towards the surrounding poverty, I also recall that just after the last meeting in July 1940, I was summoned by the Duke (as the headmaster Edgar Castle was generally called) and given a book called *Freedom* by J.C. Smuts. (Field Marshal Smuts was Prime Minister of South Africa.) The book was a transcript of Smuts's lecture at the University of St. Andrews, and was accompanied by a handwritten letter from the headmaster. I still preserve them both. He knew I was sailing back to India in the next few days. The letter said that the school would always remember me, but his parting words were, 'You have to earn to live but remember the aim must be to live to serve.' His thoughts reinforced what I must have absorbed in Vidya Bhawan. His injunction has lingered somewhere at the back of the mind throughout my life.

I was glad to get away from the undeserved career humiliation in 1979 and grateful that it was followed by acclaim in the wider arena of international academia, which gave me leisure and monetary reward. The unexpected high grading by my class and the success of the conference which I had organized were gratifying, but I had doubts about joining Seva Mandir.

Since my marriage I had felt that I did not come up to the standard of values which my father had expected from his son. My mother had passed away when he was only twenty-nine. Even though there were many possibilities, (one of which has been acknowledged in print), defying convention, my father did not remarry only because he did not want his son to have a stepmother. Living alone for sixty years may have sharpened his devotion to social work and public service, but he himself may not have realized that it also led to distortion and rigidity in his lifestyle. It made him over-dependent on a servant who performed many duties normally discharged by a wife but who also became a protective sentinel. My relations with my father were never abrasive but I could not help feeling that I did not get the confidence which he vouchsafed to other close blood-relations. My upbringing, along with his own contribution, had given me the scaffolding of independent principles. I always respected him, but I felt that he did not approve of my priorities and values.

My wife Rama was a sociologist and believed that the family permitted gradual modernization. She honestly thought that having some blood-relations around who gave him sustained affection would make her father-in-law's life more complete. After my father visited us in Bern, she sent our children—when they were just two and a half and one year old respectively—to give him affectionate distraction from his exacting duties. In 1955, when I was posted in London, Rama took all the children to Bern (by this time there were three) where he was Ambassador to Switzerland, to spend two summer months with him. Like a dutiful daughter-in-law, she tried to curb what she thought was extravagance in his household but his 'Jeeves' felt this was an unwelcome intrusion and her initiative was not encouraged by my father.

The best symbol of different approaches was when my father came back to Udaipur in 1966. Impelled with the desire to set an example of individual simplicity and sacrifice, he moved to Seva Mandir where he spent his last eighteen years in a one-room apartment. This added to my hesitation whether my father and I could work together in an institution founded by him.

After receiving Dadabhai Kesrilalji's letter, I flew back to India and at length tried to convince the trustees that I was unqualified to work as chief executive of Seva Mandir. Moreover, I did not like the taint of dynastic succession. After I had expressed my reasoned hesitation, I was taken aback when told confidentially that, though the offer had come in a letter from Kesrilalji, my father wanted me to take up the post. It was then that I decided to turn down the possibility of staying on a full-time basis at the University of Texas, and take on the responsibility of chief executive, but in an honorary capacity. I might add that, but for this express wish and six months' overlap, I might never have come to work in Seva Mandir.

As it happened, in the last few months of his life, there was no trace of the old reservations. I sensed a spontaneous trust in my counsel and also tremendous affection, which I had not known in the previous thirty years. I can only speculate as to what had brought about this sea change. Maybe because I too, was a widower; possibly he had heard of my integrity during and after the Emergency and the negotiations in which I had overcome deadlocks in national interest. It could be that he had learnt that Rama had actually encouraged her children to look upon him as a model of rectitude and social conscience. He may even have become aware that his servant had become dishonest. I was certainly stupefied when I learnt, some months after I joined Seva Mandir, that, in an interview to AIR, he had expressed the wish that 'Jagat could come back to run Seva Mandir'.

After I took over, I discovered that, after having become a near-national model of a purposeful NGO and with my father nearing ninety, Seva Mandir was in a deep crisis, causing him baffling anxiety. Let me provide a little background as this also throws light on the antecedents to my being called back.

The state of Seva Mandir in 1985

In the 1920s, my father had opened an account from his small savings in the name of Seva Mandir and in 1931 had bought a corner plot in the newly planned Fatehpura colony. However, except for the foundation stone, it remained a barren rocky space for the next thirty-five years. The construction of Seva Mandir headquarters began only after his return from the vice-chancellorship of Rajasthan University in 1966, with his accumulated savings, supplemented by the proceeds of the sale of a car which was allowed after the last diplomatic assignment as head of a mission. (It was eight years since he had come back from Bern).

Initially, Seva Mandir gave priority to adult education with volunteers going on bicycles to neighbouring villages with a blackboard and a hurricane lamp. From the very beginning, emphasis was placed on public accountability. In 1967 itself, accounts were published showing income and expenditure and a balance of Rs 2000 only. Thanks to his leadership, Seva Mandir soon won acclaim and support from many donors. By 1985 when I joined, Seva Mandir had about one hundred workers and an annual budget of approximately thirty-five lakh rupees, but the donors—nearly thirty of them—were scattered and most demanded periodic reports on its progress.

The trustees had been named in the deed itself. Chandra Singh, my uncle, and Kesrilal Bordia were the original members. Mehtab Chand, with experience as Accountant General, had replaced Chandan Singh Bhartakiya, a businessman, as financial advisor. Ela Bhatt, an eminent social worker, was trustee for a while; Narayan Desai was the son of Mahadev Desai, Gandhiji's secretary. All the trustees had unquestioned integrity, and enhanced Seva Mandir's reputation.

The year 1983 (when my father was 88) proved a crucial year. The endemic poverty was accentuated by a serious drought and government help for Seva Mandir was either inadequate or not reaching the intended beneficiaries. However, the senior persons of Seva Mandir were preoccupied with the question of who would succeed my father as President. The person who was assumed to be his successor had resigned but my father had not appointed the person next in seniority to replace him. This aggravated factionalism, which affected the constructive thrust of Seva Mandir. It was in this atmosphere of fear, uncertainty, and creeping cronyism that I was invited to join as chief executive.

I was fully conscious that my appointment was not welcome in the higher echelons of Seva Mandir. They insinuated that an ex-bureaucrat was unsuited to give leadership to an NGO. This was irritating for me as I had myself expressed my reluctance, but the decision having already been taken by the trustees, such criticism only aggravated the prevailing disenchantment. One expected full cooperation on agreed ideals. I made it clear that I was a learner and I never pontificated on development. I toured extensively, driving the jeep myself in all the four blocks and the fifteen zonal headquarters to show my face, and asked the workers about their work. I attended ceremonial functions like the opening of thatched-roof community halls and *anganwadis*. My concern was to restore unity and confidence, not to modify ongoing strategies.

Elected president of Seva Mandir

The trustees were summoned in August 1985 to decide on the successor president and they unanimously placed the mantle on me. I knew with the founder-president no more, it was going to be a challenge to prevent the virus of disaffection spreading and destroying Seva Mandir. Confidence had been shaken; I had to establish that I could be relied upon to be empathetic, fair and transparent. One also had to firmly show that I was unafraid of ulterior attempts to denigrate the institution. To relieve the pervasive fears, I made it clear that Seva Mandir expected not flattery and personal loyalties but earnestness in assigned responsibilities. I abolished the practice of everybody's annual increment, including those in a grade, requiring approval of the concerned superior.

A bigger problem for Seva Mandir was how to integrate the three strands in our personnel: (i) Those who had retired from government service but were wanting to stay in Udaipur, and were interested in our constructive programme. Some of these former officials were accustomed to the hierarchical ways of government, but Seva Mandir's ethos was one of equality. (ii) Those who had limited education but were good grass-roots communicators with villagers and showed willingness to fit in with Seva Mandir's developmental goals. (iii) Trained professionals who were generally young and educated, often motivated, and could implement developmental strategies. But they had understandably higher monetary expectations, which were commensurate with their qualifications, and also a penchant for working in the developmental sector.

Yet another problem was that of other NGOs piggybacking on Seva Mandir's patient labour. There was a rise of several NGOs around Udaipur. They were, of course, welcome, but what irked us was their pretence that they were working for Seva Mandir. They should have started in green fields and uncovered villages, but some took shortcuts by encroaching on villages which had previous association with Seva Mandir. Many experienced colleagues had collectively defected in 1986, possibly because of the belief that Seva Mandir had no future. I had decided early that Seva Mandir must not be guilty of luring people from other NGOs nor would we employ anyone unless he had voluntarily resigned from an NGO and had done so at least three months previously. Seva Mandir had to remain wedded to an exemplary code of conduct.

Seva Mandir colleagues and volunteers

Some persons from my time deserve special mention. They made an impact by their example, often resisting competitive monetary rewards. Umed Malji Lodha had retired as Joint Director in the Agriculture Department of Rajasthan. His austere lifestyle was a true example for all those who were working at the village level in restoring common lands for collective utilization and reforestation. He was distressed to lose his connection with Seva Mandir as he had to retire when he reached seventy-five. There was Rafe Bullick, who according to his mother, thought that the most dedicated NGO in all the world was Seva Mandir. She came from Edinburgh and gave us a generous endowment. Hem Rajji Bhati, a grass-roots communicator, was uniquely thoughtful. He understood the spirit of Seva Mandir and refused to join the defectors. He was an obvious choice for the post of General Secretary. Neelima Khetan, after having worked in another NGO, joined us in 1985. She had an exceptional academic record and also a broad vision on rural development. She was a worthy professional from the Institute of Rural Management, Anand (IRMA). All I could do was to let such people feel the freedom of innovation and evoke response from the people. Voluntarily, they became examples of the code of conduct which the NGO sector had to demonstrate in the national democratic progress.

We had many visitors. I remember taking Derek Bok, a former President of Harvard, and his wife Sissela, sociologist and philosopher, daughter of Gunnar and Alva Myrdal (both Nobel Laureates), to a village in Jhadol where there was a functioning gobar gas plant (fermented cow dung gas). The visit was followed by a dal-and-bati lunch. But I noticed that Sissela did not eat at all. This was surprising since all of us were hungry. However, in the evening, we realized that it was because of my confusing explanation: she thought that we kneaded gobar with the wheat flour. I clarified that though we Indians worship cows, we do not allow contamination in the food with their droppings!

Even during the Emergency, despite Intelligence suspicions, Seva Mandir always welcomed volunteers who wanted to understand and work with grass-roots development. We have had upward of 600 volunteers from abroad and over 1000 from different parts of India and their numbers keep increasing.

Soon after I joined as Chief Executive, my first preoccupation was to help Dadabhai Kesrilal plan the celebration of my father's ninetieth birthday that was due in three months. We prepared a list of speakers from among my father's friends who had won distinction in their respective fields. Not one refused, and not one asked for their travelling costs. I inaugurated it with a lecture on 'The Ascendancy of Militarism and the Failure of Diplomacy'. The other speakers—an impressive group—mostly came around 20 April. The list of speakers and their subjects are worth recapitulating: V.V. John (Education and Social Justice); B.K.

Nehru (Ethics in Administration and Public Life); E.P.W. da Costa (Social Justice and Harijan Children); Joseph Allen Stein (Habitat and Environment in 2000 AD); Rajni Kothari (Voluntary Organizations in a Plural Society); Shirley Williams (Democratic Socialism at the Grass-roots); Kuldip Nayar (Regional Identity and National Integration); Nagendra Singh (Law, Peace and the United Nations); Ashis Nandy (Images of the Indian State); Arun Shourie (Secularism, True and Counterfeited); John Kenneth Galbraith (Agriculture and Economic Development).

The lectures were brought out in book form by Somaiya Publications Pvt. Ltd. under the title, *The State in Crisis*. Arun Shourie revealed that it was Dr Mehta's initiative which had got him the Ramon Magsaysay Award for his opposition to the Emergency. The day-long function was attended by many old scouts like Sadiq Ali, Vidya Bhawan Old Boys and also Maharana Mahendra Singh, who recalled Dr Mehta's service with the Mewar government. What everybody remembers was the embrace and reconciliation between my father and Dr Kalu Lalji Srimali.

Ten days after his birthday, my father met all Seva Mandir workers and spoke about his vision that Udaipur or a small place around it could become a Greek City Republic free of hunger, oppression and deceit, where everybody had the right to education and health. In forty years, Seva Mandir has develped a reputation as being a non-corrupt, dedicated voluntary organization. Kaya, its training centre serves other voluntary organizations also. In fact, Kaya looks like a forested island surrounded by barren hills. Seva Mandir is considered a pioneer in development from grass-roots upwards by villages around Udaipur.

Soon afterwards I flew to the UK and Canada, satisfied that Bhai Sahib's meeting with Seva Mandir colleagus was good and that Seva Mandir had not become bureaucratic but would remain committed at grass-roots, and to its old ideals. However, on 25 June, Ajay rang me up informing me of the passing away of my father. I flew back. Trustees were summoned in August and the mantle of president devolved on my shoulder.

Surprisingly elected president of Vidya Bhawan

In 1993, I went to attend a conference in America and on the way back spent a few days in London. I received a telephone call from Arvind Singhal in Udaipur requesting me, rather peremptorily, to get back to India as soon as possible as they wanted my signed consent to stand once again for the presidentship of Vidya Bhawan. The nomination paper had a purposely shortened time limit. I had not known an election was in the offing.

Soon after I reached Udaipur I was visited by Dr Girija Vyas, then a deputy minister in the central government. The purport of her visit, discreetly concealed, was to ask me to withdraw my candidature. I told her that, in an earlier election, Kesrilal Bordia, an eminent educationist, had been defeated, and so I knew I had little chance of being elected, but as an Old Boy of Vidya Bhawan, I was prepared to suffer the same fate. We did not want to make Vidya Bhaan politically partisan. While I was away, twenty docile Udaipuris who had no interest in Vidya Bhawan, and overlooking the constitutional prescription of endorsement of the General Body, had been accepted as members of the Society. The Old Boys, led by Riaz Tehsin, Arvind Singhal and Harish Kapuria, with planned determination were bent on rescuing their alma mater from the doldrums into which it had fallen since my father resigned in 1978. The Old Boys had drawn inspiration from the principles of democracy which were taught to them in school. In the final result, I received one vote more than the required two-third plurality. Riaz Tehsin spontaneously declared that my election promised a resurrection for Vidya Bhawan.

Understanding the ugly legacy: tactful rectification

I will not elaborate on the reasons for the deterioration of Vidya Bhawan, but it was evident that, in 1993, the problems of Vidya Bhawan were far worse than those I had found in Seva Mandir in 1985. With the responsibility for both Seva Mandir and Vidya Bhawan Society (and its many institutions) that I had in 1993–94,

I decided to inform the LBJ School at the University of Texas that I would not be able to come back to teach even for one semester a year. I knew it would require many-sided and protracted efforts to restore Vidya Bhawan, with its extensive reach, to its earlier purposefulness. The task involved not just reversing many vicious decisions taken in the interim period, but also replacing many members of the executive as they had constitutional legitimacy, and some heads of institutions who had long tenures.

I got an opportunity to make a dramatic beginning. My election was on 12 July 1993 or 1994? The annual Sajjangarh ascent to the Palace on the highest hill in the valley had been a school tradition but it had been abandoned for many years. Despite the short notice, I decided that on 21 July we would go up again and hold an assembly of all Vidya Bhawan institutions. This would remind the staff and the students that as president I was now going to sweat literally and figuratively, and seek cooperation to climb the hill of old idealism.

I also announced that the practice of having a ten-day open air session, for which Vidya Bhawan had become famous, would be resumed. Similarly, as had been the original practice, now in alternate years, the anniversary function would be held, and a particular theme or a historic personality would be chosen to give meaningful cohesion to the senior, junior and nursery schools and other institutions. We had rejoiced in nature and history and I urged all classes and institutions to participate and learn through old experience. I contacted the Chief Minister, Ashok Gehlot, who kindly agreed to preside over the next anniversary function. I emphasized that, while the institutions had autonomy, they must have a sense of belonging to one Vidya Bhawan family.

The decisions which I took lay in the jurisdiction of the president but there were other questions which were not as easy to resolve because they had constitutional backing. To overcome long-entrenched resistance, one had to proceed tactfully to carry the sceptical staff with the new dispensation. I found that the applications of seventy Old Boys for life membership, supported by necessary advance payment, had been pending for a long time, but in the meanwhile the entrance fees had gone up; so I ordered the return of the money and requested each to apply afresh. A further 150 Old Boys' applications which had been set aside for no reason, were scrutinized by a committee as to whether, under the prevailing rules, the applicants qualified for the membership of the General Body. Some were rejected, but a sufficient number qualified, and that changed the complexion of the whole body. Therefore, when the stipulated period of the hostile members of the executive expired, they were not re-elected. No one, however, was ejected as that would have led to judicial appeals.

Vidya Bhawan: rescuing a fallen icon of voluntarism in education

I had to work hard and take some difficult decisions. The Polytechnic was separated from the main Rural Institute, ending an old feud. For the selection of a new head, I called distinguished educationists from outside Udaipur who commanded national respect. I sought the understanding and sympathy of the Education Secretary of the Rajasthan government, including approval for the maximum of the grade for the new Organizing Secretary, as his wife was working in Seva Mandir. He also allocated the establishment of a Primary School Teachers Training Centre as our vocational centre had closed down along with the one run by the state, but we had to find alternative jobs for the staff. Some old features of Vidya Bhawan, of course, could not be restored. The teachers resisted the idea of returning to a whole-day curriculum with compulsory team games, and homework being supervised in the school itself by the class teachers. The teachers had got accustomed to afternoon tuitions; the hostellers, however, were encouraged to use the playing grounds regularly.

I discouraged ulterior pressure on selection and promotion. Administrative decisions were based on open reasoning and so the old values were slowly restored.

Vidya Bhawan had a pioneering tradition. In 1954 in an official documentary, it was listed as one of the five notable public schools of India. The others were Doon, Scindia, Lovedale and Lawrence, but they all charged high fees and largely served the middle-class while Vidya Bhawan was the only one affordable by the poor. The old aims were built into the constitution but they had been ignored in practice when Dr Kalu Lalji Srimali was made the administrator of the society. He was made a deputy education minister in the central government. For a while, his affinities to Vidya Bhawan remained firm as for example, entrusting the establishment of the Rural Institute and the Polytechnic to his old institution. But over time, he developed the arrogance of political office. After Maulana Azad passed away, he was promoted to minister of state with independent charge of education. After being relieved under the Kamaraj Plan, he was Vice-Chancellor of Benaras University and later, Mysore University.

But he had got estranged from my father who, earlier, had been his acknowledged mentor. He resigned as trustee of Seva Mandir, and by the seventies when he returned to Udaipur, he had distanced himself from Vidya Bhawan.

I found that there were some fifteen or twenty legal complaints pending in court, filed by Vidya Bhawan staff against alleged wrongs. Little things had been done, which had a snowballing impact on the return to a principled approach.

Constitution modification

My real fear was that Vidya Bhawan might once again be taken over, and to prevent that, we required not just rationalizing the membership but also a constitutional amendment. For two years I consulted everybody within the institution and also outside it about my proposal, and finally got the new constitution unanimously passed. The membership was restricted to 400, to be reviewed every five years. The constitution also provided for a paid rector and an educational advisor. The aims and objectives were unchanged but the presidential choice would be by open candidature and had to be on the recommendation of the board, which would then be considered by the executive where a two-third majority would be necessary. The term of the president was increased to five years, and he could be re-elected for a second term. While retaining the president's functions as the chief executive, he could live outside and use the rector or the organizing secretary as the implementing functionary.

The other significant innovation was to ensure that the different institutions, while remaining autonomous, would all consider themselves complementary to each other.

Dr Mohan Sinha Mehta Memorial Trust and the Centenary Celebrations

After Dr Mehta passed away, a spontaneous proposal to have a memorial to his life and purposes did not fructify immediately since there were some objections. When I was elected president, I put the idea to the board of control, who readily agreed and a legal MOU was signed between Dr M.S. Mehta Trust and Vidya Bhawan for leasing a small area directly opposite Seva Mandir and in line with Sajjangarh. The trust has now become active as a forum for many voluntary organizations and a platform for lectures by those specially invited or casually visiting Udaipur.

In the absence of a building, the Dr Mohan Sinha Mehta Trust has made habitable the basement of the Vidya Bhawan Teachers College auditorium. The spruced-up basement is open to tea or coffee for visitors. It also provides a weekly forum for voluntary organizations to describe their work and to seek wider awareness and participation.

The first major opportunity to advertise that Vidya Bhawan, like Seva Mandir, had turned over a new leaf was the centenary of 'Bhai Sahib' in 1995. Two thousand villagers from the blocks of Seva Mandir came for two nights and slept in Vidya Bhawan's verandas. During the day, under a pandal, sometimes under trees in the campus, we discussed current issues. There was an exhibition of photographs and thoughtful lectures on subjects like civil liberties, gender equality and education and local self-government. The culmination was when Sadiq Sahib, one of the first boy scouts inangurated Bhai Sahib's statue.

I am connected with various other voluntary organizations in Udaipur, an important one being Jheel Sanrakshan Samity (JSS) of which I have been president for ten years. It is through my pleading on behalf of Udaipur citizens that our city was included in the Planning Commission's Lake Conservation Plan and an allocation of Rs 150 crore was made. Alas! The District Administration has excluded the cooperation of a non-official body like JSS and of the people. Our fear is that the allocation will be diverted by corruption to facilitate contracts on beautification while the lakes themselves are drying and are covered with filth.

Reinforcing grass-roots democracy on the founder's memory and revising the educational syllabi and lectures

In 1993–94, the seventy-third and seventy-fourth amendments to the Constitution were finally passed, giving a third tier of democracy to the country. No such provision exists in the constitution of any other country. I felt that we should establish an institution which could help to make it a success. On a visit to Delhi I mentioned the idea, which appealed to the visiting Council of Europe Commissioner for Human Rights. We established the Vidya Bhawan Institute of Local Self-Government and Responsible Citizenship in the guest house built by the Old Boys. In 1997 I wrote a pamphlet on 'Why Citizenship?' We have been conducting a six-day capacity-building programme ever since.

The Panchayati Raj institution has proved a huge success. Subsequent to its founding, some 320-odd six-day trainings have taken place, an average of two every month. Since it was established in 1997, the voting percentage has steadily improved. In the last one, Udaipur district jumped from fifteenth to be the first among all thirty-two districts of Rajasthan. After the grant from the EU expired, we have received support from Sir Dorabji Tata Trust. Twelve publications have been brought out by the institute, including a training manual, which is in great demand all over the Hindi belt. Women's participation has steadily increased and the total averages 40 per cent. They no longer come with their spouses or with their faces covered in veils. Most women sarpanches and wardpanches, it would seem, are more conscientious than their male counterparts. In just over ten years, some 7500 elected democrats have gone through the portals of this institution. It has been a promising beginning and so, in 1998, I was able to persuade PM Atal Bihari Vajpayee, accompanied by Bhairon Singh Shekhawat, then Chief Minister of Rajasthan, to come and bless Vidya Bhawan and give encouragement to this democratic initiative during their visit to Udaipur. I was glad to go to nearly 300 functions and get confirmation that what they learnt of their power and responsibilities had never been explained to them before.

We now have an Educational Centre, which under the direction of Dr H.K. Dewan is engaged in advising various state governments in revising their text books. It is receving support from the Azim Premji Foundation for its modern rise of approach.

In 1999 I completed six years as president of Vidya Bhawan. This was the limit prescribed in the constitution when I was elected. Though I was urged that legally I could continue on the basis of the new constitution, I insisted on giving up the post. As earlier stated, constitutionalism is at the heart of good voluntarism. A.C. Wadhawan who had known my father, was persuaded to take on the baton. He and Parvati Wadhawan were sympathetic to the aims of Vidya Bhawan. I handed over at Sajjangarh on 21 July 2000.

Voluntarism and India's future

For the seventy-fifth anniversary of Vidya Bhawan, I was asked to write a pamphlet, which I did under the title 'Responsible

Citizenship through Voluntarism in Education'. Narrowing the rich and poor divide was the original rationale of Vidya Bhawan, and now with disaffected terrorism getting internationalized. Vidya Bhawan can proudly claim that it is again propelled by its old ambitions. PM Manmohan Singh, accompanied by the Governor (now President) Pratibha Patil, kindly agreed to come for the occasion. The PM acknowledged that there were few institutions with such a steady commitment to quality education for the poor.

However, it is a difficult haul for institutions like Vidya Bhawan to remain free of political or corporate allegiance. After Independence, without request, we too became subject to uniform government regulations for non-governmental organizations; the pay structure of the government was applied to all aided institutions. This hiked our financial obligations and diluted our sense of pioneering and sacrifice. Since we only got partial aid, the enforcement of the Sixth Pay Commission with 40 per cent increase in staff salaries, and the judicial decision that uniform terminal benefits were obligatory even though they had not been promised at the time of recruitment, had a devastating effect on honest voluntary institutions like ours. In a democracy, there ought to be philosophical support for voluntary institutions which have a record of pursuing national constructive goals.

I may well be the only former Foreign Secretary who wrenched himself away from the corridors of power and came back to the place where I was born. These days my preoccupation is to build an Environmental Education Centre on the edge of the 'Beed' belonging to Vidya Bhawan, where boys and girls and even elders could spend a night or two without electric lights, feel the silent majesty of forests and wake up to birdsongs. We need to curb national selfishness and persuade the 'aam aadmi' (the ordinary citizens) to help 'Save the Earth' for our children. This would require the assistance and persuasion of worldwide voluntarism.

While the State has the primary responsibility for law and order enabling the right to education, health, shelter, safe drinking water, etc., and the market, now liberalized, is the catalyst to spur economic growth, the responsibility of ensuring a just democracy hinges on the activism of unselfish voluntary effort. Much has gone wrong in India, but largely because we did not realize that both power and responsibility devolved on our shoulders after Independence. We must find the correct blend for good governance and ensure better grassroots development. On the midnight of 14 August, Nehru's tryst with destiny was nothing more than a call to stop being a scapegoat.

19

Professionalism in Diplomacy: Bouquets and Brickbats

Apart from farewell dinners, diplomacy has its own special rituals. Each head routinely contributes a share and most must have several souvenirs of their posts. For juniors, however, such functions are optional. I wrote a parody for the farewell dinner for Martin (subsequently knighted) and Mary Ewans, when he was just a Deputy. I called it, 'Our Excellencies' Road to Samarkand'—with due apologies to James Elroy Flecker (*The Golden Journey to Samarkand*).

> 'We who, with cocktails and champagne, hawk our professional wares
> And swear that our bad livers are sacrifices to our nation's glory;
> We diplomats with our plenipotentiary titles and protocol airs
> What shall we claim at the end of our wandering story?
> We have sported bowler hats to conform to Whitehall's Establishment fashions
> And equally denounced the imperial colonialists with revolutionary zest.
> We have solemnly toasted full one hundred and thirty leaders
> And for a lifetime peacocked abroad as a cross between the country's flag and its crest.

What shall we remember? Not the protocol, the banquets
   and the proud pretensions,
But the friends we encountered, and never let go their traces.
The undoubled slams of our nightly distraction
And the trophies that the Martins monopolized at the Yacht
   Club Races.'

I am now past eighty-seven. After a life unusually rich with experience, I would like to leave behind honest thoughts to make India great—economically prosperous, distributionally just and morally respected. I do not know whether I will be around when, after editorial scrutiny, this story is published. It may evoke some plaudits, but more likely, I will not escape criticism. I am persuaded that the incidence of great power wars is less likely, and ideological agnosticism and principled non-alignment will remain universalized. However, the shadow of history will remain, and this will lead to the continuation of extravagant preparations for the next war. It would distort the world economy and could come in the way of the new dangers of global warming and terror. Democratic India has unique assets but whether they can be marshalled may hinge on professional diplomacy.

In diplomacy immediate reactions must not complicate long-term vision

Diplomacy is different from the perspective of politicians (who have only a five-year perspective); also from other civil services, where most decisions do not have to reckon with other sovereignties; historians and analysts tend to depend largely on hindsight and the nearest past parallel; and from journalists who are concerned only with instant sound bites or the next morning's headlines. Professional diplomacy requires grasping the past, present and future. He must understand the immediate situation; but it must overcome an adversary's prejudice and never compromise the long-distance solution. I have often recalled Wordsworth's poem 'Ode to Duty', in which which he qualified duty as 'Stern Daughter of the Voice of God'. I would interpret 'duty' as the promptings of a conscience, 'Who art a Light to guide, a Rod to check the erring, and reprove.'

Bouquets and brickbats are likely in the call of duty and I have had my share of both, but neither despair nor drift is satisfying in the long run.

Personal experience of trust

I had sensed empathy when senior officers tried me out as Under Secretary (Administration) in a decision-making seat. The 'reward' was the last-minute change of posting from Bonn to Bern by the Prime Minister himself. This had reinforced my confidence. The Suez Conference in August 1956 gave me a sense of 'the last hurrah' of the British empire. I learnt a lesson that the real crux of international affairs is not to live in the past but to look ahead in order to be constantly contemporaneous.

While accompanying Nehru on an election tour, I realized India's good fortune in having a man of humanity, education and dedication at the helm, but also that hero-worshipping is not always democratic; it still requires to be supplemented by the courage of dissent, which was shown by the people of Kerala.

When I accompanied the Vice-President to China, I had my first suspicions that China did not quite understand the functioning of India's parliamentary democracy. We had all but recovered from the old anti-imperialism and had chosen a system that permitted divergence, that did not smother 'a hundred flowers' from blooming. It also gave me an insight that our own senior officers were prone to 'local-itis' and to shirking from professional objectivity.

The PM's historic visit to Bhutan

Nehru's visit to Bhutan was possibly the greatest foreign policy legacy of his prime-ministership. If he had not gone in September

1958, he (or any other PM) may never have been able to go to the country. I have speculated that, but for Panditji's personal diplomacy, Bhutan would have been Tibetanized; the road from Phuntsholing would never have been built; the Chukha project (which enabled the transporting of heavy construction equipment) would not have been commissioned; tourism might have been only through Tibet. Bhutan is now on the way to becoming a democracy and that too, voluntarily with the king delegating much of his own powers as an absolute monarch. India and Bhutan are a model for relations between neighbours of unequal size and strength, united through having chosen democracy.

Professional counsel was not allowed to reach the PM; it may or may not have changed history but it was unasked

I wrote a paper on India's relations with China during Christmas 1959 but it never reached its intended recipient, which was the PM. I made bold to argue that the crisis was bigger than merely a boundary dispute. I now regret that I did not politely prod the Foreign Secretary into forwarding the paper. I do not know if my paper would have evoked a change of assessment, but professionally I had done my duty.

During the Nehru–Zhou talks in 1960 we, the 'experts', were confined to an anteroom downstairs. The Foreign Secretary should have advised against his own and our exclusion.

In my book*I have described the potentially fatal political consequences—including for Panditji himself—if he had swallowed the innocent-looking Six Points put forward by Zhou at the sixth meeting, describing it as a 'dispute'. Obstreperously I kept saying it was a 'claim'. I suspect Panditji only grasped the difference during the ten-minute drive from Maulana Azad Road to Teen Murti House. If Panditji had accepted that it was a 'dispute', his own statements and our subsequent arguments would have collapsed.

*Jagat S. Mehta, *Rescuing the Future* (Manohar: 2008) 271–278

We were very happy when eventually we got a map of China, as it implied that they had accepted traditional borders before formal delimitation. I mention all this to show that we were left to devise our own arguments. Right or wrong, S. Gopal and I gave a map defining India and got a signed map of China.

One of the most momentous decisions of my career was to show the rough draft of my final statement to Panditji on the eve of our departure for Rangoon. This enabled me to charge the Chinese with flouting the principles of Peaceful Coexistence.

The Forward Policy was the Intelligence Bureau's strategy of establishing isolated posts in the Aksai Chin area to 'fill the vacuum'. Had we had a shrewder understanding of China, we would not have been surprised and humiliated.

I came to the conclusion that the only 'ally' America had when facing defeat in Vietnam, was the Soviet Union! America was surprisingly dense not to have seen through the significance of the publicized visit of Kosygin to Hanoi. When I met Ambassador Kaul in Ulan Bator in July 1964, besides disagreeing on the state of Sino-Soviet relations, he pooh-poohed the suggestion that with competitive influence, the Soviet Union may decide to give arms to Pakistan. It did so in 1968.

Professional innovation may be a duty

I must record my gratitude to Mrs Gandhi that she herself never told me that she had expected Bhutto to come to Delhi to sign the MOU which I had signed in Islamabad.* She showed statesmanship in understanding the political difficulty of her adversary—an essential ingredient in successful diplomatic negotiations.

In making the Indo-Pakistan normalization comprehensive in 1976, I had stretched but not gone against my discretion as the designated envoy. I certainly had no authority to place a deadline of two months for the restoration of all severed links, but this dramatic innovation was in keeping with the spirit of normalization of

*Jagat S. Mehta, *Rescuing the Future* (Manohar 2008: 2008) 271–278

relations. It contributed to changing the entire climate of public opinion in Pakistan, and facilitated us in the crises which followed in the next few months.

In handling the aircraft hijack in August 1976, Mrs Gandhi had left it to officials to 'manage' the episode. It was better professionalism in that we got Pakistan officials involved against known pro-Pakistanis, so that they helped India to get back the aircraft and the passengers without any compromise of principles. (This is in striking contrast to the sluggish decision-making in the case of the hijacking of IA 814 in 2000).

It may be professionally justified to appropriate decision in national interest

It is, of course, a professional hazard to appropriate decision, even in a situation which has time constraints, as in the Raghunath–Vijay episode. It was essential to use one's judgement about wayward decision-making at the Peking end to safeguard national honour, but perhaps it was also essential to obtain permission from a senior to escort the Chinese envoy back to his embassy or to get him to make an undignified jump over the boundary wall. I had had to act similarly as the intimation that we received around 4.30 p.m. of a Chinese aircraft unilaterally threatening to violate our air space the next morning because it required a prompt reaction. I have no regrets for having taken precautions independently without observing normal procedures. In a hypothetical contingency, delay could have meant escalation or at least needless humiliation.

Professionalism always demands foresight

If the 1971 emancipation of Bangladesh had taken place in 1960, the Farakka Dam for diversion into the Hooghly would never have been politically even conceived. The Farakka barrage was really beggaring the neighbour—an example of policy without vision.

Our consolation, was getting the item dropped from the General Assembly agenda of the UN.

I acted professionally when I persisted in recommending bifurcation of the umbrella treaty with Nepal as it was a blot on Nepal's sovereignty.

Advising Vajpayee to visit Islamabad as Foreign Minister and his persistence as Prime Minister in 1999

The boldest professional initiative that I ever recommended was urging A.B. Vajpayee, an old Jansanghi, to go to Islamabad. Vajpayee's visit in 1978 has been the turning point in India–Pakistan relations. Even more credit goes to him for continuing the initiative as PM with the bus journey to Lahore in 1999.

A career naturally rich in souvenirs

Romping around the world and that too, as a diplomat, gives one unusual opportunities to pick up souvenirs, which sometimes are truly special. In writing one's story, there is an irresistible desire to advertise verbal or physical mementoes.

Some souvenirs are small but historic. In September 1960, when the entire official Chinese team came to our little flat in the Diplomatic Enclave and signed my guestbook, I was told that it was the first time that any Chinese diplomats had gone to a private house in Delhi. I treasure the 1977 Kremlin banquet menu card signed by Brezhnev, Kosygin and members of the Politburo in the Hindi section; it is individual and therefore more valuable than the signed book from Carter which was delivered after he had left.

There are, of course, more permanent souvenirs. Behind my desk in Udaipur are a few special photographs; Nehru in Bhutanese dress which he signed in Hindi, adding the words, 'Jagat ko'. I have not seen another photograph of Nehru signed in Hindi.

I also have a photograph of the heads of all non-aligned missions signed by about forty heads in Colombo in 1976. There is one of the last photographs of Kenneth Galbraith sitting on his favourite chair. The most valuable is that of the first Indo–US Cultural Agreement being signed by Panditji and US Ambassador Loy Henderson with Maulana Azad looking on, with the Joint Secretary, and the Deputy Secretary, and Rama as Under Secretary (America). I also have many photographs of world leaders. Fidel Castro is on one of the walls and on another, photos of the various negotiations in which I was involved including that with Idi Amin.

I have kept a guestbook since my first posting which has thousands of 'dhobi' marks of persons who came to my parties. Some left with flattering remarks. They are all reminders of an exciting life abroad and in India. These books also have thumb impressions of my children when they were toddlers. My most prized souvenir is that of Charlie Chaplin's signature, when I had brought him to meet Pandit Nehru in Burgenstock in 1953. He drew his famous floppy boots along with crooked walking stick! That itself is worth a whole career. The next page has the signature of Tenzing Norgay, one of the first two ever to climb Mount Everest. Gopalaswami Ayyangar, then Defence Minister, during a break in discussions in Geneva on the Kashmir question, had dinner with us when I was the Chargé. The delegation included D.P. Dhar, General Thimayya, V. Shankar and B.L. Sharma. Dr Radhakrishnan as Vice-President had come for a meal after attending the UNESCO Board Meeting in Paris.

My guest book is enriched with the signatures of Amartya Sen, V.S. Naipaul, Marti Artissaria, Joseph Stiglitz and Henry Kissinger—all of whom got Nobel Prizes. But I know these were rewards of being in the Indian Foreign Service.

My father was High Commissioner in Karachi, and Rama's father was a UP civilian and they both knew Nawabzada Liaquat Ali Khan. Rama and I were touched when, in 1953, Begum Ra'ana Liaquat Ali Khan, the widow of the first PM of Pakistan, along with her two sons and a secretary, insisted on staying in our flat with its single bathroom, preferring it to an invitation from the British Ambassador in Bern.

I felt privileged to meet with memorable leaders. Baba Amte came to Seva Mandir, planted a tree in Kaya and blessed our NGO.

Siddharth Daddha named the meditation centre in Kaya Mohan Kunj because it carried the first name of both Mahatma Gandhi and my father.

While I was going in and out of academic institutions, I also went to Ditchley House where Churchill used to spend the night when he did not want to be in his Cabinet War Room bunker in Whitehall. During the same visit, I had dinner at All Souls College, Oxford where Robert Wade-Gery wanted me to become a Fellow. It was overruled on the grounds that I was over seventy years but it was an honour even to be considered.

I have heard some colleagues confess that they did not tender honest advice as they were not asked to do so, but it is implicit in our long tenures, where all instances of professional duty need to be honest but, at the same time, never renege on the vision for the long term. I took risks in higher civil service but not in perceived national interests.

Prime Ministerial 'Shabashi' (Encouragement)

Ambassador Gharekhan revealed only last year (in 2008)—I had never heard it before—that the then Foreign Secretary, Rajeshwar Dayal, had told him, 'The UN members led by the US do not know that we have a secret weapon—Jagat Mehta.' This could have been no more than good humour!

Despite my grandchildren's justification in criticizing me for vanity, I cannot but recall some of the encouraging remarks which gilded my career. PM Nehru, in February 1961, while presenting our official report to Parliament, paid a warm tribute to S. Gopal and me for our six-month-long exertions—the most intense in diplomacy with China—when we had improvised to the best of our ability in defence of the frontiers of India.

What I cherish most is a note dictated, *suo moto*, by PM Lal Bahadur Shastri on 24 September 1965, the day after the Indo-Pakistan ceasefire. He asked the Foreign Secretary to convey his gratitude and appreciation for my volunteering the analysis that the Chinese ultimatum was for political purposes only and at midnight, when it was due to expire, it would not be translated into any military action. Like George Kennan's 'Long Telegram' from Moscow in 1946, warning of Stalin's Cold War postures. I had tried at length to explain the logic of China–Pakistan relations. Senior officers in MEA, the Defence Ministry and the general staff were expecting a second front would be opened in Sikkim or NEFA. The telegram was sent against the advice of all my colleagues and I knew I was staking my reputation and career, but I felt I was doing my duty. I learnt afterwards from L.P. Singh, who was then Home Secretary, that the PM was quite amazed that I had had the courage to send the message before being asked for my assessment. When I met the PM two weeks later in his office, he got up and embraced me for what he thought was exemplary professional duty. Shastri added that the safest thing for me would have been to remain silent and, at best, prepare for the consequential action in the Embassy.

I must also take the bold liberty of reproducing the remarks by Manmohan Singh, when he was leader of the Opposition and came to have dinner in our house in Udaipur (17 October 2003). It would be churlish to pretend that I did not feel honoured. 'What a great sense of joy I experience visiting Jagat in his home grounds. He has been a role model for many of us. My best wishes for his continued good health and happiness.'

A.B. Vajpayee kindly gave me four volumes of his speeches (19 October 2004), with the inscription, 'To the professor of international politics and successful diplomat, Shri Jagat Mehta, with whom I have spent memorable and happy times.'

I am also tempted to quote the first paragraph of PM Manmohan Singh's speech when, in 2006, he kindly launched my book, *Negotiating for India*.

'I have learnt a great deal from Jagat and it is my proud privilege to acknowledge that fact. Jagat is the quintessential civil servant, outstanding diplomat, complete patriot and thorough professional. The likes of him are not found everywhere and blessed is the land which has given birth or nurtured men of his vision, men of his integrity and men of his courage.'

All this may signify occasional poor judgement in high places but, nevertheless, one feels flattered by the recognition. It confirms that in a democracy, honest opinion in national interest has its own reward, and spurs civil service integrity: 'to thine own self be true.'

Brickbats

Let me, however, also confess honestly to some brickbats, which came my way.

Being summarily removed from the post of Foreign Secretary was humiliating and unwarranted. Even now I see it as a left-handed recognition of my independence. Obviously they did not know that the only country which suggested to me to come as ambassador was the USSR, but conventional wisdom said that I was pro-America. To remove somebody who was not known to be pro-Soviet Union would, it was believed, automatically yield dividends to the party in power! As I say in the next chapter, wishfulness on Russia has been one of our worst professional failures. I am not ashamed of being prematurely defrocked.

I should never have persisted with my candidacy for the position of Commonwealth Secretary General, but the real brickbat was not personal—it was a matter of policy. On Afghanistan, if I had continued for another six weeks, I would have been in a position to offer my advice to the re-elected PM, Mrs Gandhi. India remained marginalized and could play no constructive role for the next twenty-one years. We could return to Afghanistan only after 9/11. Thankfully, our aid has not been military. The present Pak–US relations are a monument to Cold War fallacies, and Afghanistan is, in my view, one of the greatest avoidable blunders of the twentieth–twenty-first century.

The results are national, regional and global. The challenge is to blend national and planetary interests. We diplomats are not just national civil servants but also world citizens.

National gains and penalties of diplomacy

In my experience, in independent India, the crucial role of MEA has all too often been downgraded, and we have tended to go by the projections of the military and the intelligence organizations. There is a fundamental difference in the institutional approaches of these agencies. For the military, it is understandably essential to have 'an enemy', the preparations are based on capability calculus and, after the start of operations, the aim is unconditional surrender. For the intelligence organizations, the assessment is that the hostility of the adversary is permanent, and so, large-scale covert efforts are made to undermine the strength of the hostile power. Diplomacy, however, has always been a matter of negotiated compromise for reasonably safeguarding national interests. It has become even more important because of nuclear weapons. However, we tend to be conditioned by the worst-case scenario of history. We do not consider the fact that, following the information revolution, we have o take into account the unprecedented national sensitivities of small countries with their immense capacity for defiance. MEA, in pursuit of diplomacy, has to strike a balance between military and intelligence aims and the economic imperative of maximizing growth. Many of our envoys were imprisoned by the past and tended to rely on size and firepower, discounting people's rising consciousness.

The old habit of adversarial suspicion has continued between India and Pakistan even after there was a sea change in governmental approaches. With the overlap of the Cold War, non-alignment accustomed us to a kind of blackmail leverage—presuming on the West and tilting towards the East. Professional diplomacy should have corrected this myopia, but often did not.

Constructive diplomacy that involves problem-solving without conflict is not easy but for a democracy there are special difficulties. There are legislatures and public opinion on both sides, and neither side's unilateral interpretation can prevail, even if compromise is deemed preferable. The 'mood' of the country tends to influence governmental thinking and we resort to making excuses. Consequently, we often argue that our flaws and failures were imposed. We should remember how Mrs Gandhi resisted the US threat in 1971. Professionals must not take the media at face value.

There are many examples of professional hesitation in giving advice against public opinion. Our policy suffered by a kind of 'Panditji knows best' thinking. It is true he had a notorious and sometimes frightening bark, but it is also true that it seldom ended in a bite. Decision-making has now become simply career-husbanding and ambivalence. Civil servants have been guilty of showing politicians how to magnify their corruption potential. This is not so frequent in the Foreign Service, but I wish I could say that we have expressed seemingly unpopular views, and objectively reminded the political leaders of the country's long-term interests. We were wrong about China, too wishful over Russia, and not discriminatory on the US. Some colleagues were irrevocably anti-Pakistan; some of our envoys behaved like Viceroys towards our neighbours. Professionally, we must recognize that we contributed to these errors.

Let me mention that the challenge of diplomacy is aggravated when we do not recognize that postponing solutions can be costly. I have recalled my own initiative earlier which led to the resolution of the deadlock on Salal which had persisted for eight years. It probably cost us hundreds of crores in power and, indirectly, in productivity. Let me give another example. I happened to be in Delhi late in December 2001. I had sought an appointment with the then Foreign Minister, Jaswant Singh, but I could not see him as he had been called away by the PM. So I chatted with his Special Assistant, and repeated more or less what I was proposing to say to his chief. I told him that it would be a great mistake if we succumbed to the popular demand for retaliation against Pakistan for the terrorist attack on our Parliament by abrogating the Indus Treaty. (This had been publicly recommended by some of my erstwhile and eminent colleagues.) While four rivers in the Punjab (which are all tributaries of the Indus) originate in India, two (the Indus and the Sutlej) start in Tibet. The Brahmaputra (called Tsangpo in Tibet) like the Indus, rises near Lake Mansarovar. (Many tributaries of the Ganges rise in Nepal while the rivers coming from Bhutan flow into the Brahmaputra). The flow of the rivers makes India an upper riparian but in some cases, a middle or a lower one. In other words, our interest is best served by the consensus of International Law Association that the rights of an upper, middle and lower river, and their present and future potential should be considered all together, not in national compartmentalization. Terminating the Indus Treaty in the exercise of upper riparian rights on some rivers in the Punjab would provide China with legal justification for diverting the main Indus and the Brahmaputra from flowing into the subcontinent with disastrous consequences, including the risk of turning Assam into a near-desert. Also, the upper riparian logic would further delay the availability of hydel power surplus from Nepal.

That night, the Foreign Minister rang me up and thanked me for my input. Apparently, a Cabinet Committee had on its agenda the repudiation of the Indus Treaty as a response to public outcry. Our knee-jerk reaction would have been a disastrous impetuosity. It would incidentally have foreclosed the improvement in Indo–Pak relations, which started after the SAARC communiqué in January 2004, just two years later. It is yet another proof that diplomacy has to have a long-term vision and, at times, override public opinion.

It was a similar professional oversight in MEA to have accepted the proposal—perhaps it emanated from Tamil Nadu or RAW— to send the Indian Peace Keeping Force (IPKF) into Sri Lanka. It alienated Sri Lankans and culminated in the killing of a prime minister, Rajiv Gandhi.

Officers fall into three categories: the first consists of those with ultimate concern for national interest regardless of immediate consequences and who say so whether asked or not; the second category is of those who worry about their careers or, at best, follow orders or answer questions. The third, a largish group falls in between: they give of their best if leadership or directions so demand but in the absence of a positive atmosphere, coast along and pass the buck without taking risks. Ultimately, it is a question of character and values which determine the choice of how you define duty and do not become simply a subordinate lackey.

The only test which I have applied to myself is whether, after forty or fifty years, one can re-read one's own assessment and recommendations and not feel too embarrassed. Obviously the circumstances and the world situation keep changing but the fundamentals of geography, people's welfare and a strengthening civil society must be abiding and permanent for national stability. The nation-state has to get in tune with the present environment and climate change. India should not aim to be an overarmed modern Sparta; a more appropriate purpose would be to imitate Athens which, while adequately armed, had its citizens' confidence in their democracy and by implication, of planetary interdependence. Al Gore calls it 'the inconvenient truth'. My own career may not always have had optimum rewards but it has given me great satisfaction.

20

Why has India underperformed after Independence

Retrieving our standing through diplomacy

India was a pioneer in the long quest for emancipation from European colonialism and self-government. But at rank 132 in the Human Development Index, in social justice, we lag behind many countries which became independent as a result of our having led the way. In 1905, separate electorates were first accepted. The year 1916 is held up as a highpoint in Hindu–Muslim unity. Another moment came during the Round Table Conference in 1931 when India nearly accepted—Mahatma Gandhi was inclined to do so—Dominion Status which would have forestalled the division of an area united by geography and culture. However Nehru, then back from Europe and the Soviet Union, wanted nothing short of complete independence to fashion a progressive future for India. The subcontinent and indeed, world politics, might have been different as it would have stymied the British policy of 'Divide and Rule'.

What followed may be briefly recalled. Provincial autonomy was embodied in the 1935 Act, but federal integration—incorporating the 'native princely states'—could not take place because of the declaration of World War II. Following the sweeping Congress victory in the polls in 1937—and the example of Westminster single-party rule—coalition governments were not tried in the provinces. The Nazi victories on the continent created overweening anxiety in Whitehall. In 1940, the 'Pakistan Resolution' was passed by the Muslim League. The Americans, however, continued to press HMG to broaden the war effort and make it 'our kind of war' for democracy. The Cripps Mission (1942) followed but it failed to reach an agreement with the Congress. The Quit India resolution meant that Gandhi and other Congress leaders spent the war years in jail. In 1946, a Cabinet Mission sponsored by the Labour Party made efforts to keep India united. A Congress-led interim government was formed in September and the Constituent Assembly started its deliberations in December, pledging that India would be a Sovereign Democratic Republic. The three-leader negotiations were held in London in December 1946, but they too, could not hammer out an agreement. Finally on 20 February 1947, British PM Attlee announced the appointment of Mountbatten, 'as the last Viceroy with authority' to transfer power to responsible Indian hands not later than June 1948. After his arrival in March 1947, Mountbatten held a round of consultations with the Indian leaders. On 3 June Mountbatten announced the preponement of the transfer of power to 15 August 1947. A wholly unexpected holocaust ensued, with twenty million involved in two-way migration and about 5,00,000 killed, in the first months after the dominions of India and Pakistan were created.

However, some facts have not received sufficient attention in the mountains of literature on the Independence of India and Pakistan. On 21 February—the day after Attlee's announcement—the same British government informed the State Department in Washington that it would not be possible for it to redeem the pledge voluntarily given by Churchill as PM at Yalta in 1945 that in the post-war dispensation, the UK would undertake to support the governments of Greece and Turkey (and incidentally, Libya), which lay astride the route to much of the British Empire. Considering the alarm with which the US regarded Soviet military might and ideological global intentions, the British statement implied that the US would have to take over the burden being vacated by HMG if the 'Containment' Policy of the West announced in the Truman Doctrine, was to be implemented. The US had never before given aid except during an ongoing war. When the Democratic Administration urged, the proposal met with reluctance as the Republican Party was committed to returning to pre-war 'isolationist' normalcy. However, after sustained persuasion of the US Congress, two days after Mountbatten's announcement preponing the transfer of power in the subcontinent, in George Marshall's Harvard commencement address, in June 1947, the 'Marshall Plan' was announced.

The coincidence, between Mountbatten's announcement and the Marshall Plan, was accidental but it led to escalation of the Cold War and confrontation between NATO and Warsaw Pact-dominated politics for the next forty years. As a result, the process of decolonization initiated by the Labour government was subordinated. The advent of Weapons of Mass Destruction had also heightened alarm as their destructive capacity exceeded all previous weapons of war. Moreover, a civil war was raging next door to the subcontinent, but there is little mention of this development in China in the literature of the period. This too was surprising as the People's Liberation Army (PLA) would overrun the whole country in two years and change world politics. The combination of these unexpected developments, both positive and negative, was however, interpreted in familiar nineteenth-century analogies.

Let me digress and indulge in some speculation. What if the 'centripetality' around ideology had not coincided with the 'centrifugality' of decolonization? If Jawaharlal Nehru and Sardar Patel had not accepted the preponement to 15 August as announced by Mountbatten, what might have happened? By December 1947, it had become widely known that Jinnah was suffering from terminal tuberculosis. When Gandhiji was assassinated in January 1948 by a Hindu for his efforts to defend Muslim rights, there was visible shock all over Pakistan. I happened to ask Lord Nicholas Mansergh, the editor of the twelve volumes on the transfer of power (*The Transfer of Power, 1942–47*), would Britain have gone ahead with Partition if the crystal ball of HMG had shown the communist victory in China? It would be plausible to argue that if the date of transfer of power had not been changed, there might have been no Partition of India!

I am, of course, discounting the views of people like Sir Olaf Caroe, an expert on the Pathans, and Sir Francis Tucker (Commander-in-Chief of Eastern Command in India until 1947), who were confident that the 'Muslims would be better allies' against the communists than the 'Hindus' who were more sympathetic towards the USSR. But these were all mindsets carried over from the nineteenth century. Lord Salisbury, the British PM, with the self-confidence of an Empire where the sun never set, could claim in the last decade of that century that 'British Foreign Policy was like sailing majestically down the Thames: only occasionally a boat hook was required to avert a small collision.' It reflected a Western arrogance, evident since the Reformation, which was going to be shattered in the post-imperial world. In 2009 such predictions invite only mockery. When I was teaching a post-graduate seminar at the LBJ School in Austin, Texas, my first sentence every year was the same, 'On behalf of the non-existent international guild of Foreign Service officers, we have almost invariably been wrong in the twentieth century in anticipating the future'. The fact of the matter is, in our times, while technology has galloped we, the decision-makers, have been generally on a slow trot, and the gap keeps widening.

Jawaharlal Nehru and, indeed, Jinnah were patriots but both were schooled in European notions of modernization—social justice, industrialization, self-government and institutionalized Westminster democracy. It was predicated on the nation-state as the main actor and did not envisage the rise of people's power. The League of Nations was based on the membership of a handful of states, mostly European. Although the UN Charter starts with 'We the people', it still revolves round the state system. Hiroshima and Nagasaki were the greatest moral outrages in history, but they were supposed to enhance state power. However, so far their use has remained paralysed. The illusion of unmatchable destructive power was also short-lived. Within four years, the USSR had its own atomic explosion and brought about the Mutual Assured Destruction (MAD) strategy. The Cuban missile crisis demonstrated the danger of nuclear war through miscalculation and quickly led to the Partial Test Ban Treaty (1963). It was the first-ever agreement restricting weaponization between adversaries. Although the blocs continued with their sophisticated nuclear armouries, they slowly recognized that they faced a common peril of accidental conflagration, and so they negotiated a broadened approach on non-proliferation (1967–68). However, it incorporated a distinction between the five 'responsible' countries and all the others. When the British carried out their own explosion they made WMD a symbol of 'great power' status and this only provoked competing aspirations. The UK was only extrapolating from the inherited notions that a government must continue preparing for retaliation on the assumption that the 'other side' may yield to nervous impetuosity and initiate a nuclear attack. No one anticipated that war was no longer politics by other means and that Carl von Clausewitz would stand belied so soon.

In fact we have had unprecedented 'peace' amongst the great powers for over sixty years and annihilation has proved the twin child of survival. Strategists are belatedly beginning to recognize the logic of nuclear disarmament. There is an emerging horizontal bipolarity with all governments—democracies and dictatorships, capitalist and communist—developing an unspoken, shared interest in fighting terror as threatened by non-state actors, some of whom even believe that suicide against historic inequities is a justified short cut to Heaven. Thoughtful observers are now conceding that the forty-year Cold War was no more than mutually reinforced paranoia. In 2008, four old American hawks, on a bipartisan basis, urged steps to a nuclear-free world. The competitive universalist ideologies have also got diluted or been nationally domesticated. The technological revolution has not brought about the end of history, but spread political awareness of the inequities and irrationalities like Islam phobia, and revulsion against the abuse of military power, as with the US.

Mahatma Gandhi was unique in his political sagacity. It was not just that he eschewed violence and disarmed hard-headed imperialists by moral persuasion, but that he always had faith in diplomacy for resolving conflict. He always believed that the people were the ultimate repository of power, and that progress would be only through participation and transparency. India's special asset was that despite its continuing social rigidity, its heritage contained the ingredients of tolerance, which is essential to globalization and modernization. Our Constitution embodies the elements of a just, modern, human society as does no other first-generation, post-colonial country. We never accepted the clash of civilization, the superiority of European and Christian experience.

There are many reasons for our underperformance but the root cause was the carry-over of European ideas of the nation-state which overlooked the unique character of South Asia. It is still entrenched in prejudice. Even though there were civil tensions in the domestic body politic resulting from the decolonization of an undivided country, India might have developed more rapidly. Partition was retrograde.

In Nehru's speech on 22 March 1947 at the Asian Relations Conference, there was no mention of the Truman Doctrine although it had been proclaimed days earlier and implied the threat of communism was global. Nehru believed that decolonization and the Cold War would get enmeshed. Had he not done so, he might not have considered Partition as the lesser evil.

The penalty for Partition must run into billions if not trillions of dollars. Partition aggravated Third World militarization and diverted resources from development. The Foreign Policy of both India and Pakistan got conditioned by competition especially in the Muslim and other Third World countries. Let me try to encapsulate the specific consequences which can be traced to, or were prolonged by, Partition.

We know it led to four wars and inculcated the poison of hate which still persists. Interest in prosperity and functional relations between neighbours was shelved. The common Himalayas, the monsoon, the evolved common culture, the southbound flow of rivers and traditional civilizational homogeneity in South Asia were forgotten. Gandhiji and Maulana Azad opposed Partition; but only Aung San, a cabiet minister and independence leader of Burma, on 4 June 1947, the day after Partition was announced, foresaw its terrible consequences. But for Partition, South Asia would have dominated the Indian Ocean, which laps the shores of South-east Asia, the west coast of Australia, the Gulf with its oil production and vital trade, and the east coast of Africa.

Consequences of the self-hypnosis that 'Panditji knows best'

Panditji was the greatest democratic dictator in history, but twelve years of his prime-ministership were largely wasted. He did not realize that he could not be replicated. Of all our PMs, Shastri alone knew how to ask an unloaded question, then take bold decisions and face the consequences. (Alas! his term was too short!). We shall never again have the likes of Nehru and we, the professionals, lacked the courage to offer him timely corrective counsel. Panditji could call one a 'damn fool', but if one stood one's ground, he was willing to change his own opinion in pursuit of the national interest. His bark was frightening but I know of only one case where he ordered disciplinary action, and that was temporary.

Acquiescence in Panditji's misjudgement on China

Panditji's anti-imperialism was the springboard of his greatness and place in history, but he thought that, after the humiliating experience at the hands of the European powers, the communists would appreciate India's non-hostility through non-alignment.

Nehru had raised the question of erroneous Chinese maps in 1956–57 but Zhou had deflected a straight reply by saying they were based on KMT surveys but they would be resolved through India–China friendship. Not seizing this opening was a professional failure in India.

India's wishfulness on the Soviet Union was based on taking its ideological rhetoric seriously

Apart from the pre-war civilizational appeal of socialism, the concept of the Soviet Union as a time-tested friend was based on the presumption of the permanence of the Cold War. We felt obliged to the USSR for the supply of arms, the support for and the veto on Kashmir and Bangladesh, but it was poor professionalism not to note the element of commercialization in its arms and civil supplies, the change of attitude on the India–China conflict during the Cuban missile crisis in 1962, the significance of the Partial Test Ban Treaty (1963), the objective neutrality at Tashkent (1966), and the strong commitment to the Non-Proliferation Treaty (1968). The fact is that we were not prepared for enlightened Soviet neutrality outside the Cold War. We failed to grasp that fundamentally, the USSR was for reconciliation on the subcontinent rather than supporting a counter-tilt against Pakistan.

Afghanistan

European politics mattered only marginally to India, but due to the spontaneous self-denying initiative in 1978, the anxiety in 1979, and following my premonition in January 1980, we lost the respect of Afghan nationalism for twenty-one years. Afghanistan best illustrates the penalties of misjudgements in diplomacy. I have written about Afghanistan at different places, after retirement, starting in 1981. In subsequent developments, and in varying degrees, Brezhnev, Carter, Brzezinski, Zia-ul-Haq, Musharaff and, of course, Hafizullah Amin and Najibullah in Afghanistan, will be blamed in history books. So will G. Parthasarthy (Sr) and T.N. Kaul for wrong advice given to Mrs Gandhi in 1980, and B.K. Nehru for not transmitting the caution of confronting Sanjay.

The misperception on this question became the turning point in regional and global politics as it seeded terrorism. From different Cold War angles, neither the US nor India understood that nationalism was now stronger than military power. Pakistan must now regret being taken in by the US fallacy, which turned a blind eye to the military training of the Taliban and the funnelling of support to the Mujahideen. Osama bin Laden was installed in the caves of Tora Bora by the CIA and with the connivance of Pakistan. In his latest book *Second Chance*, written after 9/11, Brzezinski does not mention that it was US policy which had helped arm Al Qaeda. Nationalist militancy is now bogging down the well armed NATO forces. The people of Pakistan have turned rabidly anti-American. The best Indian analysts also ignored the cost of our falling out of step with Afghan nationals with whom the Congress had been friendly up to 1947.

The US returned to Afghanistan after 9/11 and Pakistan is now considered the epicentre of terrorism. General Musharaff was given an ultimatum by the US President, 'Are you with us or against us?' Having earlier created the Taliban, Pakistan suddenly abandoned them. The Afghan tribals have turned against Pakistan. There can be few other instances of comparable dialectical nemesis in history.

In the eighties I had shown my Texas Conference paper to William Bundy, then editor of *Foreign Affairs*. He had initially evinced interest in publishing it but, eventually informed me that Afghanistan had faded from public attention! When the Conference was held in Austin, it was four months after Tiananmen and a few days before the Berlin Wall was dismantled with pickaxes and nails. A little perspicacity could have given a better insight into the ferment brewing in Eastern Europe which called for greater respect for the people's feelings. One cannot help regretting that our book on the Austin Conference did not come out in 1990 or 1991. If either the article or the book had been published, it might have refocused attention on the crisis developing in the region. India was able to go back to Afghanistan only by going piggyback on the Americans after the attack on the twin towers of the World Trade Center. Fortunately, our present substantial assistance is entirely humanitarian and non-military, but twenty years of 'hate' still manifests itself.

Analysis of 'what might have been'

What follows can neither be proved nor disproved. On the basis of information which is on our records, we should have told Pakistan that the Soviet Union had no intention of invading Pakistan to cut off the oil artery of the Gulf; the purpose was limited to dislodging Hafizullah Amin, who had precipitated the insurgency and alienated the Afghan people by his ideological militancy. Unlike the Prague Spring in 1968, (which was to install humane communism), the Soviet Union intervened in Afghanistan against ideological militancy. There was absolutely no reason to take at face value—as did most of our professionals and non-official intellectuals—the explanation that the CIA had been active in the soft belly of the USSR and so it warranted having recourse to an invasion. (Babrak Karmal, a Soviet puppet after his installation in Kabul, actually revived the practice of religion in the country in 1980.) Functional normalization between India and Pakistan had actually got underway in Mrs Gandhi's time in 1976, and was continued by Morarji Desai's government. Though the LOC was not internationalized at Simla (1972), till 1979 not a single rifle had been dispatched nor had any cross-border violations occurred. In fact, in 1979, Kashmir was moving towards rationalization. (I had urged on PM Morarji Desai in 1978 that the old problem of Jammu and Kashmir was on the way to settlement, but I requested him not to claim it publicly.)

Tensions developed internally in J&K through the eighties but vicious violence only developed in the nineties. The ISI fuelled and armed militants after the breakout in the Valley. Incidentally, there were Afghans with the Pakistani troops in Kargil (1999).

It is also worth recalling that in 1978 Pakistan had been admitted to the non-aligned group. Our objective should have been to keep the whole of South Asia 'non-aligned'. Had we had a little more professional foresight, we could have (at least should have) prevented the remilitarization of Pakistan. The CIA operations to help the Mujahideen and turn it into a Soviet 'Vietnam' were wholly ill-conceived. The Russians did not really withdraw because of the supply of 'Stinger'(homing surface-to-air missiles) or the CIA military help, but because they faced the manifestation of the old Afghan love for their homeland, which flowed from the tradition of fearlessly harassing 'foreigners'. Now, seven years after the NATO operations, Afghanistan still reels under instability. It is financed by narco-terrorism and uses safe routes along the border with Pakistan. There are millions of internal and external refugees, rampant destruction and terrible social problems in the country.

If we assume that the US would still have gone into Iraq and prematurely declared victory, as President George W. Bush did in 2003, the entire scenario of anti-Americanism, which has gripped the people of Pakistan like those in the rest of the Muslim world, may still have emerged. On the other hand, if Afghanistan and Pakistan had been left alone and the Soviets allowed to withdraw as they did in 1989, and India had voted with the non-aligned in 1980, Osama bin Laden may not have gone back to Afghanistan in 1996. It is also plausible that there would have been no Taliban in Afghanistan. Instead of having a confederation with Afghanistan for 'depth security', Pakistan is now deploying half of its army reserves in Waziristan to fight the Afghans. It has forgotten that India alone used to be its enemy! Pakistan might have been saved from being flush with small arms; Siachen hopefully might not have been militarized in 1984; the brigade should have been at least partly withdrawn in 1988. Brzezinski who, as National Security Advisor, advised President Carter that the Soviet Union was a menace to world peace, now appears as one conditioned by a Cold War mindset and, professionally, not an updated one. If we analyse ruthlessly, it all goes back to Partition. In the twentieth century, as the present tensions in South Asia show, there should be better understanding of the coincidence of 'centrifugality' and ideological 'centripetality'.

If only Mrs Gandhi had remained principled and non-aligned, Afghan nationalism would have never been alienated from India; the irrationality of Islam phobia might have been moderated in South Asia; Pakistan would have been saved the humiliation of President Pervez Musharaff being perceived as a dutiful surrogate of the US. While the people in Pakistan have turned anti-American, the process of normalization which was resumed in 2004, when the governments of both India and Pakistan declared that their common interest was in combating terror, might have begun in 1980. Mrs Gandhi would then have had a more honoured place in South Asian annals and world history.

Let me repeat that, while these are all speculations, they had been realistically projected at the time. The rise of terrorism in South Asia can be plausibly traced to the linking of three independent developments—the hostage crisis in Tehran in early November 1979, the Soviet invasion of Afghanistan in December, and our general elections on 3 January 1980—and together, generating a quadrilateral of mistakes by the USSR, the US, India and Pakistan. The twin towers of the World Trade Center may or may not have been attacked, but suffice it to say that the lesson in twenty-first century diplomacy is that it should not be based on knee-jerk, inherited, historical paranoia.

One speculates that if, in 1980, the whole of South Asia had remained non-aligned, cross-border terrorism in Kashmir might not have started. It has cost the Indian taxpayer perhaps fifty billion dollars. Pakistan might not be agonizing whether or not to shoot at an American helicopter in Waziristan! The hypnosis of the Cold War has wreaked terrible needless retribution.

Alienation of neighbours was always bad diplomacy

The fact is Pakistan, Sri Lanka, Nepal and Bangladesh—not Bhutan—look upon India as inclined to exercise hegemonic control over them. SAARC was, in fact, born of the unity of the apprehensions of neighbours of India. There is no greater example of the squandering of permanent and beneficial interdependence in all history as between India and Nepal. Farakka was conceived on the basis of the two-nation theory but the emergence of Bangladesh should have been anticipated. India's relations with its neighbours is its greatest failure in foreign policy.

Nuclear myopia and contradictions

One major misjudgement, at least in my view, has been the virtual retraction of our commitment on nuclear disarmament. We forgot that Nehru was the first to see the dangers of nuclear explosions and shared Gandhi's belief that nuclear weapons would lead to the atrophy of 'great power' militarism, especially if it is divorced from people's well-being. The universality of principles was our special asset, but it was compromised when we found ourselves in a minority of three who stood aloof from the 1968 Treaty. Nehru's anxiety over development and opportunity costs is as valid now as before. Nehru felt that even a partial step towards disarmament, like the Partial Test Ban Treaty, was consistent with our internationalism.

By falling out of step with enlightened internationalism, we have had to make excuses to justify our 'exceptionalism' on disarmament. It is significant that four small democratic countries—Austria, Ireland, Switzerland and New Zealand—at first hesitated to approve the 123 Agreement (between India and the US regarding transfer of technology for civil nuclear energy) in favour of India. Our declared policy of 'No First Strike' has made us vulnerable to the malice of nuclear neighbours. The Chinese will have their own hesitations because of the uncertainty of superpower retaliation. As a poor country, India has overlooked the enormous social agenda confronting it. MEA should, in its professional capacity and competence, advise on the difference between a *possible* and *probable* threat to India.

Canvassing for veto-carrying membership of the Security Council

Professionalism must resist the populist demand for national prestige when success is doubtful. Improvement in our standing has come with our economic growth, which has given us prestige equal to that of some great powers and permanent members. In the fifties, even without a veto, we commanded international respect for our leadership on decolonization, and as an open democracy.

Better governance in the Foreign Ministry

When I was working, we had branches of the EA Ministry scattered in six different locations in Delhi. We have an excellent library and reading room next to Patiala House, but it was seldom used by the senior officers. I could not help believing that, if Nehru had also not been Foreign Minister, long ago, we might have built a low-ceilinged foreign office with an underpass which would not obstruct the view of the main South Block. Nehru probably hesitated because he did not want to appear to be favouring his own Ministry, and we professionals did not tell him that scattered locations caused serious delays, inconvenience and inefficiency.

Nehru could have insisted that after ten or fifteen years of service, by objective selection without involving any politicians, one or two officers from every batch be put on the fast track. The selection would be reviewed, not just for additions but also for subtractions, after five years. All officers, especially the Foreign Secretaries, should be assured of three to five years' tenure, but without expectations of post-retirement cadre appointments. This would ensure integrity and the proffering of independent advice. The Foreign Secretary (and also the Cabinet Secretary) could be nominated senior governors or members of the Rajya Sabha, but they would not be entitled to any cadre appointments at home or abroad. (Purely political appointments with no pension benefit would not fall into this category.) The system of reward should be completely depoliticized so that the low-level nexus between party politics and governmental institutions is ended.

We can retrieve our standing

Having acknowledged that we ourselves have departed from our 'Tryst with Destiny', I still believe that a fresh optimization of our governance and Foreign Policy is not impossible. We must curb the cancer of corruption. We must go back to our civilization's assets and regain confidence in the principled vindication of 'non-alignment'. While we should have confident functional relations with the great powers, we must repose trust in the nationalism of our neighbours regardless of the nature of their domestic regimes. We have to get out of the hypnosis of the intervening overlap of Cold War paranoia and its perceived blackmail advantage. Alexis de Tocqueville discovered that volunteerism was an essential ingredient of functioning democracy and must always supplement the role of the state.

Before World War II, and to some extent even afterwards, the US was the only 'City on the Hill'. In spite of a defence budget of 580 billion dollars—equalling the defence allocations of the rest of the countries put together—political respect for the US has declined round the world. The refusal to sign the Bali declaration and objecting to the Kyoto declaration are the most recent examples of unforgivable national self-righteousness in the face of the new challenge to international environmental interdependence. Contrary to Leslie Gelb's analysis in his recent book, *Power Rules*, power only holds sway if it is combined with social justice for the people.

*Leslie H. Gelb, *Power Rules: How Common Sense Can Rescue Foreign Policy* (Harper Collins: March 2009)

There is hope around the world that the thumping victory of Barack Obama will be a turning point, and that we will see a new 'John F. Kennedy' and this time a black one. In the context of the recent terrorist attack on Mumbai, we should have linked it to show that terrorism is a worldwide phenomenon and not a threat just to India and Pakistan. It has manifested itself in the USA, the UK, Spain, etc. Terrorism poses a threat to all governments favouring orderly development. Indeed, the present financial crisis, though it resembles the Great Crash of 1929, is not confined to the US and Europe but has spread around the world. It is hoped that the emerging consumer economies of Asia, including China and India, will help the recovery.

Barack Obama is striking enlightened blows, but the ingrained American arrogance and unilateralism will require sustained efforts especially in Iraq, Afghanistan, Palestine, etc. No doubt the US remains the strongest economy in the world but, to borrow a phrase from Fareed Zakaria, there must be a change in the equations with the rest. Mahatma Gandhi and Martin Luther King were prophetic in their dreams of the power of the people which is capable of fighting against injustice.

We had reservations towards the US in Nehru's time, but in the post-Nehru period, we flattered ourselves that, after Chile, India would be subverted. We did not realize that our democracy had become well grounded. The elections of 1977 confirmed this. The fear of the CIA undermining the loyalty of Indians was as far-fetched as thinking of members of the communist party as KGB agents! Our greatest and most plausible security threat is internal terrorism, not a nuclear attack by neighbours. The risk must be taken. The Naxalites—the domestic equivalent of the Taliban and the Al Qaeda—must be allowed to enjoy the benefits of democracy which provide a better safety valve than insurgency. We must make much greater efforts—and be seen doing so to reduce effectively the chasm between the rich and the poor.

We should have stuck to our principles of non-intervention in Goa and Sri Lanka, and non-conquest in Sikkim. We should not have fuelled 'Pashtunistan' nor militarized Siachen. (Sustained military operations at that height are considered, even hypothetically, not feasible.) Billions spent in importing fuel would have been saved if our diplomacy had been more sensitive in Nepal. (MEA should have anticipated the disenchantment over the consequences of the flooding of the Terai.) Nepal can prosper like Bhutan with the joint exploitation of its natural resources. Our youthful trained workforce may be sought even in advanced countries, but we must not minimize the challenge; we must ensure a greater focus on primary education and accessible village clinics.

Massive resources will now be needed to build a wall to prevent seawater intrusion into Bangladesh and West Bengal against an environmentally vulnerable coastline posing a danger to East and South Asia. (It might prevent or diminish the threat of twenty million infiltration from the endangered low-lying delta region into the uplands of India, Bangladesh, Bhutan and Nepal.) It is ideal as a combined SAARC project.

My vision, though distant, is not unrealistic. A large regional fund with the Gulf states leading but with India more openly taking a part might end the dependence of Afghanistan on the sale of hashish. Pakistan, on the other hand, could help India to regain the confidence of Nepal and Bangladesh. It could thus dismantle the old anti-India pockets behind terror outrages. We must give Nepal access to Chittagong to prove that being landlocked is not a handicap, and to show Bangladesh can benefit from BIMSTEC (Bay of Bengal Initiative for Multi-Sectoral Technical and Economic Cooperation) and the vast market in India. It all requires diplomacy in recognizing the equality of nationalisms to ease the old and persisting suspicions. The whole of South Asia must graduate to functional relations between independent nations so that one day South Asia can match the European Union.

A further word about China, our neighbour. The Chinese are, no doubt, more diligent, but they have to understand that historical national pride may have to be adjusted to twenty-first century human beings for individual freedom and aspirations to equal fulfilment. The lesson of Tiananmen or the recent upsurge of protests in Tibet and Sinkiang for real autonomy were really a craving for democracy. It is hard for the world to understand why Tibet's autonomy and religious system cannot be accepted when the Dalai Lama has accepted that Tibet is part of China. Tibetan civilization poses no threat to China. India accepted Bhutan's autonomy and even its experiment of institutional democracy. Globalization is not only economic but also political. China cannot, for ever, use the argument of internal sovereignty to suppress democracy and yet use the world as a market for its manufactured wares.

India now has the experience of fifteen general elections and can muddle along positively as only democracies can. The world respects us for producing Gandhiji. We have to demonstrate that we still cherish Gandhi's idea of secularism as embodied in our Constitution. As a principled country we must recognize, the way we did in 1946, that world cooperation is an asset for worldwide peace and that freedom can no longer be compartmentalized.

This is the swansong of somebody whose career started with Indian Independence. I have not glossed over personal disappointments, but I never despaired of the potential of our 'Tryst with Destiny' or our professional diplomacy. We still have many current shortcomings, but in my view, the one overriding weakness has been of us civil servants abdicating the obligation to volunteer advice in the long-term interests of the country. But in the twentieth century, advance in technology has vindicated post-nationalism and climate interdependence.

The future aim for India's policy should be to revert to a pioneering role domestically and in foreign policy. We should remind ourselves that our narrow national interest was not repugnant but coincidental with international moral imperative and planetary health. We should seek to lead in global environmental interdependence and with R.K. Pachauri (and Al Gore) getting the Nobel Prize for work on climate change, we may have the burden of setting an example. Neither Sweden nor Finland has ever voted except with the majority. Also, though within range of nuclear powers, both Sweden and Finland have prophetically believed that social security is a better insurance against possible, but improbable, nuclear attacks in the modern world. Both countries are in the forefront of aiding the Third World and supporting universalist environmental targets. India should be seen as helping to rescue the planet's future. We know that we have 'miles to go', as Nehru read every night from Robert Frost's poem before he slept. Gandhiji constantly chanted *Vaishnav jan to tene kahiye jo pid parayee jane re* (Men of God are those who feel the pain of others). Gandhiji was an Indian. We may have to modify him to modernize him but we must not disown him at home when he is being increasingly respected as a true rationalist of the new century.

Index

Abbas, 220–21, 223, 231
Abdullah, Sheikh, 39
Acharya, B.K., 106
Acheson, Dean, 250
Adenauer, 'Der Alte' Chancellor, 125–27
Adenauer, Max, 126
Administration, 199–209, 251–52
African Liberation Movements, 188
African Survey, 95
Afro-Shirazi Party (ASP), 196
Agate, N.V., 78
Agrawal, Bina, 57
Agreement on Tibet, negotiations for, 104
Ahmed, Mahboob, 43, 124
Ahuja, Vishnu, 211
Aircraft imported probe, 247–48
Ajmani, Jagdish, 211
Akshay Singhji, 12
Albrecht, Madeleine, 39
Albright, Madeleine, 261
Alexander, P.C., 239
Al Gore, 302, 320
Al-Hashmi, 221, 234
Ali, Aruna Asaf, 82

Ali, Asaf, 38–40, 79–82
  death, 80–82
Ali, Sadiq, 11, 278, 284
Ali, Yusuf, 104
Alienation of neighbours, 315
Alirajpur, Surendra, 94
Ali Zaheer, 23
Al-Qaeda, 318
Amin, Hafizullah, 246–47, 311–12
Amin, Idi, 184, 192, 207, 256
Amte, Baba, 296
Annals and Antiquities of Rajasthan, The, 8
Anne-Marie, 173
Arlington, 132
Around the Cragged Hill, 4
ASEAN countries, 244–45
Attlee, Clement, 36, 46, 304
Aung San, 309
Austin, life in, 267–69
Austin, US Senator, 38
Auswartiges Amt, 57
Avtar Singh, 122, 199
Ayyangar, Gopalaswami, 35, 80, 98, 295

Azad, Maulana Abdul Kalam, 53, 81–82, 282, 294, 309

Bachchan, Harvansh Rai, 25
Bag couriers, use for morale and national advantage, 140–41
Bahuguna, Hemvati Nandan, 26, 257
Baig, Rashid, 121
Bajpai, Girja Shankar, 6, 31, 33, 36–40, 42, 45–47, 64, 79, 232
Bajpai, K. Shankar, 216
Bajpai, K.S., 85
Baker, 210
Balbir, 7
Bandhopadhyay, 105–06
Banerjee, Amitabh, 203
Banerjee, P.K., 132
Banerji, P.C., 22
Bangladesh, 184–89
Bannerji, S.K., 174
Bansilal, 216
Bara Hoti pasture issue, 106–07
Barnala, Surjeet Singh, 231
Batlivala, Soli, 74–76, 80
Beaumont, 31
Bernstein, 148
Bertoli, Gianni, 89
Bevin, Ernie, 44, 95
Bhadkamkar, Ashok, 18, 24, 171
Bhadwar, Mary, 34
Bhagat, Usha, 174, 177
Bhagawat Singh, 121
Bhalla, Bhupi, 24
Bhalla, Hardev, 50
Bhandari, P.L., 45

Bhandari, Romesh, 98, 252
Bharati, 205
Bharatram, 50, 104
Bhartakiya, Chandan Singhji, 274
Bhartiya, Shri Ram, 22
Bhasin, Om, 53
Bhati, Hem Rajji, 276
Bhatt, Ela, 274
Bhim Singhji, Maharana, 7
Bhopal Singhji, 14
Bhutan, policy towards, 108–11
Bhutto, Benazir, 57
Bhutto, Z.A., 154, 156, 158–59, 212–16, 219, 228, 292
BIMSTEC (Bay of Bengal Initiative for Multi-Sectoral Technical and Economic Cooperation), 319
Birendra, King, 234, 239
Bissell, Bim, 59
Blitzer, Charles, 243
Bobbit, Philip, 267–68
Bok, Sisela, 277
Bordia, Kesrilal, 272, 274, 277, 279
Bose, Subhas Chandra, 69, 74
Bowie, Robert, 181, 262
Bowles, Chester, 254
Boys Scout Troop, in old Rajputana, 11
Brajesh, 96–97
Brandt, Willy, 124
Brar, General, 258
Brezhnev, 150, 235, 247, 294, 310
Brzezinski, 236, 310–11, 313
Brown, Ben, 182, 260
Buch, N.C., 34

Bucharest Conference of
    Communist Parties, 1960,
    147
Bum Suk Lee, 61
Bundy, MacGeorge, 177
Bundy, William, 311
Bunker, Carol Laise, 54–56
Bunker, Ellsworth, 54–56
Bunker, Harriet, 54
Bunker, Sam, 55
Burgenstock, PM's visit and Heads
    of Missions conference,
    84–86
Burgi, Maria, 53
Burki, Hamidullah, 213
Bush, George W., 313

Cadogan, Alexander, 38
Caleb, Coral, 25
Caledonian Society, 195
Caroe, Olaf, 306
Carter, Jimmy, 61, 240–42, 265,
    294, 310, 314
    visits India, 235–38
Carter, Rose Mary, 61
Castle, Edgar, 271
Castro, Fidel, 255, 295
Catlin, George, 95
Cecil, William, 259
Chakravarty, B.N., 42, 69–70, 76,
    92
Chakravarty, Kashi, 53
Chakravarty, K.N., 78
Chakravarty, Nikhil, 5
Chamberlain, Neville, 156
Chanda, Anil, 98
Chandralekha, 49, 74
Chandra Shekhar, 61

Chandra Singhji, 17, 22, 274
Chang Wen-chin, 118–20, 262, 268
Chaplin, Charlie, 87–88, 295
Chaplin, Claire Bloom, 88
Charan Singh, 231
    as Prime Minister, 251, 257, 260
Charat Ram, 50, 236
Chatterji, P.C., 15
Chattopadyaya, Kamla Devi, 92
Chavan, Y.B., 208–09, 221, 248
Chayet, Claude, 135
Chellam (personal assistant), 33
Chenevix-Trench, 15, 96
Chen Yi, 146, 162
Chiang Ching, 147
Chiang Kai-shek, 136
Chieh, 262
China
    collateral support to Pakistan,
        153–55
    De Gaulle's recognition, 135
    diplomacy of walking out of
        banquets, 157–60
    import of technology, 160–61
    Indian diplomatic expertise,
        141–43
    Legation Street monuments of
        Imperial Peking, 132–35
    missionary school for diplomatic
        corps, 139–40
    Nkrumah visit, 161–63
    political belligerence and
        military prudence, 151–52
    pre-cultural revolution, 146–47
    professionalism demanded risk-
        taking, 155–57
    social life of Diplomatic Corps
        in, 136–39

Soviet relations
  debate on shared ideology, 147–50
  and Vietnam conflict, 150–53
China Pictorial, 115
China Quarterly, 136
Chopra, Brigadier, 83
Chopra, I.S., 53
Choudhary, Dileep, 36, 39
Churchill, Winston, 21, 47, 93, 145, 250, 295, 304
Civil & Military Gazette, 45
Clinton, 39, 254
Coelho, V.H., 74
Cohen, Stephen, 268
Commonwealth conference, 1948, 43–46
Commonwealth Prime Ministers' Conference, 1977, 232, 255–56
Communist Party of China (CPC), 148–50
Communist Party of India (CPI), 246
Communist Party of Japan, 150
Communist Party of Soviet Union (CPSU), 148, 150
Conquest, Robert, 94
Cook, Hope, 110
Courtney, 68
Coutts, Anne-Money, 122
Cox, Archibald, 181
Creigh-Cohen, 34
Creighton, 2, 33, 40
Cripps, Stafford, 44
Cripps Mission (1942), 304
Crispin, 122
Crossley, 40

Cuban missile crisis, 128, 148, 169, 307, 310

da Costa, E.P.W., 278
Daddha, Siddharth, 296
Daisy, 60
Dalal, K.L., 211
Daljit Singh, 18
Damodaran, A., 141, 155
Damodaran, Ramu, 203
Danger in Kashmir, 39, 261
Dar, Avtar, 74, 77
Dastoor, Phiroze, 25
Dastur, Nari, 83
Daud, 216, 242
Davenport, Hugh, 34
Dayal, Bhagwat, 24
Dayal, Harishwar, 32, 109
Dayal, Rajeshwar, 6, 177, 180, 296
Dayan, Moshe, 243–44
Deb, S.C., 25
de Bolívar, Simón, 175
Defence Plan proposals, 248–49
De Gaulle, 100, 127, 135–36, 152–53
Delhi Declaration 1977, 238
Delhi Durbar of King George in 1911, 10
Delhi Golf Club, 34
Deng Xiaoping, 160, 245–46
Denise, 173
Deo, Arvind, 223
Derk, 277
Desai, Bhulabhai, 41
Desai, Dhirubhai, 41, 45, 74–75, 82
Desai, Madhuri, 75–76, 80
Desai, Mahadev, 274
Desai, M.J., 91–92

Desai, Morarji, 6, 33, 58, 128, 250–51, 312
  at Commonwealth Prime Ministers' Conference, May 1977, 232
  Farakka negotiations, 229–32
  as Prime Minister, 226, 229–32, 255, 313
  visit to
    USSR, 234–35, 246–47
    Washington, 240–41
Desai, Narayanbhai, 274
Desai, Niranjan, 243
De Tocqueville, 317
Dhar, D.P., 80, 167, 295
Dhar, P.N., 6, 200–01, 209, 213–14
Dharm Vir, 23
Dhawan, R.K., 33
Diplomacy
  brickbats, 298
  career rich in souvenirs, 294–96
  foresight in, 293
  justified appropriate discretion in national interest, 293
  in London, 92–94
  national gains and penalties of, 298–302
  performance, 303–21
    alienation of neighbours, 315
    analysis, 311–14
    avoidable consequences traced to Partition, 303–09
    consequences of hypnosis, 309
    governance in foreign ministry, 316–17
    nuclear myopia and contradictions, 315–16
    re-optimization of governance and Foreign Policy, 317–21
    veto carrying membership of Security Council, 316
    wishfulness on Soviet Union, 310
  personal experience of trust, 290
  PM's historic visit to Bhutan and, 290–91
  Prime Ministerial encouragement, 296–97
  professional counsel not allowed to reach Prime Minister, 291–92
  professional innovation in duty, 292–93
  professionalism in, 288–302
  recommending Vajpayee to visit Islamabad as Foreign Minister and Prime Minister's persistence in 1999, 294
Diplomatic Corps, *See also* Foreign Service
  expertise in China, 141–43
  Portuguese speaking professionals, 206–07
  social life in Peking, 136–39
Diplomatic networks in India, *See also* Foreign Service
  recruitment and initial seniority of over age selection, 43
  seniority on interleaving Foreign Service after initial constitution, 42–43
  setting up, 41–42

Diplomatic rigidity and over-reaction, 221–22
Divide and Rule policy, 303
Doshi, Kiran, 204, 215
Doshi, Razia, 53
Dr Mohan Sinha Mehta Memorial Trust, 283, 286–87
Dubey, Muchkund, 231
Dulles, John Foster, 99
Dutt, R.C., 69
Dutt, S., 6, 40, 64, 258
Dutt, Subimal, 104

Economic development, logic of, 178–80
Eden, Anthony, 93, 101
Education, voluntarism in, 281–82
Eisenhower, 80, 120–21
Elections and service reactions, 225–26
Elizabeth II, Queen, 80, 232
Elwin, Verrier, 104
Emergency proclamation, 205–06, 222–23
Engel, 144
Erhard, 128
Europe–India aid negotiations, 125
Ewans, Martin, 288
Ewatt, Australian Foreign Minister, 45
Experiments with Truth, 3

Fairbanks, John, 181
Farakka negotiations, 220–21, 229–32, 234, 293, 315
Fateh Singhji, Maharana, 10, 14

Federal Public Service Commission in, Simla, 27
Fernandes, George, 239
Festival of India, origin of, 243
Feuz, Erust, 89
Feuz, Maria, 89
Firyubin, 223
Foot, Michael, 222
Foreign Affairs, 311
Foreign Policy, 262, 266
Foreign policy, re-optimization of, 317–21
Foreign Service
 expertise in China, 141–43
 foreign minister's impact, 233–34
 post categorization to ensure rotational fairness, 70–72
 preserving morale of, 233
 seniority on interleaving after initial constitution, 42–43
 social life in Peking, 136–39
Foreign Service 'B,' constitution of, 68–70
Freedom, 271
Freeman, John, 95
Frelimo, 188
Friday Club, 23, 25
Frost, Robert, 321

Galbraith, Catherine, 56, 186, 237
Galbraith, John Kenneth, 56, 177, 262, 266, 278, 294
Galbraith, Kitty, 57–58
Galbraith, Peter, 265
Gandhi, Indira, 5–6, 24, 33, 55, 85–88, 129, 163, 205, 207, 209,

214, 224–26, 228, 233, 238, 241, 243, 254, 257–58, 260, 291–92, 298–99, 311–12, 314
Emergency proclamation, 205–06, 222–23
as Prime Minister, 214–17, 220
visits to Eastern Europe and Latin America as Prime Minister, 174–77
Gandhi, M.K., 3, 20, 97, 274, 303–04, 308–09, 315, 318, 320–21
assassination of, 36, 121
Gandhi, Rajiv, 85, 87, 117, 177, 301
Gandhi, Sanjay, 24, 85, 87, 248
Gandhi, Sonia, 177
Gangaramji, 62
Gharekhan, 296
Garner, Joe, 94
Garvey, Rose Marie, 136
Garvey, Terence, 136
Gavshon, Arthur, 95
Geheeb, Paul, 85–86
Gehlot, Ashok, 280
Gelb, Leslie, 317
Gan island, Maldives, 242–43
George, King, 10
George VI, King, 47
Gery, Wade, 296
Ghani, 185–86
Giri, V.V., 192–93
Goheen, Robert, 237, 242
Gonsalves, Eric, 245–46, 252
Gopal, S., 296
Gorakhpuri, Firaque, 23
Gore-Booth, Paul, 149–50
Gould-Adems, 95
Governance

in foreign ministry, 316–17
re-optimization of, 317–21
Government of India Act 1935, 303
Govind Narain, 23
Grassroots democracy, reinforcing of, 284–86
Gromyko, 228–29, 234–35
Gruber, 86
Guardian, 142
Guillebaud, Claude, 28
Gujral, 223
Gulab Singhji, 25
Gundevia, Rokshi, 88, 90, 92
Gundevia, Yezdi, 40, 84, 86–88, 90, 94, 138
Gupta, Hansarajji, 33
Gupta, J.P., 24

Hadow, Marie, 3
Hadow, Michael, 3
Haider, Col., 24
Haider, Salman, 25, 53
Hailey, Malcolm, 95
Haksar, Ajit, 50
Haksar, P.N., 5, 85, 94
Hallstein Doctrine, 125
Hamir, Rana, 9
Han Nien-lung, 246
Hardgrave, Robert, 222
Hardinge, 95
Harish Chandra, 23
Harriman, Averill, 58
Harris, Richard, 95
Harrison, Agatha, 20
Hartley, Anthony, 95
Harvard Centre for International Affairs (CFIA), 260

Index   329

Hasan, ambassador of Qatar, 259
Hathingadi, 194
Heillemann, Kathrine, 19
Heine, 118
Helen, 41, 50
Henderson, Loy, 53, 294
Henderson, Nicholas, 267
Hijacking incident, August '76, 217–18
Hillary, Edmund, 88–89
Himalayas, as strategic barrier/bridge of friendship, 105–07
Hindu, 95
Hindu Divorced Women, 58
Hindu Family and Modern Values, The, 58
Hindu Reform Act of 1955, 58
Hindustan Times, 95, 206
Hitchcock, 178
Hitler, 21–22, 201
Hobson, Donald, 136, 162, 172–73
Ho-Chi-Minh, 113
Hoffman, Stanley, 181
Holyoake, 46
Hope Cook, 201
Horton, Alfred, 128
Hunt, John, 88
Huntingdon, Samuel, 181
Hussain, Mubashir, 219
Hussain, Tabarak, 230
Hydari, Akbar, 31
Hypnosis, consequences in diplomacy performance, 309

Ibrahim, Hauwa, 57
Illustrated Weekly of India, 248
Imperial Delhi Gymkhana Club, 34

Inder, 62
India-China crisis, 117–18
India–China treaty of 1890, 201
India-Nepal relations, 111–12, 238–39
Indian Express, 206
Indian Frontier Administrative Service (IFAS), and tribal NEFA, 102–05
India Now and In Time, 58
India-Pakistan relations, 212–220, 228–29
India-Tanzania relations, 188–93
Indo-German economic relations, 123
Ingle, 260
In search of old Peking, 132
Inside the Haveli, 59, 62–63
International conference on water, 223–24
International Law Association, 301
Israel, bipartisanship on, 243–44
Iyengar, H.V.R., 33

Jagjivan Ram, 220, 223, 229–30, 251
Jain, N.P., 234
Jaipal, 221
Jamal, 191
Jam Sahib, 45
Janata coalition government, 226
 Farakka negotiations, 229–31
 prophylactic diplomacy towards Afghanistan, 242
 USSR and Pakistan, 228–29
Japan Times, 142
Jaswant Singh, 13, 17, 217, 300

Jayakar, Pupul, 92, 243
Jha, Amara Nath, 22–23
Jha, B.N., 23
Jha, C.S., 6, 53, 164, 179–80
Jha, L.K., 23, 128, 179
Jinnah, M.A., 23, 29, 73, 305–06
John, V.V., 278
Johnson, Lyndon, 54, 151, 267
Joint communiqués hypocrisy, 175–76, 237–38
Joint Intelligence Committee (JIC), 166
Jones, Gregory, 270
Jones, Rodney, 265
Jordan, Barbara, 268
Jung, Ali Yawar, 98
Jurgensen, Rose, 56

Kahn, Hermann, 181
Kalidas, 114
Kamaraj Plan, 282
Kandahar Club, 89
Kanwar, Baiji Sobhag, 45
Kanwar, Pratap, 59
Kao, R.N., 230
Kapuria, Harish, 279
Karanjia, Rusi, 75
Karmal, Babrak, 312
Karstens, Frau, 57
Karume, Abeid, 196
Kashmir issue
  tribal intrusion into, 35
  in UN, 35–39
Kaul, Brahma, 25
Kaul, M.G., 25
Kaul, T.N., 5, 104, 106, 153, 210, 292, 311

Kaunda, 188, 256
Kautsky, 148
Kellas, Arthur, 195
Ken, 177
Kennan, George, 4, 166, 296
Kennedy, John F., 126–27, 317–18
Kennedy, Paul, 269
Kewal Singh, 85, 198, 208–09, 211, 253
Khan, Admiral, 220–21, 231
Khan, Ayub, 154, 156, 159
Khan, Fakir Aizuddin, 159
Khan, Liaqat Ali, 44, 295
Khan, R. Axel, 69
Khan, Yunus, 205
Khan, Zafarullah, 40
Khanna, Vinod, 141
Khanna, Wadchu, 53
Kher, B.G., 85, 91
Khera, Col., 154–55
Khetan, Neelima, 277
Khrushchev, 115, 147–50
Khubchand, 72
Khurana, M.M., 43
Khushwant Singh, 18, 55, 209
Kibe, Sardar, 18
Kim Il-sung, 144
King, Martin Luther, 318
Kissinger, Henry, 159, 177, 181
Kochar, Manorama, 50
Koirala, B.P., 111
Koirala, M.P., 111
Kongka Pass incident, 115
Korbel, 39, 261
Kosygin, 150–51, 178–79, 235, 246, 294
Kotelawala, John, 44

Kothari, Daulat Singh, 25
Kothari, Rajni, 278
Kotlewala, John, 108
Krishna, 3
Krishna Iyer, V.R., 253
Krishna Menon, 41, 91, 96, 98–99, 112, 157
Krishnan, N., 255
Krishnaswamy, K.R., 77–78, 81–82
Krishnaswamy, S., 77
Kumar, Lovraj, 24
Kundan Singh, 67
Kundu, 208

La Condition Humane, 136
Laden, Osama bin, 311, 313
Laise, Carol, 54–56
Lake Conservation Plan, 284
Lal Bahadur Shastri Academy, Mussorie, 202–05
Lall, Dewan Chaman, 41
Lall, K.B., 125, 239
Lamb, Alistair, 36, 105
Lambert, 89
Lamping, 49
Latif, Air Chief Marshall, 249
Lee Kwan Yu, 179
Legation Street, China, 132–35
Lei Feng, 146
Lenin, 144, 148–49
Lewisham, 132
Liu Shao-ch'i, 114, 133, 146–47, 162
Li Zhisui, 113
Lodha, Umed Malji, 276
Lohia, Ram Manohar, 82
Luebke, 128

Machel, Samora, 188
McMahon tripartite negotiations, in Simla, 201
McMahon, Henry, 52
Macmillan, Harold, 94, 101
Madan, Nanna, 205
Mahendra, King, 111, 172
Mahendra Singhji, Maharana, 278
Mahindra, Keshab, 50
Majumdar, Ajit, 205
Makonde carvings, 196
Malhotra, Inder, 55
Malik, H.S., 41, 96
Malraux, Andre, 136
Manchuria, 145–46
Mandela, Nelson, 3
Manekshaw, Field Marshall Sam, 35, 199
Manmohan Singh, S., 28, 66, 248, 286, 297
Mansergh, 305
Mao Zedong, 113–14, 117–18, 133–34, 137, 141, 146–50, 153–54, 157, 159
Marchel, Samora, 207
March of Folly, 263
Marshall, Alfred, 28
Marshall, David, 179
Marshall, George, 165
Marshall Plan, 166
Marshal Plan, 305
Martin, Kingsley, 95
Marx, 144, 148
Mathai, Dilip, 197
Matthai, John, 50
Mathai, M.O., 33, 44–45, 85, 88
Matthai, Ravi, 50

Matthai, Valsa, 50
Maynes, Charles, 262
Mazumdar, Chitra, 28
Mehta, Ajay, 62, 90–91, 123, 130, 278
Mehta, Ajit, 22
Mehta, Arun, 50
Mehta, Ashok, 74
Mehta, G.L., 85
Mehta, Jagat S.
  accusations of gender bias, 252–54
  administering lower deck of ministry, 66–68
  administrative responsibilities, 201–02
  aide to V.L. Pandit, 95–96
  ancestors, 7–10
  as Assistant Foreign Secretary, 208
  birth, 11
  change of governments, 225–54
  as Chief Executive of Seva Mandir, 272, 275–76
  chief guest at Caledonian society dinner, 195–96
  civil services ethics approaches, 105–07
  commission in Royal Indian Navy, 26–28
  Commonwealth conference, 1948, 43–46
  constitution of Foreign Service 'B,' 68–70
  defeat in election for post of Secretary General, 255–56
  diplomacy
    brickbats, 298
    career rich in souvenirs, 294–96
    foresight, 293
    justified appropriate discretion in national interest, 293
    in London, 92–94
    national gains and penalties of, 298–302
    personal experience of trust, 290
    PM's historic visit to Bhutan and, 290–91
    Prime Ministerial encouragement, 296–97
    professional counsel not allowed to reach Prime Minister, 291–92
    professional innovation in duty, 292–93
    professionalism in, 288–302
    recommending Vajpayee to visit Islamabad as Foreign Minister and Prime Minister's persistence in 1999, 294
  education
    at Allahabad University, 22–26
    at Leighton Park, Reading, 20–21
    in Modern School, 18
    at St. John's College, Cambridge, 28–30
    in Vidya Bhawan, 18–20
  on family bond to Mewar, 7–16
  family pride, 12–16
    association with administration, 12–13
    commitment to public interest, 13–14
    empathy for people, 13–14

never compromise on principles, 15–16
pioneer of education, 13
farewell to Foreign Service, 258–59
on father, 10–12, 271–73
father's death, 278
at Harvard under fellowship with intellectuals, 260–62
Himalayas as strategic barrier, 105–07
holiday in Spain, 96–97
India-China crisis, 117–18
India stays in Commonwealth, 46–47
interlude in Harvard, 180–82
joined Foreign Service, 32
Kashmir issue in UN, 35–39, 97
leading Indian team defending frontiers, 118–20
on life in Austin, 267–69
marriage, 51
on ministry in 1947–49, 39–41
mother's death, 11–12
naval interlude, 26–28
Partition and, 33–34
post categorization to ensure rotational fairness, 70–72
postings
  Additional Secretary (Administration), 199–209, 251–52
  Deputy Secretary (East), 102–21
  Deputy Secretary (Personnel), 98–101
  First Secretary in Bern, 73–91
  First Secretary in Bonn, 72
  as Foreign Secretary, 209–56
  head of embassy in Peking, 128–63
  High Commissioner to Tanzania, 183–98
  Minister Political in Bonn, 122–30
  Policy Planning Division in Ministry, 163–82
  PPS to London, 91–98
  as Private Secretary to Secretary General, 32–47
  Under Secretary (Ad), 64–72
President of Seva Mandir, 275–76
President Vidya Bhawan, 270–71, 278–87
Professor of World Peace at Austin, 263–69
Queen's visit, 120–21
rationale for posting to eastern division, 102–05
removed as Foreign Secretary, 257–58
sabbatical exposures in Harvard, 180–82
scrutinized by Jawaharlalji, 32
secret resistance to promotion, 208–09
selection for ICS, 28
setting up diplomatic networks in India, 41–42
at Seva Mandir, 271–76
skiing in Bern, 89–90
souvenir from Nehru, 129–30
special tours accompanying Nehru on election tour, 112, 290
PM in trek to Bhutan, 115–17, 290–91

PM to Eastern Europe and Latin America, 174–77
Vice President, 112–15, 290
Suez nationalization issue, 98–101
supersession and notice of transfer, 197–98
as Tom Slick Professor at LBJ School, 263–66
visit to
  Bhutan, 177–78
  DPR Korea, 144
  Dublin with High Commissioner, 97–98
  Eastern Europe and Latin America with PM, 174–77
  LBS Academy in Mussorie, 202–05
  Makonde tribals, 196
  Manchuria, 145–46
  Nyerere's tribal village, 193–94
  Szechuan and Yangtze, 144–45
  Washington with PM, 240–41
on wife Rama, 48–63
Mehta, Khimjibhai, 53–54
Mehta, K.L., 104*
Mehta, Megnaa, 50
Mehta, Mohan Sinha, 15
Mehta, N.C., 48
Mehta, P.S., 24
Mehta, Rama, 48–63, 76, 80–83, 86, 88, 90–91, 97, 121, 154, 156, 158–59, 185, 192–93, 205–06, 209, 237, 272–73, 295
  an intellectual, 56–58
  education, 50–51
  friendship with Carol Laise, 54–56
  heart attack and death, 60–63, 240
  marriage and compulsory resignation, 51
  in and out of diplomacy, 52–54
  in purdah household, 51–52
  a sociologist, 58–60
Mehta, Saraswati, 53–54
Mehta, Sheila, 50
Mehta, Uday, 12, 60, 122, 131, 138–40, 240, 244
Mehta, Vijay, 22, 52, 55, 60, 62, 76, 91, 95, 122, 240, 243
Mehta, Vikram, 61, 91, 95, 122, 240
Mehtab Chandji, 274
Mela Singh, S., 67
Memoirs, and egotism, 1–6
Menon, K.P.S., 31, 40, 50, 53, 64–65, 75, 86
Menon, P.A., 39, 123
Menon, P.N., 40
Menon, Shivshankar, 40, 141
Menon, V.P., 4, 34, 43, 108
Menon (Sr), K.P.S., 50
Menzies, 46, 99
Ministry of External affairs (MEA)
  in 1947–49, 39–41
  governance in, 316–17
  Policy Planning Division, 164–74
  post Emergency problems in, 247–50
Mir Qasim, 216
Misra, S.N., 251, 256–57
Missionary school for diplomatic corps, in Peking, 139–40
Mochulski, 135

Mohini, 56
Molotov, 86, 115
Montgomery, Field Marshall, 89, 136
Monuments of Imperial Peking, 132–35
Morin, Mme, 20
Mountbatten, Edwina, 2, 44–45
Mountbatten, Louis, 33, 35, 45, 254, 304–05, 309
Mountbatten, Pamela, 2
Moynihan, Elizabeth, 56
Moynihan, Pat, 269
Moynihan, Patrick, 56, 181
Mozambique, Portuguese speaking professionals for, 206–07
Muelleium-Rechberg, Frecherrovon, 195
Mukherjee, Nirmal, 248, 257
Mukherjee (Ms), 55
Mukti Bahini, 229–30
Mulgaonkar, 95, 206
Munshi, K.M., 22
Musahib Ala, 15
Musharaff, Pervez, 310–11, 314
Muslim League, 304
Muthamma, 252–53
Mutual Assured Destruction (MAD) strategy, 307
Myrdal, Alva, 263
Myrdal, Gunnar, 263

Najibullah, 311
Nambiar, A.C.N., 73–75, 77, 85–86, 88
Nandy, Ashis, 278
Narain, Jai Prakash, 82, 205, 251

Narain, Prakash, 24
Narasimha Rao, P.V., 245
Narayanan, K.R., 211
Narayanan, M.K., 42, 69
Narsimhan, 28
Nasser, 86, 99, 178
National Development Corporation (NDC), 194
National Environment Development Centre, 184
Natwar Singh, K., 114, 174, 224, 233, 256, 258
Naxalites, 318
Nayar, Kuldip, 206, 278
Negotiating for India, 115, 207, 297
Neguib, 86
Nehru, B.K., 2, 4, 55, 224, 278, 311
Nehru, Fory, 2
Nehru, Jawaharlal, 2–3, 6, 32–33, 41–42, 79–80, 91, 99, 107, 109, 111, 115, 118–19, 127, 129, 135, 157, 159, 181, 186–87, 190, 225, 227, 245, 250, 256, 262, 287, 290–91, 294–96, 303, 305–06, 308–09, 315–16, 318, 321
assassination of Gandhi and, 36
attitude towards tribal belt, 102, 107
Austrian foreign minister calls on, 86–87
Charlie Chaplin calls on, 87–88
Churchill relations, 47
at Commonwealth conference, 43–46
consequences of hypnosis, 309
election tour, 112

Kashmir issue, 35
misjudgement on China, 309–10
on Suez nationalization issue, 99–101
on top of Engelberg Peak, 86–87
trek to Bhutan, 115–17
as Vice Chairman of the Governor General's Council, 32
visit Allahabad University, 25
visit to Burgenstock and heads of Missions conference, 84–86
Nehru, Kamla, 41
Nehru, Rajan, 132
Nehru, R.K., 81, 113–14, 116, 132
Nepal, policy towards, 111–12, 238–39
separate trade and transit treaties with, 238–39
Neutralists Koreans issue, 103–04
New Statesman, 95
Nina, 89
Nixon, 159, 177, 235, 238, 268
Nkrumah, 161–63
Noel-Baker, 35
No First Strike policy, 315
Non-aligned summit, September 1979, 255
Norgay, Anglahmu, 89
Norgay, Tenzing, 88–89, 295
Nuclear Disarmament Committee, 200
Nuclear Non-Proliferation, 179–80, 200
Nujomo, 188
Nurul Hasan, 23

Nye, Joe, 181
Nyerere, Julius, 57, 184, 186, 191–93, 196, 198

Obama, Barack, 5–6, 317–18
Obote, Milton, 184
Observer, 95
O'Meally, 65, 70
Operation Gibraltar, 154
Ottunu, Olaru, 265
Oza, Bhupat, 141, 143, 160

Pachauri, R.K., 320
Pakistan resolution, 1940, 304
Palliser, Michael, 216
Pandit, A.D., 181
Pandit, Vijaya Lakshmi, 40, 45, 49, 74, 92–93, 95–97, 158
Panna Dhay, 7
Pannikar, K.M., 79
Pant, Apa, 183
Paris Harold Tribune, 142
Parthasarthy, G., 132, 167, 211, 220, 229, 311
Parthasarthy, Shanti, 53, 211
Partial Test Ban Treaty, 150, 307, 310, 315
Partition, 33–34
avoidable consequences traced to, 303–09
Patel, C.C., 229
Patel, H.M., 31, 239
Patel, Sardar Vallabhbhai, 3, 28, 108–09, 305
Pathak, R.S., 24
Patil, Pratibha, 286
Patten, Chris, 113

Peaceful Nuclear Explosion (PNE), in Pokhran desert, 200
Pearson, Lester, 47
Peking
   missionary school for diplomatic corps, 139–40
   monuments of, 132–35
   social life of Diplomatic Corps in, 136–39
Peking Review, 117
Pem Pem, 89
People's Daily, 142, 157
Philip, Prince, 121
Pierre, Andrew, 265
Pillai, N.R., 31, 41, 85
Polak, Henry, 20
Policy Planning Division (PPD), in Ministry, 164–74
   coping with public and Parliamentary anger, 169–72
   hazard of impetuosity and constriction, 172–73
   marginalization of, 166–67
   operational role, 168–74
   professional sagacity imperative, 173–74
   Raghunath–Vijay episode, 168–74
   structure for, 165–66
   utilization of, 167–68
Portuguese speaking professionals, for decolonized Mozambique, 206–07
Power Rules, 317
Prem, 22
Private Life of Chairman Mao, The, 113

Prophylactic diplomacy towards Afghanistan, 242
   USSR and Pakistan, 228–29
Puri, Y.K., 69
Purushottam, 223, 237

Queen's visit, to India, 120–21
Quit India resolution, 304

Radcliffe, Cyril, 31
Radhakrishnan, S., 40, 80, 112–15, 133, 245, 295
Raghavan, Nedyam, 78–79
Raghunath, K., 53, 141
Raghunath–Vijay episode, 168–74, 293
Raghuvir Singhji, 18
Rahman, Ishi, 33, 199, 258
Rahman, Sheikh Mujibur, 185, 220, 231
Rai, Mangat, 181
Raina, General, 203
Rajagopalachari, 75
Rajan, K.V., 211
Rajaram, 52–53
Ramphal, 232, 255–56
Ram Rao, Santa, 59
Ram Singhji, Mehta, 8–9, 12, 14
Rana, Kishan, 137, 141
Rana Kumbha, 7
Rana Pratap, 7
Randhawa, M.S., 177
Ranganathan, C.V., 53, 141
Rani Amma, 62
Ranjit, 27
Rao, A.N., 204
Rao, Nirupama, 141

Rao, Shiv, 45
Rasgotra, M.K., 253
Ratnam, S., 40, 64, 69
Rau, B.N., 42, 88
Rauf, Ambassador, 40
Ray, A.N., 181
Raza, General, 137, 154, 156, 159
Reddy, G.K., 95
Reischauer, 181
Rescuing the Future, 264
Rise and Fall of Great Empires, The, 269
Roach, Jim, 263
Roberts, Frank, 94
Robertson, Denis, 31
Rockefeller, Nelson, 177
Roosevelt, Elenaor, 92
Rostow, Watt, 263
Roy, Sunil, 43
Roy, Tarachand, 74
Runganathan, Samuel, 41
Rup Chand, 41

Sabry, Ali, 99
Sadaat, 238
Safrani, Abid Hasan, 43, 69
Sahay, Bhagwan, 111
Sahib Pannalalji, Mehta
Sajjan Singhji, Maharana, 9, 12
Salal hydel project, 218–20, 300
Salisbury, 306
Sanyal, Bimal, 190, 209, 211
Sarabhai, Vikram, 177
Saran, Shyam, 211
Sarila, Narendra Singh, 64
Sarlaji, 19
Sarma, Hella, 53, 74, 84
Sarma, Krish, 74

Sathe, Ram, 40, 168, 171, 208–09, 258
Sathe, Shaila, 209
Satish Chandra, 24
Saunders, Harold, 236, 265
Saxena, R.R., 39
Schlesinger, 127
Schumann–Mollet Plan, 127
Schwartz, Ben, 181
Second Chance, The, 311
Secretary General election, for Commonwealth Prime Ministers' Conference, 255–56
Security Council, veto carrying membership of, 316
Selassie, Haile, 188
Seminar, 236
Sen, Amartya, 57
Sen, Geeta, 57
Sen, P.C., 71
Sen, Usha Nath, 34
Seshan, N.K., 33
Sethi, Rajiv, 243
Sethi, Ranjeet, 141
Seva Mandir
  code of conduct at, 276–77
  colleagues and volunteers, 276–78
  state in 1985, 273–75
Seva Samiti Scout Association, 11
Shah, Zahir, 216
Shah Banu, 58
Shah Commission, 247–48
Shahi, Agha, 212–14, 217–18, 228–29, 242
Shah Nawaz, 43, 217
Shakuntalam, 114

Shankar, V., 80, 235, 295
Shankar Lalji, 11
Shanti Bhushan, 24
Sharda Prasad, 174
Sharma, B.L., 97, 295
Sharma, Kukoo, 53
Shashank, Kalpana, 53
Shastri, Lal Bahadur, 154, 158–59, 227, 247, 296–97, 309
Shekhawat, Bhairon Singhji, 285
Shelvankar, K.S., 95
Sherman, Max, 266
Sher Singhji, Mehta, 8
Shield of Achilles, A, 268
Shourie, Arun, 278
Shri Ram, Sir, 50–51
Shroff, Manu, 179
Shukairy, 151
Shyamaldas, 8
Siddiqui, Tiger, 229
Sikkim
  annexation of, 200–01
  policy towards, 108–11
Simla Agreement (1972), 212, 238
Singapore PM's initiative, on South East Asia, 179
Singh, C.P.N., 111
Singh, Dinesh 96–97, 129, 181
Singh, L.P., 23, 158, 181, 297
Singh, Nagendra, 278
Singh, S.K., 174
Singhal, Arvind, 279
Sinha, Satya Narain, 77
Sino-Soviet friendship treaty, 128, 134, 292
Sir Dorabji Tata Trust, 285
Smith, Constance (Connie), 56, 58
Smuts, J.C., 271

Sobani, Lt., 27
Sobha Singh, 18
Socialism and non-alignment, 178–80
Sorensen, Ted, 126
South East Asia, Singapore PM's initiative on, 179
Spectator, 95
Srimali, Kalu Lalji, 11, 278, 282
Srinagesh, J.N., 31
Srinivasan, Thampi, 141
Srivastava, Kailash, 53
Stalin, 86, 124, 144, 147–48, 155, 166, 296
Stalin, Marshall, 97
Standstill Agreement with Kashmir, 35
Stangate, 96
Stein, Joseph Allen, 278
Stracey, C. J., 43
Strauss, George, 96
Subhan, 45
Subramaniam, K., 249
Subramanyam (stenographer), 33
Sudarikov, 223, 247
Suez nationalization issue, 98–101
Sukarno, 100, 161
Sukhadia, Mohan Lalji, 184
Sultan Singhji, Lala, 18
Suri, Nalini, 141
Svetlana, 97
Swamy, Subramaniam, 206, 248
Swaran Singh, 171, 198, 254
Szechuan, 144–45

Taliban, 311, 313, 318
Tanganyika African National Union (TANU), 186

340   Index

Tanzania
    China relations, 197
    development aid to, 187–88
    Indian naval squadron visit, 194–95
    India relations, 188–93
    India to take-over running cement factory, 194
    Milton Obote refuge in, 184
    negotiating compensation for Indians, 207–08
    under Nyerere's leadership, 186–97
    President V.V. Giri visit to, 192–93
    Zanzibar relations, 196–97
Tara Chand, 53
Tarlok Singh, 32, 74
Tata, J.R.D., 89, 127
Taylor, John, 36
Tehelka, 121
Tehsin, Riaz, 279
Tej Singhji, 14–15
Temple of Service, *See* Seva Mandir
Terror and Consent: Wars of the 21st Century, 268
Terrorism, 5, 286, 311, 313–14, 318
Tewari, N.D., 26
Thakur Singh, 53
Thapar, Mala, 236
Thapar, P.N., 31
Thapar, Romesh, 236
Thatcher (Mrs), 222, 256
Thermo-nuclear war, 181
Thimayya, Gen., 55, 80, 295
Third World militarization, 264–66

Thomson, John, 259
Thornton, Tom, 237, 265
Thoughts of Mao Zedong, The, 146
Thousand Days, 127
Tikhvinsky, 94
Times, 95, 141
Times of India, 95
Tito, 178, 255
Tod, James, 8
'Tonkin Gulf' incident, 151
Tonpe, 33, 128
Trevelyan, 96
Trevelyan, Humphrey, 32, 39
Trivedi, Chandu Lal, 24
Trivedi, V.C., 94
Truman doctrine, 308
Tryst with Destiny, 127
Tsang, Ambassador, 38
Tuchmann, Barbara, 263
Tucker, Francis, 306
Tully, Mark, 222
Twelfth Night, 25
Tyabji, Badrudin, 64, 121
Tyabji, B.F.H.B., 2

Uday Shankar, 15
Uday Singhji, Rana, 7
Ulam, Adam, 181
University Training Corp (UTC), 24
Urquidi, Victor, 265
US–German relations, 127

Vaidyanathan, 204
Vajpayee, Atal Bihari, 6, 59, 61, 174, 226–29, 231, 233–35, 238, 240–41, 245–47, 249–50, 297

Index   341

defence plan proposals and, 249
as foreign minister, 226–28, 231, 233–35
reassurance to Muslim countries, 241
visit to
China, 245–46
Islamabad, 1978, 238
Vidya Bhawan, 285
Vance, Cyrus, 236–37
Vasundhara Raje, 240
Veer Vinod, 8
Vellodi, M.A., 77, 288
Vellodi, M.K., 41
Venkateswaran, A.P., 40
Venkateswaran, R., 125
Venkatraman, Dharma, 24, 28
Vernon, Ray, 181
Vidya Bhawan, 270–71, 278–87
boarding school, 18–20
Vidya Bhawan Institute of Local-Self Government and Responsible Citizenship, 285
Vidya Bhawan Society
constitution modification, 283
Dr. M.S. Mehta Trust and, 283–84
Prime Minister visit to, 285–86
reinforcing grassroots diplomacy at, 284–85
rescuing of, 281–82
tactful rectification at, 279–81
Vietnam conflict
and Sino-Soviet differences, 150–53
USSR secret well-wisher of USA in, 153–54

Vijayraghavachari, T., 15
Voluntarism
in education, 281–82
and future of India, 286–87, 317
Voronstov, 94
Vorontsov, 245
Vyas, Girja, 279

Wadhawan, A.C., 285
Wadhawan, Parvatiji, 285
Warsaw Pact, 125, 305
Watch on the Rhine, 118
Wazir Hasan, 23
Weapons of Mass Destruction (WMD), 180, 305, 307
Wedgewod-Benn, Tony, 96
Weightman, Hugh, 31, 33
Western Educated Hindu Women, 58
Western India Automobile Association, 26
Whitehall Establishment Code, 68–69, 205
Wilhelmina, Queen, 73
Williams, Baroness Shirley, 267
Williams, Bernard, 95
Williams, Shirley, 95, 278
Willingdon Club, Bombay, 74
Wilson, David, 136–137
Wilson, Harold, 152
Woodrow Wilson Centre for Scholars (WWC), in Washington DC, 261

Xuecheng Liu, 267

Yang Kung-su, 155
Yangtze River, 144–45

Younger, Kenneth, 95
Younger, Lucy, 95
Younger, Sam, 95
Yunus, 142

Zafar, 23
Zafrullah, 35
Zakaria, Fareed, 318
Zalam Singh, 9, 12
Zanzibar
  beating the retreat in, 194–95
  relations with Tanzania, 196–97
Zheel Sanrakshan Samity (ZSS), Udaipur, 284
Zhou Enlai, 114–15, 118, 120, 133, 135, 139, 146, 152, 157, 159–60, 162, 188, 291, 310
Zhu De, Marshal, 114
Zia-ul-Haq, General, 228, 310
Zia-ul-Rahman, General, 230
Zulueta, Philip, 94